Organize, Fight, Win

Organize, Fight, Win

Black Communist Women's Political Writing

Edited by
Charisse Burden-Stelly and Jodi Dean

VERSO

London • New York

First published by Verso 2022
Collection © Verso 2022
Contributions © Contributors 2022

3 5 7 9 10 8 6 4

Verso
UK: 6 Meard Street, London W1F 0EG
US: 388 Atlantic Avenue, Brooklyn, NY 11217
versobooks.com

Verso is the imprint of New Left Books

ISBN-13: 978-1-83976-497-4
ISBN-13: 978-1-83976-498-1 (UK EBK)
ISBN-13: 978-1-83976-499-8 (US EBK)

British Library Cataloguing in Publication Data
A catalogue record for this book is available from the British Library

Library of Congress Cataloging-in-Publication Data
A catalog record for this book is available from the Library of Congress

Typeset in Minion by Hewer Text UK Ltd, Edinburgh
Printed and bound by CPI Group (UK) Ltd, Croydon CR0 4YY

Contents

Section II:
Organizing, Labor, and Militancy   41

Section III:
Fighting Fascism   123

Acknowledgments

The bulk of the work of identifying, locating, compiling, and transcribing the contributions to this collection was carried out during the spring and summer of 2020, the first year of the COVID-19 pandemic. Many people provided generous assistance and support; the volume could not have existed without their work. We are especially grateful to Sadie Kenyon-Dean for transcribing each of the texts. We extend our thanks to Adam McNeil for his work securing permissions. We appreciate the Faculty Research Grant from Hobart and William Smith Colleges that let us pay Sadie and Adam for their work. Special thanks go to MaryLouise Patterson and to the Communist Party of the United States of America for publication permissions. Additional thanks go to Carrie E. Hintz and Rachel Detzler from the Rose Library at Emory University and Jennifer Nace from the Warren Hunting Smith Library at Hobart and William Smith Colleges. A number of scholars shared their invaluable time, expertise, and enthusiasm; we are especially grateful to Gregg Andrews, Melissa Ford, Erik Gellman, Sean Guillory, LaShawn Harris, Gerald Horne, Zifeng Liu, Erik McDuffie, Minkah Makalani, and John Munro. Finally, the book is also the product of the labor of the talented and committed workers at Verso, especially Rosie Warren, Jeanne Tao, and copy editor Steve Hiatt.

Introduction

Charisse Burden-Stelly and Jodi Dean

At the founding convention of the National Negro Labor Council on October 27–28, 1951, Black Communist women received emphatic applause as they asserted their importance in and to the labor movement. Throughout the meeting, they emphasized that as long as Black women were locked out of significant sections of US industry, reduced to domestic service, and marginalized in or left out of unions, the labor struggle as a whole would be weakened. The refusal to fight against the abuse of domestic workers and to organize this section of oppressed laborers rendered the union movement incomplete at best. Women such as Helen Lunelly and Viola Brown pointed out that a key struggle of the Labor Council was to open the doors of factories and industry to Black women while simultaneously struggling for livable working conditions and wages for domestics.[1] By offering this powerful critique, Black Communist women redefined who counted as a worker, shed light on the intersections of oppression and exploitation that needed to be addressed by the labor movement, and presented the necessary actions for launching a truly representative labor struggle.

This analysis did not originate after World War II. At the first meeting of the National Negro Congress (NNC) from February 14 to 18, 1936, Black Communist women helped to shape a resolution for a national movement, under the direction of the NNC, to organize domestic workers—85 percent of whom were Black women—to regularize their hours, raise their wages, and improve their living conditions. Such a movement would elevate the conditions of Black and working people as a whole. It was out of this meeting that Louise Thompson Patterson wrote her pivotal article "Toward a Brighter Dawn," in which she laid out how Black women, in the Northern "slave markets" and on Southern farms, were "severely exploited" as workers, as women, and as "Negroes." This superexploitation was exacerbated by their high rate of unemployment, discrimination in relief programs, exorbitant rents, and terrible housing, all of which Black women endured while maintaining and rearing their families (see chapter 10). Black women's plight was not only the plight of the Black community; it was the plight of all workers struggling against the intensification of subjection in the throes of the Great Depression.

This astute analysis of the structural and material conditions of Black women had been articulated even earlier by Grace Campbell, one of the first women to join the Communist Party of the United States of America (CPUSA). In 1928 Campbell wrote:

> Negro women workers are the most abused, exploited and discriminated against of all American workers, not only by the capitalist system and the employers, but by unenlightened race prejudice which is found even in the working class, and is used by the employers to drive a wedge between the black and white workers and thus destroy their unity and fighting power.[2]

Campbell was ahead of her time in using the realities of Black women workers to illuminate the importance of struggling against capitalism and racism simultaneously to shore up interracial worker unity. Black Communist women understood that satisfying the material needs of the most bitterly exploited group would strengthen the labor movement and its ability to struggle against class domination and its intensification by imperialism, war, racism, and fascism, which combined all of these. This was not least because, as Claudia Jones put it, Black women were the "real active forces—the organizers and the workers" in the institutions and organizations that were central to the economic, political, and social life of Black people; addressing their special oppressed status would help to bring their militant energy to even greater heights in the fight for peace and socialism.[3]

For several decades in the early to mid-twentieth-century United States, Black Communist women organized, fought, and led mass campaigns against national oppression and economic exploitation. Within and adjacent to the CPUSA, they highlighted the conditions facing Black women workers, placed the abolition of white supremacy at the center of the class struggle, and viewed the achievement of socialism as necessary for full social and economic equality. Their explorations of racialized domestic, agricultural, and industrial labor demonstrated the necessity of unionizing all workers, with a special consideration for those who bore the brunt of racism and capitalism—and their experiences as organizers taught them just how challenging this task is. Black Communist and Communist-adjacent women's analyses of the economic bases of racist segregation, discrimination, and violence also generated a compelling theorization of fascism as the way capitalists held on to power via white supremacy, militarism, male supremacy, and imperialism.[4] Engaged in international struggles against fascism and colonialism, they built new organizations and created an international movement for peace. Yet their work forging the CPUSA and envisioning an international socialism dedicated to Black liberation— and Black liberation with socialism at the center—has been largely excluded from popular visions of twentieth century radical left politics. This "intellectual McCarthyism," or erasure, suppression, and forgetting of the contributions of these theorist-organizers, distorts our understanding of organized radical politics. In restoring the likes of Grace Campbell, Williana Burroughs, Maude White Katz, Thyra Edwards, Ella Baker, Marvel Cooke, Louise Thompson Patterson, Esther Cooper Jackson, Thelma Dale, Claudia Jones, Vicki Garvin, Dorothy Hunton, Lorraine Hansberry, Eslanda Goode Robeson, Dorothy Burnham, Yvonne Gregory, Charlotta Bass, and Alice Childress to their rightful place in radical left political history, this volume seeks to expand our understanding of what radical left movements have been, and what they can be.

Scholars such as Dayo F. Gore, LaShawn Harris, Gerald Horne, Robin D. G. Kelly, Lydia Lindsey, Minkah Makalani, John H. McClendon III, Erik S. McDuffie, Mark Naison, Mark Solomon, and Mary Helen Washington have done crucial work bringing to life the activist milieu of Black women in and around the Communist Party in the first half of the twentieth century. Likewise, Horne, Gregg Andrews, Carole Boyce Davies, Keith Gilyard, Imani Perry, Barbara Ransby, and Sara Rzeszutek, among others, have written indispensable biographies of Shirley Graham Du Bois, Thyra Edwards, Claudia Jones, Louise Thompson Patterson, Lorraine Hansberry, Eslanda Goode Robeson, and Esther Cooper Jackson, respectively, excavating how these women shaped and were shaped by the CPUSA.[5] *Organize, Fight, Win: Black Communist Women's*

Political Writing builds on these scholarly contributions by compiling, for the first time, these women's political writing into a single volume. It aims to support and supplement the path-breaking research that has challenged liberal reductions of Black politics to the National Association for the Advancement of Colored People, other mainstream organizations, and the civil rights movement; left reductions of Communist politics to white male workers, industrial and trade unionism, and Cold War stereotypes of domination from Moscow; and feminist reductions of women's politics to white, bourgeois, idealist preoccupations with attitude, identity, and privilege. Black Communist women theorized capitalism's investment in dividing workers by race, sex, occupation, skill, and even region. They sought to build power through unity and unity through equality.

Organize, Fight, Win also aims to inspire contemporary activists and organizers committed to internationalist anticapitalist, anti-imperialist, antisexist, and Black liberation struggle. One of the most striking features of Black Communist women's political writing is the way they consistently link specific issues and local conditions to international, historical, and structural patterns. Their focus on local community and domestic politics is inextricable from their understanding of what was occurring in other parts of the world. What's happening in Ethiopia, Spain, China, and Korea matters for struggles in the US; struggles in the US—the "belly of the beast"—matter for the rest of the world. In short, in their writings, building socialism and defeating fascism are international projects. Moreover, Black Communist women's analyses emphasize the historical nature of conditions confronting Black working people, which continue from the relations, degradations, and terror of trans-Atlantic slavery. As such, resistance and fightback are neither new nor unique; they extend back through history and across the globe to the anticolonial struggles of people on the dark side of the color-line. Black Communist women were inspired by a range of struggles, from Harriet Tubman's defiance of slavery to the Russian working women's ignition of the February Revolution in 1917.

Seeing the Patterns, Fighting the System

A deep sense of the patterns of oppression and resistance guided Black Communist women's activism. Their analyses made connections and their organizing reinforced them. Specific issues—for example, the campaign around the "Scottsboro Boys," nine Black youth who were wrongfully convicted of raping two white women in a freight train boxcar in Alabama in 1931—served as a catalyst for bringing more people into organized struggle. Through its militant defense of these young men, the Communist Party established itself among Black people as a leader in the struggle against Jim Crow, lynching, and white supremacy. Attention to a specific crime exposed a general, structural injustice. The Scottsboro Boys crusade brought national and international attention to the white supremacist violence and economic deprivation of the Jim Crow South. It also brought more Black women and men into the party, building their capacities for ongoing political work. Black Communist women likewise highlighted similarities between the situation of Black people in the "Black Belt" of the southern United States and in Ethiopia when that country was invaded by Italy under Benito Mussolini in 1935. In each instance, defending the safety and freedom of Black people was necessary for the defeat of fascism—and neither the US government nor the League of Nations found Black lives worth defending.[6]

Black Communist women's political writing can teach contemporary organizers valuable practical and theoretical lessons. Practical lessons include going directly to the people to learn about their experiences, creating opportunities for people to speak and advocate for themselves, and building and using organizations to amplify power. The writings in this volume prioritize the creation of groups and associations as tactics of struggle. Operating within a horizon opened up by the Bolshevik Revolution, on the one hand, and the rise of New Negro militancy as a result of Black participation in World War I and the flourishing of the Harlem Renaissance, on the other hand, Black women in and around the CPUSA saw the party as an alternative to the Republicans and Democrats, the capitalist duopoly, both of which oversaw Jim Crow segregation, overlooked lynching and racist violence, and facilitated the rise of monopoly-finance capitalism.

Theoretical lessons recognize the centrality of capitalism to white supremacy and national oppression and the imperative of unity in the struggle for liberation at the same time that the special character of anti-Black oppression is acknowledged. Rather than emphasizing separate axes of difference or domination that they then attempt to bring together, Black Communist women in the first half of the twentieth century analyzed the ways capitalism incites race hatred and sex chauvinism in order to fragment workers and maintain class power—and how the participation of the working class in these forms of discrimination undermines worker unity. The power of the capitalist class was always and necessarily raced and sexed, as was clear to those trying to organize workers and fight for relief aid. Shedding light on Black women's experiences as racialized and sexed workers, Black Communist women's political writing avoids identity reductionism—the assumption that a particular confluence of identities objectively renders one the most oppressed, on the one hand, and inherently radical or revolutionary, on the other hand. Rather, their speeches and articles highlight the interests and experiences of Black women and men workers, analyze them in terms of patterns of exploitation and oppression, and propose strategies for organization and agitation based on these analyses. The goal was building collective power capable of winning the struggle for liberation.

About the Collection

Organize, Fight, Win compiles speeches, writings from Black and Communist publications, political reports, proclamations, and memoirs. We include writings focused on the period spanning roughly from 1919 to 1956, an era bookended by Black women such as Grace Campbell and Williana Burroughs joining the US Communist Party in its formative stages, and the mass exodus of Black and white Communists from the CPUSA in 1956 after Nikita Khrushchev, the general secretary of the Communist Party of the Soviet Union, gave his "Secret Speech" in February of that year condemning Joseph Stalin and revealing a number of atrocities committed under his leadership that were previously unknown to Communists. For women such as Vicki Garvin and Maude White Katz, these revelations were compounded by the rise of particularly vicious anticommunism in the form of McCarthyism, and the perception shared by a number of Black communists that the CPUSA was no longer at the forefront of the antiracist and anticolonial struggles.[7]

This collection is not exhaustive; it is a contribution, not a culmination. For reasons of space and accessibility of primary texts, not all of the influential Black women working in and around the Communist Party in the first half of the twentieth century are featured (for example, the volume does not include pieces from Audley Moore or Shirley Graham Du Bois). Not every significant piece of writing is included. Most noticeable is our omission of Claudia Jones's influential "An End to the Neglect of the Problems of the Negro Woman!" Given that this article has been widely anthologized and is easy to find online, we feature some of Jones's lesser-known pieces. We also chose not to include poetry and literary writing, though these are important sites of Black Communist women's theorizing and knowledge production. Furthermore, *Organize, Fight, Win* focuses on work *by* named authors rather than writing *about* the organizing and struggles of Black women that appeared in the Communist and Black presses during the period on which this volume focuses. We hope that future volumes will fill in these gaps.

The chapters in this collection are organized chronologically rather than thematically for two primary reasons. First, the chronology makes it easier to contextualize Black Communist women's writings in twentieth-century history, especially the first Red Scare, the Great Depression, the Spanish Civil War, World War II, the Korean conflict, and the Cold War/McCarthy era. Struggles for unions and against exploitation, for basic rights and against violent oppression, and for internationalism and against fascism persisted across these moments. Second, because their analyses use specific cases and campaigns to expose the broader patterns of economic and social subjugation, nearly every piece opens up multiple themes, revealing the interactive structure of capitalism and white supremacy. The campaign on behalf of Rosa Lee Ingram illustrates this point. In 1948, Ingram and two of her sons were sentenced to death for the self-defense killing of John Ed Stratford, a white landowner who had assaulted Ingram. For over a decade, Black women in and around the Communist Party fought a campaign in their defense, drawing attention to "legal lynchings," the lack of justice available to Black people in the Jim Crow South (especially when juries were all white), the denial of Black women's basic right to defend themselves from various forms of violence and assault, the deep inequity of the death penalty, the superexploitative conditions sharecroppers faced, and the failure of the United States to respect the basic human rights of its citizens. Internationalism was central to this case, with a letter-writing campaign bringing it to the attention of the United Nations.[8]

To organize the pieces thematically would unravel the patterns the analyses knit together. The power of the collected writing increases with the repetition and development of themes over time insofar as they elucidate the *persistence* and *durability* of state-sanctioned white supremacist violence against Black people, of a political economy reducing Black women to domestic and personal service, and, most important, of enduring collective courage and resistance.

Communists Against White Supremacy and Fascism

One of our most pressing concerns in collecting these texts is the continued need to combat anticommunism and the constraints of Cold War binaries on contemporary political thinking and action. Anticommunism in the United States has long been tied to antiforeignness and white supremacy. In the first Red Scare of 1919, fears of anarchism emanating from a slew of anarchist bombings and anxieties about Bolshevism intensified by rising labor militancy and the Seattle General Strike combined with the nationalism, anti-Germanism, and anti-immigrant sentiment of World War I. Unwarranted arrests and illegal search and seizures led to the deportation of hundreds of noncitizens. This antiradicalism also manifested in the related "Black Scare" in which Black soldiers returning home from the war and Black workers occupying "white" jobs in industrial centers encountered savage white mobs. During that violent Red Summer of 1919, Black people resisted white terror, fighting back against race rioters and lynchers. Instead of acknowledging justified Black outrage, white newspapers blamed the Bolsheviks and "outside agitators" for inciting revolt.[9]

Over subsequent decades, the US State Department consistently depicted Black internationalists as subversives, enemies of the state, and prone to foreign inspiration, presenting Black resistance not as the logical response to lynch law but as a manifestation of Black disloyalty.[10] The McCarthy era is widely known as a period in US history when a paranoid fear of communism was unleashed. During this second Red Scare, state repression damaged the lives of thousands of people. Communists were arrested, imprisoned, and deported. Anticommunism knit together and intensified anti-Blackness and antiforeignness and justified the violent repression of Black political leaders. Because anticolonialism, the peace movement, and desegregation were construed as dangerously un-American, leaders of the Black liberation movement came under particular attack. When communism—because of its mobilization for economic redistribution, racial equality, and Black-white labor solidarity—is presented as antithetical to legitimate political struggle, when it is rendered as totalitarian, antidemocratic, and criminal, anything that can be construed as even potentially communist, not least Black militancy, becomes akin to sedition.

Anticommunism is a key plank of white supremacy because it articulates democracy with liberal capitalism and white class rule while rendering Black struggle and its challenge to racial hierarchy as a threat to the "American way of life." These tropes are alive and well today: from the liberal and right-wing attacks on "wokeism" to the far-right scapegoating of "cultural Marxism" and "Critical Race Theory" as violent and dangerous movements undoing the fabric of US society.[11] Here anticommunism persists through the association of Black radical fightback with criminality, destruction, outside agitation, and subversion.

Another version of anticommunism manifests in the refusal to acknowledge that Black people were founding members of the CPUSA, visible leaders of the party, candidates for office, and respected theoreticians, as well as leaders in party-backed mass organizations. It is assumed that such acknowledgment would stain or tarnish the legacy of these Black leaders, since communism is understood as bad or illegitimate. At the same time, such erasure allows for critics to misconstrue the CPUSA as constitutively racist and antithetical to Black interests by obscuring the central contributions of Blacks organizers and theoreticians to its program and positions. Anticommunism also manifests in the overemphasis on cracks in, and disagreement with, party positions as indications of Black integrity, independence, and innovation *despite* the party. This interpretation construes the latter's platforms as necessarily incorrect, and responsible thinking—especially on issues of Black liberation—as only possible in opposition to them.

The scholarly or activist attempt to hold communism and the CPUSA at arm's length has sometimes been a well-meaning effort to protect people from false accusations inasmuch as Red Scare persecution menaced Communists and noncommunists alike. Yet avoiding communism to proffer a more "acceptable" progressive, democratic, left politics dishonestly severs communism from that very politics, presenting it as the opponent of democracy rather than as the opponent of fascism. Even worse, the separation of Black Communists from their own party work generates a mistaken view that all the communists are white and all the Blacks are liberal, and breaks the links between the Black liberation struggle in the United States and international movements against fascism, colonialism, and imperialism.

Indeed, antifascism—and its strong links to anti-imperialism, anticolonialism, and peace—was a key component of Black Communist women's political work. Williana Burroughs made Black women's knowledge of lynch mobs, their confinement to "the kitchens of the South under slave conditions," the contemptible treatment of Black soldiers, and the "studied degradation of Negro Gold Star mothers" a basis for bringing Black women into the movement against war and fascism.[12] Esther Cooper Jackson presented anti-Black discrimination as a direct threat to the survival of the nation as it played into the hands of the Axis powers (see chapter 17). Thyra Edwards and Louise Thompson Patterson were committed advocates for the antifascist struggle in Spain, visiting Republican Spain and writing and speaking about the war. Edwards declared, "No Force in the world today so threatens the position and security of women as does the rising force of fascism. Fascism degrades women."[13] Charlotta Bass, a newspaper editor and publisher and the Progressive Party's candidate for vice president in 1952, observed that Black Americans had fought to "destroy Hitlerism," but its doctrine of "race superiority and the oppression of other peoples" had taken root in the US and was justifying the oppression of people of color all over the world.[14] A war to make the world "safe for democracy" had in fact made "Africa safe for exploitation by . . . European powers."[15]

As demonstrated in the texts included in this volume, Black Communist women's theory of fascism deepened and extended the CPUSA's analysis of the oppression of Black people in the United States as national oppression. The "Black Belt" thesis held that Black people were an oppressed nation with a right to self-determination, a view Vladimir I. Lenin had already proposed to the Comintern in 1920. As theorized by Harry Haywood, Black people in the US met all the criteria for a nation: they had a common territory (the "Black Belt" in the US South, called "black" because of the dark soil), common economic life, common historical experience, and common culture. Black oppression in the US was thus a function of imperialism, as it was throughout the world. Objectively revolutionary, the Black struggle for liberation required the overthrow of imperialism and the establishment of socialism. Haywood argued that treating the Black struggle as a problem of racism downgraded its revolutionary nature, ignored its economic basis, and reduced a struggle for equality to a struggle against prejudice.[16] Under party chair Earl Browder, US Communists retreated from this position, adopting the view that Black people in the US preferred integration to self-determination.

Together with Thelma Dale and other comrades who excoriated such revisionism, Claudia Jones pointed out that it was the party's thesis on national oppression that put it at the vanguard of the fight against the "imperialist ideology" of white supremacy.[17] It was the basis for white workers' recognition that joining the fight against racism was in their self-interest insofar as "white chauvinism" was how the ruling class kept workers weak and divided. Defense of Black people's right of self-determination was likewise central to confronting "petty-bourgeois nationalism" and building proletarian internationalism.

To the core premise of Black oppression as national oppression, Jones added a theorization of the impact of growing reaction on the material conditions of women following the end of World War II. She noted the "tremendous ideological campaign" put forward by Wall Street imperialism to influence popular perceptions of women.[18] With its "Hitlerite" slogan that "a woman's place is in the home," this campaign cloaked social and economic inequalities, obscuring how the postwar push of women out of industry and into the domestic sphere was undermining gains made during the war. Working-class women were being relegated to low-paying clerical, sales, and service work. The first to be fired from industry jobs, Black women were the most heavily impacted by the reactionary intensification of a sexual division of labor. Cuts in social services, particularly of the childcare centers available for wage-earning mothers during the war, accompanied the attack on women, rendering it an attack on the whole working class. Jones argued that employers were trying to create a "sex antagonism," to divide men and women workers as part of a large-scale offensive against wages.[19] Men were encouraged to support the return of women to the kitchen because that would free up more jobs for men. Through this characteristically fascist offensive, the ruling class also attacked women's social participation in the peace movement, not to mention their engagement in economic struggle. The more confined women are to the household, the less free they are to participate in politics.

Jones's treatment of "sex antagonism" as fomented by bosses in an effectively fascist drive to divide working-class women and men troubles readings of Black Communist women as primarily feminists. The Black women organizing in and around the Communist Party in the first half of the twentieth century did not use the term "feminist" to name their politics. They were deeply engaged in what the socialist tradition had designated the "woman question," sharing the socialist view that "feminism" was the politics of bourgeois, typically white, women. Those in the party pushed the CPUSA to undertake special efforts to recruit Black women and develop them as party leaders. Louise Thompson Patterson reminded her comrades that welcoming Black women into the party required that party members transform their personal as well as their political lives: they needed to challenge social oppression by not only inviting Black women to dances and events but also dancing with them, making sure they weren't wallflowers (see chapter 13).

Black Communist and Communist-adjacent women also focused on Black women's working conditions, whether within or blocked from industry; in unregulated domestic day labor; as sharecroppers in the slave-like, "semi-feudal" conditions of the US South; or as primary providers for their own families, concerned with housing, rents, and a sufficient supply of healthy food. Black working-class women's social and economic position primed them for organizing; they were an intensely exploited and intensely militant segment of the labor force ready to challenge fascism, imperialism, war, and economic exploitation alike. Black Communist women organizers also appealed to Black women's knowledge of and experience with violence, whether of lynch mobs, police, or the imperialist state. They organized Black mothers to speak out against the attacks on their sons and the disrespect leveled at their husbands. Particularly as attacks on Communist leaders intensified during the Red Scare, some Black Communist women organized specifically in defense of their husbands and comrades, using this defense as a tactic of movement building. The vocabulary associated with contemporary feminism—"gender," "standpoint epistemology," or "intersectionality"—did not figure into, and does not map neatly onto, their analyses. Nor did an emphasis on a division between men and women. The goal was organizing the Black working class in order to liberate Black people and the whole working class; Black women, as a key sector of the working class, were essential to this aim. Black Communist women's attention to concrete material conditions drives an analysis that demonstrates—in theory and practice—that "there can never be real equality for all women until Negro women are also given equality," as Thelma Dale argued in 1947.[20]

Claiming radical left Black women for feminism does important work toward dismantling myths of a hegemonic white bourgeois feminism and complicating understandings of Black women's activism. It also opens up to a better, internationalist feminism that rejects its capitalist and imperialist constraints. At the same time, describing the Black Communist women's organizing up through the 1950s as "feminism" risks a certain anachronism as it sweeps aside the raced and classed dimensions of their interactions with non-Black women. For example, in "The Bronx Slave Market," Ella Baker and Marvel Cooke present lower-middle- and working-class white and Jewish women as exploiters trying to get domestic help as cheaply as they can. Depression-era conditions forced Black women who had previously held better-paid jobs in industry or in the homes of the wealthy to accept cleaning jobs in lower-class white houses for below-subsistence wages as white housewives insisted on paying them less and less (a point Louise Thompson Patterson and Esther Cooper Jackson would also go on to make). That Black women seeking housework were sometimes pushed into sex work amplified the continuity with slavery. For Baker and Cooke, the "real significance of the Bronx slave market" is its implications: "the 'market' is but a miniature mirror of our economic battle front."[21] Their materialist analysis focuses not on the singularity of the experience of Black women looking for work but rather uses a presentation of this experience to bring out the power differential between employers and job seekers. Baker and Cooke's recommendation is neither to convince the white women to recognize ties of sisterhood or pervasive gender stereotypes nor to criminalize sex work. Their solution is to organize the domestic workers so that they can build the collective power necessary for fixing wages and abolishing the "existing evils in day labor." This organizing task requires both combatting domestic workers' continued attachment to the "American illusion" that determination is all it takes to get ahead and remedying organized labor's all too limited concept of exploitation.

As mentioned above, in "Toward a Brighter Dawn," published less than six months after "The Bronx Slave Market," Louise Thompson Patterson offers her theory of "triple exploitation." Black women are exploited "as workers, as women, and as Negroes."[22] Combatting this exploitation demands organization and unity, the "keynote" of a broader program addressing women passed by the National Negro Congress at its assembly in Chicago in February 1936. The program emphasized unionizing domestic workers, creating housewives' leagues, and organizing professional women. These would join together "to work for adequate social legislation, for better relief, and against war and fascism."

Claudia Jones echoes and amplifies Thompson when she calls on Communist men to combat male supremacy. "Failure to recognize the special social disabilities of women under capitalism is one of the chief manifestations of male supremacy," Jones writes. "These special forms of oppression particularly affect the working women, the farm women, and the triply oppressed Negro women; but in varying degrees, they help to determine the inferior status of women in all classes of society."[23] In contrast to those feminists who foreground divisions between women and men, and for whom race and gender tend to outweigh class, Black Communist women's attention to Black women's triple exploitation and oppression was situated within analyses of capitalism and white supremacy. Overturning them depended on liberating Black women.

Anticommunism did not come to an end with the dissolution of the Soviet Union in 1991. It continues to animate fascist mobilization around the world, as is apparent in Ukraine, Hungary, Poland, and Brazil. It is also apparent in the assault on the US Capitol on January 6, 2021. Attention to the political writing of Black Communist women helps unravel anticommunist and Cold War assumptions and the stunted political imaginary that accompanies them. When one begins from the writings of Black Communist women, one sees a Communist Party being created at the branch and neighborhood level, through local organizing that recognizes itself as part of an international struggle. The party is perpetually responding and changing, assessing its failures and pushing itself to be better. The caricature of an all-powerful political monolith falls away before the appreciation of a vibrant organizational ecosystem, with new groups and organizations and conferences and campaigns created to bring ever more people into the struggle. The Black Communist women of the early to mid-twentieth century have a lot to teach the contemporary radical left about concrete, action-oriented, materialist analysis—and about organizing to fight, build, and win.

SECTION I

Struggle in the Early Years

The first section features pieces from two Black women, Grace Campbell and Williana Burroughs, who were instrumental in building communism in the United States. Campbell was a leader and cofounder of the African Blood Brotherhood (ABB), one of the few Black Socialists organizing in Harlem in the wake of the riotous Red Summer of 1919. Together with ABB cofounder Cyril Briggs; Richard B. Moore, who at different times belonged to the Universal Negro Improvement Association, the Socialist Party, and the Communist Party USA (CPUSA); radical New Negro poet Claude McKay; and Otto Huiswoud, "the first black charter member of the Party," Campbell formed the West Side Harlem Branch of the Workers Party in 1922.[1] Throughout the first Red Scare of the 1920s, Campbell was heavily monitored by the state. One government informant reported that at a political forum in Harlem Campbell "devoted about twenty minutes to condemning all other forms of government but the Soviet, which she claims is the only hope of the workingman."[2] Later in the decade, Campbell helped lead the Harlem Tenants League (HTL). The group's tactics included establishing tenants' committees that would pressure landlords to make repairs and lower rents and organizing "protest marches, rent strikes, and boycotts to galvanize the community."[3]

Like Campbell, Burroughs was involved in the HTL. Joining the CPUSA in 1926, she was a delegate to the Comintern's Sixth Congress in 1928.[4] Burroughs brought her two children with her to the USSR and subsequently enrolled them in a boarding school near Leningrad; the children remained there for fifteen years.[5] Burroughs continued to do political work in Harlem, running as the Communist candidate for New York comptroller and then lieutenant governor, playing a leading role in the League of Struggle for Negro Rights (LSNR), and organizing around housing and the Scottsboro case. She returned to the Soviet Union in 1935 and worked for Radio Moscow.

Two of the articles by Campbell describe day courts as sites of inequality and injustice, particularly for Black women facing charges of prostitution. The deck is stacked against women in general as police and informants work together to railroad this vulnerable class of women. The law itself humiliates the woman charged with prostitution while ignoring her "willing partner," who is not accused of any crime. Black women face the additional degradation of being sentenced to the workhouse. Unlike white women, Black women are rarely granted probation. Campbell analyzes this fact institutionally: there are fewer Black probation officers and social workers assigned to the Women's Court, and the segregated private institutions for women and girls on probation accept white women while barring Black women.

This section also includes Burroughs's reports on organizing Black workers, both in unions and in the party. She attends to the concrete material challenges facing organizers as well as to the impact of those challenges on morale. How is work to be coordinated, funded, and directed? What are the specific tasks to be undertaken? How will comrades be prepared and how will they be held accountable? Burroughs presents the organization of Black women workers—in Africa, in the colonies, in the United States—as an indispensable component of the organization of all Black workers. She challenges the party to connect its platform to the concerns of Black women workers and become a channel for their militancy and dissatisfaction. She argues that the party—including white comrades—needs to concentrate its efforts on organizing the masses of Black workers, recognizing that it will take a special effort to reach them: "White comrades must be active in Negro work just as Negro comrades should take place in general party work."[6]

1

Two Articles on the Women's Day Court
Grace Campbell

"Women Offenders and the Day Court"

New York Age, April 18, 1925, p. 3

(Editor's note: Miss Campbell is court attendant at the Court of General Sessions, N.Y. For seven years she was parole officer with the Municipal Parole Commission of New York. A few years ago she had under her supervision the Empire Friendly Shelter of New York which housed thousands of wayward colored girls, and sent most of the re-[text missing] For Lack of funds the Shelter closed.)[1]

The 9th District Magistrates Court, commonly known to the city of New York as The Jefferson Market Court, or, The Women's Day Court, located at 6th Avenue and 10th Street, is that branch of the Magistrates Court used exclusively for the prosecution of women, including girls who have barely reached their sixteenth year who are accused of prostitution soliciting and kindred offences in Manhattan.

Through this court, day after day throughout the year pass hundreds of women defendants, most of them young, many of them attractive and intelligent. In appearance these women do not differ materially, if at all, from the average women of the rank and file whom one passes on the streets of New York.

For many a girl this court is a Gethsemane. When arraigned for final disposition some faint, some scream and fall and are carried out by court attendants; others suffer in silence and still others hear their fate stoically or even with callous indifference.

The accused woman is brought before the court upon the complaint of a plain clothes officer of the special service squad whose work it is to hunt down women offenders. His statement against the woman defendant is invariably corroborated by his brother officer. The woman rarely has a witness. Her word, if ventured at all, is rarely corroborated save by chance by a woman co-defendant who, like herself stands accused. Thus the odds are against the woman.

The officers frequently do not accuse the defendant of the commission of the act of prostitution, but rather of the suggestion of the act to them or some other male person. The testimony in the various cases is much the same, and often bears a rubber stamp likeness. In numerous cases an informant, not an officer, is used for the purpose of obtaining evidence. Such informant is known in the language of the street as a stool pigeon. The informant, who is said to enter a flat, doorway, basement or a taxi-cab as the case may be, with the woman defendant, is not brought into court. Hence he may not be questioned by the woman's attorney, if she has one. His name is mentioned in the complaint, and an address given, but court investigators rarely seek to locate him, his status being understood. The writer has on some occasions, however, sought to locate such informants but with poor success. At times she has found the address incorrect, and on other occasions found the name fictitious, or no such person known on the premises. A few informants or stool pigeons are publicly known characters and abhorred, but they like others, are conspicuous by their absence at court at the time of the woman's trial.

In cases of actual prostitution the offence against the law is made possible only through participation of men, but our man-made law does not consider the man who is the actual partner in the offence with the woman as her accomplice, although the violation of the law could not be accomplished without the willing consent of the man. The woman alone is accountable, and she alone bears the humiliation and punishment.

(One remedy suggested by Miss Campbell is an amendment to the law making men co-defendants in prostitution cases equally guilty with the women, and that stool-pigeons employed for the purpose of trapping women be brought to face the accused women as a matter of common justice.)

(To be continued next week with "The Colored Girl in Court.")

"Tragedy of the Colored Girl in Court, Suffers as the Girl of No Other Race by Lack of Interest of Her Own People"

New York Age, April 25, 1925, p. 3

(Court Attendant at the Court of General Sessions, N.Y.)
For 7 years Parole Officer with the Municipal Parole Commission.

The number of colored women and girls convicted of prostitution, Violation of the Tenement House Law, etc., is relatively larger than white; but when it is considered that the colored woman, and especially young colored girls, are the least protected group, this can be understood.

There are fewer protective homes for them before they fall. No woman's hotel or public lodging places under social supervision where the lone girl or woman may live at a moderate rate.

The Weight of Economic Pressure

The average colored woman's wage is less than that of the white: there is but small or no margin to cover periods of unemployment or sickness. While the economic problem cannot be looked upon as the sole factor in the question of prostitution among colored girls, or indeed any girls, yet it must be faced as a prime factor in their fall. Especially is this true when the standard and cost of living is understood and duly considered.

Moreover, even the most law abiding citizen who looks closely into the matter of arrests among colored women must admit that many are unwarranted.

In the course of investigations the investigator frequently will see doors of private apartments marred and broken and is told by other tenants that these marks were the results of arresting officers entering private homes by force and without a warrant.

When the accused colored woman or girl is brought into court, if convicted as she generally is, her chances of escape from a workhouse sentence is less than that of the white offender for as stated in chapter 8, in *A Study of Women Delinquents*, by Mable R. Fernald, Mary S. Hayes and Amelia Dawley, referring to the very high percentage of colored women in the workhouse, it is said.[2] The probation group has a small percentage of colored because of meager facilities for supervising colored girls on probation. Only the most promising colored girls are considered for probation instead of an institutional sentence because of the difficulty of looking after them with an inadequate staff of probation officers.

Is this another way of stating that white probation officers do not care to give close probationary care to colored girls and women? or, Do they in some way feel themselves unfit to cope with the task? If this be true, there should certainly be colored probation officers of the Women's Court, and experienced colored social workers placed there by colored people to co-operate with the court in the care of colored girls and women.

White women offenders are not infrequently given probation even when second offenders, and if young or particularly unfortunate, even though committed, are oftimes sentenced to private institutions which refuse colored girls—as they might have to occupy the same dormitories, or eat at the same table.

If the girl is white, and Catholic, she may be sent to the House of the Good Shepherd.

If Protestant, to some private institution, but if colored and committed however promising her case, she is sent to the workhouse.

The practice of giving short sentences in the workhouse to young colored girls is undoubtedly the cause of the high percentage of colored women in that institution.

The degradation of putting unfortunate young colored women in the workhouse with hardened offenders can hardly be over-estimated. The loss of self-respect and vice learned by them are appalling.

Even in the workhouse segregation is rife, and that institution known as Grey Court, which is a woman's farm colony, is used for white women only, while the colored women are kept in the old fashioned workhouse prison.

In the words of many colored women inmates, strict segregation seems the idea of the present Commissioner of Correction.

2

Negro Work Has Not Been Entirely Successful
Williana Burroughs

July 3, 1928[1]

A   Negro Work has not been entirely successful because:

I   We had so few workers.

These workers, if they were white comrades had to learn about the problems and if they were colored, were new to revolutionary methods and organization.

II   We could not find concrete tasks. We did not know where to take hold in this very complex situation. We have been groping for points of contact with the masses in the rural South and in the industrial centres of the country.

Today, however, we see many concrete tasks. The fact can be stressed again that the Negro is such an integral part of American life that almost every struggle of the workers has its Negro side. At the present time each and every campaign carried on by party has a vital interest for the Negro masses.

For Example:

1   Women's Work (a vast field for organization as colored women are nearly all gainfully employed.)

2   Miner's Relief (Negro miner is an important factor in this basic industry throughout the country.)

3   Foreign-Born (Thousands of Negroes from West Indies, South America, Cape Verde Islands, Africa.)

4   Unemployment (Negro is last to be taken on and first to be fired.)

5 Organize unorganized (Almost virgin field. Negroes north and
   south belong to unskilled and semi-skilled. Some small unionization in North, almost none in South with its new industrialism and tenant farmer, share cropper, agrarian problems. –
   Concrete tasks – Laundry workers, miners in West Virginia,
   etc., Textile workers in New Bedford, Pullman Porters.)
6 Anti-Imperialism (Thousands of Negroes from Haiti, Cuba,
   British possessions, Virgin Islands and Puerto Rico have felt the
   iron heel of British or American Imperialism.)
7 Youth Work (Hampton, Fiske and Howard all have had recent
   student revolts. A ripe field. We have a comrade who knows the
   field situation.)
8 I.L.D. (Can make a drive for members on basis of treatment
   meted out to a militant Negro furrier.)
9 W.I.R. (Method of doling out relief to Negro Sufferers in the
   Mississippi flood raises the question of workers' relief among
   Negroes.)

III Lack of co-ordination – Work has suffered from the fact that no
systematic program or information is regularly sent out from Negro
Offices. – Reasons for this are very plain.
   10 Negro Dept. is most undermanned of any party Dept.
   11 Lack of mechanical equipment, and office help.
   12 Vagueness of organization. The organization of Negro Dept. is
       not clear. That the comrade at the head of A.N.L.C. is head of
       Negro work is not definitely understood.

IV Loose connection between leading party committees and D.N.C.
Much time and energy has been wasted by D.N.C. trying to present
decisions to responsible committees. There seems to be no set time
when demands can be presented. This defect in organization is so glaring and its effects so paralyzing that the failure to remedy it has made me
wonder if the party actually wants to do the difficult job of Negro work.
V Failure to get Negro members for party. – There seems to have
been a lack of ability or effort to draw Negroes to the party. Our tasks are
out of all proportion to our small forces. An analysis of the situation is
needed, in order to remedy this fatal weakness in our work.
VI Lack of money – The work in this district suffers from having no
definite income. We can not plan ahead. We have no money except

specific sums issued on request for a particular purpose. We were compelled at one time to do without a local organizer for lack of money. We are working without a place for the same reason. Our forum and classes run because they are self-supporting. We need advice on ways and means of raising regularly sufficient funds.

VII Lack of publicity – We do not get and keep our program and point of view before the masses. From the favorable response to our miners' relief campaign I am convinced that the people are ready for message. We need –

13 Literature

14 News bureau — sending releases to all papers.

15 Speakers bureau — To route speakers to clubs, lyceums, forums, etc.

16 Articles by our comrades in Negro periodicals.

The inability to state our point of view on race and economic questions on peonage, share cropping, tenant farming, on new industrialism etc. is most deplorable. The bosses are paying teachers, ministers, lecturers, organizations and Negro press to issue poisonous propaganda which does get a constant hearing.

B Lack of a centre has kept back the work. Another major defect. Insofar as an unhealthy condition exists in our work it is due entirely in my opinion to the smallness of our Negro party membership. This makes

17 Our work appear too difficult and breeds discouragement.

18 It difficult to allot tasks.

19 It difficult to hold Negro comrades responsible.

20 For tendency to relax party discipline in case of Negro comrades.

There are three signs of poor condition of work

21 A disposition to keep active comrades from conferences on Negro work. I and other active comrades were called to none of recent conferences with O.E.C. members on Negro work. This is to be combatted, as in this complex situation we especially need clarity. Small unofficial talks are a criminal waste of time.

22 Smoldering dissatisfaction with conditions as they affect Negro work, which has resulted in dividing the group into cliques. Grievances should be taken seriously, presented, analyzed and threshed out in full committee. With a majority opinion

arrived at as to the best way to remedy matters, there would be no opportunity to range comrades on different sides and disaffect new members, as has been done.

23 A determination to keep white comrades from important places or prominence in Negro work is a wrong attitude. We need the help of white comrades for many reasons. White comrades must be active in Negro work just as Negro comrades should take part in general party work.

C To cure unhealthfulness and insure success of our future work suggest

I Immediate drive for Negro party members – using medium of street meetings. Utilizing:

1 Party political campaign.
2 Classes and Forums.
3 All party campaigns mentioned above.
4 Left wing org., I.L.D., W.I.R. etc. to be used for party.
a- Set new members to work. Have a program and definite tasks assigned.
b- Hold comrades accountable for tasks.
c- Show newcomers a united fighting front. No airing of differences to them as in past.

II Colored and white comrades both in Negro work.

III Perfect and tighten our organization of Negro Dept.

IV Negroes on leading committees, local and national.

V Require regular detailed reports from responsible department heads.

VI Put and keep our program and position before Negro masses by Publicity

1 News Bureau
2 Speakers Bureau
3 Bulletins
4 Literature
5 Newspaper

VII Negro Help wherever possible in party and sympathetic org. offices. The F.O.R. has Negro help in both offices. – Has large Negro liberal following.

VIII Conference (Party) on Negro work.

a- Stake out minimum program.
b- Budget for Negro work.
c- Organization.

    d- Publicity.

    e- Lay plans for industrial Conference (Working toward reorgani-
       zation of A.N.L.C.)

IX Labor Centre – to house all Negro work.

X The minimum number of full time workers to make this program a success.

I feel sure with this machinery working to its full capacity we can do the necessary work instead of simply scratching the surface as we are doing now.

3

How Shall the Negro Woman Vote?

Grace Campbell (writing as Grace Lamb)

Chicago, Ill., *Daily Worker*, October 29, 1928, p. 5

But One Party Favors Racial Equality

Colored women, like other voters during the present campaign, are being swamped with campaign literature and letters from the capitalist parties requesting votes for their candidates. It must therefore be borne in mind by colored women voters, that the function of the vote is to give opportunity to a citizen to register his or her opinion as to which parties will best protect his interests and those of his respective group.

The democratic and republican parties have been in power through Negro votes since the close of the Civil War. Negroes have voted for both parties during this long period. Out of democratic and republican administrations alike, have come Jim Crowism, mobbing, segregation, lynching, southern disfranchisement, and general terrorism; lack of opportunity of making a living and poor educational facilities. At the same time a stamp of inferiority has been placed on all Negro people. This is the past record of the capitalist parties. In the present campaign they promise nothing better.

Only the Workers (Communist) Party stands for full social and racial equality, equal opportunity to earn a living, fair and square treatment before the courts of law, and general racial emancipation. A vote, therefore, for the Workers (Communist) Party, its platform and its candidates, is the only vote which can serve the interests of the Negro woman voter as a worker, and which expresses her struggle to gain for her posterity an equal opportunity for life, liberty, and normal human development.

4

Trade Union Work Report

Williana Burroughs

September 17, 1929[1]

The net result of our trade union work among Negroes has not been large and in some cases we have suffered a distinct loss. This has been due to insufficient Party support, lack of direction, no clear objective, wrong policy, inadequate forces, poor organization.

In 1926 we had between 20 and 50 members men and women in the Furriers Union. The A.N.L.C. began to make this group the base of its organization work. There were also several hundred members in the Dressmakers Union. These members were active, attended meetings, though these were separate, because of language difficulties it was claimed. Both these unions have lost all of the Negro members when the break with the rights came, due to the inability or failure of the Left wing unions to give them jobs. Two members remain in the Furriers Union and a handful in the Dressmakers Union. The Negro members complain of segregation, language barrier, lack of support by Union in grievances, not generally given active position in union.

In the two Left wing unions mentioned and in the Left wing Miners' Union there is complaint of lack of support on the part of Communist elements. There is general complaint of Right opportunist tendency in these unions. A disposition to make deals with bosses, and support and pushing to prominence other than Communist elements in the organization.

The failure on the part of the Lefts to get Negroes jobs in shops where they do control explains in large measure the loss of membership. A

Negro's idea of a union is a force which can procure a job for him and protect him in it. The Rights give jobs, pay dues, etc. for their members. Many Negroes are working in unorganized shops. This matter of a job is very vital to the Negro as he has no reserve and no friends in business to refer to specific cases. The two Negro members of the Furriers Union are Party members. Only after Party pressure were they put on the Executive. They are not called to small fraction meetings. The business of the Executive is carried on in Yiddish and they are only asked to vote. One of the members is referred to as an organizer, but he is not paid, has no job either. There are 30 people on the payroll of the Union. In last winter's strike he was seriously injured on the picket line and has been refused medical aid by Union.

The one active member of the Dressmakers' Union has served always on the picket line during strikes. She is well qualified to be an organizer.

In my opinion in every Left wing Union there should be a Negro organizer. Also besides the T.U.E.L. functionary in the N.O. there should be a Negro in every T.U.E.L. local.

The Negro T.U.E.L. organizer should work in closest cooperation with the A.N.L.C. This work of organizing the Negro unorganized should be the joint work of the two groups.

The Negro and strikes. Of all workers in America the Negroes have the largest percentage of constant unemployment. This makes a vast reserve labour army, always available in strikes. They were used to break the steel strike, the dock strike in New York, the coal strike in Pennsylvania, the paper box strike and many others.

Our Left wing unions have not succeeded in rousing the Negro masses so that they would refuse to so serve during an industrial crisis. They have neglected to draw them into active duty on strike committees. At the mass meetings the Negro worker is conspicuously absent from the halls during strikes. During the recent strikes in New York a strike committee of union members was hastily formed. It did not function because of poor coordination. Though we have had several conferences on organizing we have worked out no definite plan.

Since last report have made contacts and done some work in Teachers' Union, and E.W.I., the Seamen's Union, Baltimore local, Window Cleaners', Textile Union in South Women's Days Workers' Union, Longshoreman's Union, and with laundry workers.

Among this last mentioned group there are great possibilities, as all over the country there are a great proportion of Negro workers in laundry mostly women. Incidentally would like to mention that Chinese workers in California were able to persuade coloured women not to serve as scabs during a recent strike.

The women in the laundries work under frightful conditions for long hours, with overtime and speed-up for very low pay. They are ripe for organization. Formation of shop committees was going on and an effort made to get a good representation at the Cleveland Convention.

There is still much disagreement however as to the methods of organization to be employed by the members of the fraction.

The Left wing of the Teachers' Union functions through a Progressive Club. Members of this group with aid from the Union were instrumental in getting 20 Negro teachers into Union last year. Plans are being made now by the Left group to call an Eastern Conference at Xmas time. One of our main tasks is to get Negro teachers to this Conference.

In order to successfully organize the exploited Negro workers we must crush whatever white chauvinism that appears in the Left wing movement. We must have a good organizational structure for work. Shop and mill committee industrial organizers in each unit of Party— T.U.E.L. representation on district and section committees, fractions that function in unions.

Negro representation in fraction. Negroes in local T.U.E.L., A.N.L.C. coordinating their work, working in closest harmony. Campaign by T.U.E.L. and A.N.L.C. in press and from platform to combat pessimism on part of Negro worker towards union. Protection by union of Negro worker in job. It is only by hard honest intelligent work we can organize this reserve body of labour which is deliberately kept by the bosses as a weapon against the workers.

Fraternally submitted,
    Adams.
W.S. Burroughs Teachers' Union.

5

Three Reports on Negro Women Workers
Williana Burroughs

"Work Among Negro Women," June 17, 1930[1]

We have made some attempt to work among Negro women, but with small success, due mainly to lack of forces. It is imperative that the work be started energetically as soon as possible. These workers are increasingly important in industry, because the rationalization schemes of the bosses substitute cheaper and cheaper labour, because of the growing militancy of Negro women, and because now there is a deliberate attempt by the social reformists to draw these thousands of unorganized workers into their boss controlled unions. Our industrial work must have definite plans for the organization of these grossly exploited workers. We must formulate demands in our propaganda, as to hours, conditions, wages for Negro women.

Up till now we have developed no machinery for the winning of the domestic workers. Conditions in domestic work are changing, to the disadvantage of the worker. Our work of organization must be extended to include the domestic worker and day's worker.

The bulk of Negro women are still in the South where a large number work on the land. We have not entered this field at all. Our programme should hold plans to get our message to these widely separated workers, through our literature. A magazine for the rural South dealing with the problems of woman land labour, such as child labour, illiteracy, school, home, peonage, relief would be one means. The "Liberator" should have a woman's page. The "Working Woman" should begin to deal with the problem of the woman peasant.

The use of the cooperatives as an organizing factor especially in the rural districts should be considered at this time.

The Southern Negro masses are used to schools started by individuals and societies. This method of penetration is worth consideration.

Many of these women workers are members of mass organizations. We should make contacts with these groups through lectures and moving pictures of Soviet Russia, through individual contacts within, and united front, drawing them into our campaigns, and into our federation.

The Negro masses of the South are the main sufferers from natural disasters, such as floods, hurricanes, etc. The WIR must be developed among the Negro masses as a relief organization of the workers in sharp opposition to the Jim Crow Red Cross of the bosses.

The work of the Anti-Imperialist League must be extended to the Negro women among whom are a large number of foreigners from the Caribbean, themselves sufferers from imperialism. These workers must be drawn into the joint struggle of the colonial masses and of American workers against imperialism.

Every party campaign must have its appeal to Negro women workers emphasized. We must quickly draw into the work the new elements and must train cadres. The Party must carry on constant agitation against the discrimination in industry practices towards the Negro woman. Never omit slogans for support of this most exploited section. They must be drawn into every struggle and must have Party support in all their struggles.

Proposals:

1 Build Party apparatus for Negro women.
2 Build TUUL apparatus for same.
3 Tour of country by Negro women comrades.
4 Organize in Left wing unions where large numbers of women.
5 Concentrate on railroad yards, laundries, tobacco and canning factories, stock yards.
6 Negro women on strike committees.
7 Make programme of work among domestic workers and day workers.
8 Make contacts in workers' mass organizations.
9 Make contacts in rural South.
10 Draw women into ILU-Anti-Imperialist League, WIR.
11 Speed up training of cadres.

12 Plan programme for Tenants' League, strengthen League, strengthen factions.

13 Campaign against religion.

14 Campaign against reformists.

"Woman and Child Labor in the Colonies," July 30, 1930

Through slavery the Negro group has been scattered from Africa in the Eastern hemisphere to both continents and the islands of the Caribbean in the Western hemisphere. In capitalist countries this proletarian mass is at the bottom of the economic scale. In the colonies they are subjected to such ruthless exploitation as baffles description. Imperialistic greed pays such miserable wages to Negro men that women and children also are forced to work.

Well over 90% of Negro women are wage earners. Of these the largest number work in the fields. Fruit plantations in Colombia and Honduras, Jamaica, sugar plantations in Guadeloupe and Cuba, cocoa and coffee estates in Portuguese Africa, Belgian and French Congo, farms of South Africa, cotton and tobacco fields in the U.S. all utilize the low paid labour of Negro women. From sun up to sun down they toil, sometimes for no wages at all, as in French West Africa, in the other colonies for less than a shilling a day and in the US for 10¢ an hour.

Domestic workers are the next largest category among coloured women. As general houseworkers they slave 14 and 16 hours a day for $10–12 a week in America, for $3–8 a month in the Southern states and the West Indies and for less than 25¢ a day in all parts of Africa. Industry—In the US thousands of Negro women work in the tobacco, canning, box, rag, textile and clothing factories and laundries. In South America and the West Indies a heavy work is done by women such as coaling steamers and breaking stones. They work also in the canning factories. Though portions of Africa are being rapidly industrialized there are few enterprises that employ women. They have been used as porters in caravans and as workers in the mines, clothing and canning factories. Hours of work are from 9–12. There are instances of a 14–16 hour working day. There is frequent night work even in dangerous trades as glass, of 8–12 hours. Wages vary from $4 to 12 a week in America, to 50¢ a day in the West Indies and less than 25¢ a day in Africa.

Working conditions for coloured women are extremely bad. Employers in America make little provision for the health, comfort or decency of their workers. In communities where there is protective legislation it is often violated in the case of these workers. Many sections have no legislation. Safeguards for women workers are lacking in the West Indies. All the African colonies have a large body of labour regulations. That part which protects the worker remains a dead letter for the most part. Throughout the colonies the other part which penalizes the labourer for any infraction and regulations is rigidly enforced. Workers must carry a card which identifies them. They are beaten and flogged for petty offenses. They often work under the lash of the over-seer who bullies them. They are victimized and frequently defrauded of their money. Any attempt to escape from these intolerable conditions is punished by arrest, followed by the jail or fine. In prison they are chained in some places or have halters put round their necks. In Africa the practice of taking gangs of labourers from one section of the country to another is common.

Recruiting agents scour the country for workers, whom they obtain by fraud or force if necessary. When whole families are so conscripted the women and children must work often without wages. Deliberate mutilation and murder of workers has become an established custom in Africa.

Forced labour—All labour in Africa is brutal slave labour. In all the colonies, by depriving him of land by hut tax; by law of compulsory public work (which however, is used by private individuals and industries) through contacts which bind him for two and three years, the native is compelled to work for the invader. Women are forced to work through conscriptions of families or a contract which includes the whole group or by the imposition of a poll tax.

Though it has never been so characterized, nevertheless America has forms of forced labour also. Through the arrest of unemployed workers under vagrancy laws, through arrest for debt and other minor offense the Southern ruling class keeps a continual supply of labour. These unfortunate workers become the peons of contractors who hold them indefinitely on farms and plantations by withholding their wages. Sharecroppers are the victims of this form of peonage also because of their indebtedness to their landlords. Workers who must serve out a sentence in the chain gang, perform public work on road or rock-pile.

Expropriation of land—Imperialists throughout Africa have stolen the major portion of the land from the natives and reduced millions to the position of a landless proletariat. They have seized for themselves the best land (fertile and grazing) leaving the Negro insufficient and barren land on which to support himself and family. These native locations and reserves are subject to constant encroachment on part of the Europeans. The land thus alienated, has been given to settlers to companies for enterprises and large portions held by crown or government.

Living conditions — An inquiry into the housing of labourers on African farms reveals much overcrowding and lack of sanitation. The quarters where natives live at the enterprises and in urban centres are a disgraceful collection of hovels fitly called slums. Women workers with difficulty maintain a decent standard of living under these conditions. Employers have not made efforts to cope with the situation arising from their practice of handling of labour in masses. Conditions are equally bad for the Negro proletariat in America, who are forced to live in segregated, discarded, unsanitary houses in undesirable sections in every town.

Death rate—The Negro death rate all over the world is much higher than that of white neighbouring group. This is true also of infant mortality. The slums of Africa and America are breeding death traps for Negro workers. War, murder, harsh labour and diseases of civilization have reduced the population of Africa by tens of millions.

Women and children have died like flies on porterage trails, in rubber hunts and other tasks set by greed of whites. Africa has been made a shamble by the cupidity of the imperialists.

Child Labour—Among this low paid and unprotected group child labour is widespread. There is a good deal of child labour in the Congo in the industries and on the plantations. They work as porters, fuel cutters and rickshaw boys. In the West Indies they work on plantations, on dock and at breaking stones. In America hundreds work in the fields and some in bag and canning factories. For all this they are paid a few cents a day.

Education—A deliberate policy of neglect has been pursued by the exploiters in the education of Negro workers. Education in the colonies has been left to the missionaries who have placed the emphasis on religious instruction. The rate of illiteracy is high, only 43% of native population are in school in South Africa. In East Africa (British) 26,000£ are spent on schools for whites and 36,000£ on schools for natives and Arabs.

Education in the French colonies is planned to undermine the native social structure and customs. Teaching of native language is forbidden. All training is directed toward serving the whites. America also makes poor provisions for the workers. Separate schools, badly equipped, and staffed, a short school term explain the large amount of illiteracy in that country. The prevalence of child labour is another factor.

Vote—Only a small proportion of Negro workers have the franchise. In the North in America, at the cape in South Africa, and in Senegal some workers can vote. Most are disfranchised by law. In those democratic (?) communities these workers have no voice.

Legislation—Each year sees an increase in the amount of hostile and repressive legislation toward Negro workers. Recently residential segregation laws have been added to vagrancy, disfranchisement, and intermarriage and Jim Crow laws already in effect in America. Throughout the African colonies pass and curfew laws, land acts, the Colour Bar Bill, labour regulations and now the Riotous Assembly Act strangle the Negro workers and render him a helpless vassal.

Organization—The leaders of organized labour in America have neglected the Negro masses. So these thousands of unorganic workers lack this protection. Very few Negro women are in the trade unions in the US. There is more organization in the West Indies and Africa, in the form of trade unions and nationalist organizations. Hundreds of women in the Caribbean and thousands in Africa are in some one of these organizations. But the masses, the millions of workers are practically unorganized. The drive against workers organizations and for the open shop is going on in the colonies. The Riotous Assembly Bill mentioned above shows the determination of the master class to prevent the organization of the Negro workers. Beside such stringent laws the bosses are using reformists and liberals among the Negro intellectuals to stop the growing movement of the workers toward unity.

Struggles—Despite the savage repression used against them, Negro workers are resisting. Revolts have broken out in Haiti, Nigeria, South Africa. Strikes have occurred in Guadeloupe, Cuba and America. In all of these outbreaks women have fought militantly. They were conspicuous for their courage in the fruit strike in Colombia and in Durban. In Nigeria the women began the attack. Their active opposition to the hellish tax system of the imperialists has challenged attention. Native women are very positive factors in the ferment that is stirring in colonial Africa.

Our tasks in the revolutionary trade unions are to lead these struggles of the masses and direct them into the stream of world revolt, to put up a programme of immediate demands and organize them into workers and peasants unions. We must put up a determined fight for their rights as a national group, fighting for their self-determination. To do this we must strengthen the work already begun, find new forms of penetration and carry on constant help from the metropolitan countries.

"Negro Women in Industry," December 25, 1930

In America, the continued search of the bosses for cheap labour, has produced a considerable body of Negro proletarian women. Though the movement of the group into the factories had started before the war, that upheaval gave the impetus which drew thousands from the farms and domestic service into the shops and mills. From the fields and homes of the South they came to fill vacancies in varied industries of the North. Tobacco, textiles, canning, clothing, box, rag, food, cigars, paper, auto, glass, iron, steel, toy and notion factories, railroads, laundries, stores and offices utilized this cheapest and most viciously exploited form of adult labour. The number of coloured women workers in industry was perhaps highest during this period.

Work for wages is the rule among the Negro women of America. According to the last census (1920) 39% of all Negro women over the years and age were gainfully employed. For years the overwhelming majority have been rigorously confined to two easily exploited branches, domestic services and agricultural labour. Of the small proportion which had penetrated into industry before the war, the greater number were in industries listed as woman-employing, namely textiles, clothing, food, products, tobacco and hand and footwear. The low-paid, unorganized tobacco and peanut industries of the South absorbed thousands of these workers.

Though she had become a necessary factor in the economic life of the country during the war, the position of the Negro woman worker in the factory was by no means secure. She had been used chiefly for heavy and unskilled labour and could easily be replaced when man power became available. There was a marked tendency to dismiss those workers who had served in an emergency. On the return of the forces from overseas employers began to let out the Negro women workers. This movement was offset however by the rationalization projects of the factory owners. They were able by the retention of the labour of Negro women workers to maintain the huge profits of the war period, to push down the wage level of the workers and to make a drive for the open shop. There are no figures available to show the number of women in industry at the present time. The latest figures which we have (1920) show a decided increase in Negro women in industry over 1910. We must await the next census report, which will be ready in 1931–32, for such statistics, which will record this decided shift to the industrial field.

Several problems have arisen from the entrance of these totally unorganized workers into factory life. In all industries the dirtiest, hardest, most dangerous jobs fall to the lot of coloured women. Their pay is invariably the lowest given any adult workers. Employers are sometimes brutally frank in maintaining two wage scales and sometimes resort to subterfuge. The result is the same, wages below the subsistence level. In the canneries, box, rag, tobacco and peanut factories, and laundries of the south and west, women get as low as four and five dollars a week, for the most exhausting labour. The slightly higher average wage of [$]12–14 a week is entirely inadequate, because of higher living costs. Even this meager pay is uncertain however, as the bosses take advantages of the weak position of these workers to withhold on various pretexts. Piece work has been introduced into many industries, as tobacco, laundries and needle trades, toys, notions. Here the pay is steadily pushed down as the workers acquire speed. As a result coloured girls are working today under sweat shop conditions to maintain a bare existence.

Investigators find that Negro women workers are subjected to extremely long hours. A day of 10 or 12 hours is general in many states and 14 and even 16 is not uncommon in some places. In most factories employing Negro female labour the 50–55 hr. week is the rule, though the canneries of Florida and tobacco factories of Virginia lengthen this to 60 hr. Night work with unbelievable shifts of 9, 10 and 12 hours is the practice in some industries, even dangerous ones like glass. Overtime is frequent in exhausting labour like laundries.

Provision for rest, for necessary decent sanitation, or for comfort are almost never provided for women workers if they are coloured. The accommodations are in the majority of cases either lacking entirely or very elementary. These workers often have no place for their clothing, no dressing rooms, no place in which to eat lunch, no towels, no seats, no cool drinking water and no medical attention.

It is obvious from the facts cited above that this group of workers lack the slight protection which the little labour legislation of the country gives. The bulk of coloured workers still live in the south where laws safeguarding workers are not favoured. Several states in this sections have no laws at all limiting the daily or weekly hours a woman may work, and also none prohibiting night work. However, where such laws exist they are broken continuously through the greed of the bosses.

Among Negro working women there is a much higher percentage of married women than among the white. These working mothers have the added problems of home and children. Racial discrimination forces coloured people to live in segregated quarters in every city. These sections are always undesirable, dirty, often unsanitary, without paving or sewerage. For poor housing in these ghettos coloured workers who receive least pay are charge higher rent than others. In their attempts to pay these exorbitant rents the homes of the workers are filled with lodgers. The resulting overcrowding is disastrous to both health and morals. For a number of years the Negro death rate has been abnormally high.

Parks and playgrounds are never planned for these restricted Negro territories and the children are forced to spend their spare time in the streets. Separate schools for Negro children are likewise small, inadequate and ill-equipped. Throughout the south in these make-shift building poorly paid teachers instruct the workers' children. In the North the coloured children receive the same poor treatment as the children of the other workers crowded schools, large classes, part time sessions and steadily lowering standards of teaching.

Negro women workers are totally unorganized. The present helpless position of these new proletarian forces is the result of the policy of both the reactionary leaders of the AF of L and the bosses. It is to the interests of both that she should be outside the labour movement. The labour bureaucracy has steadily refused to organize these workers. The extreme victimization pictured above is possible because she lacks this protection.

However in view of their intense exploitation the bosses have thought it advisable to make some efforts to keep these workers docile. Many agencies, subsidized by the rich, such as the church, YMCA and the Urban League perform this task.

Through industrial clubs and conferences which preach a policy of friendship between workers and boss they have established a hold over the workers. Leaders are being trained through all their agencies and at the reformist labour college, Burkurd, a representative from the coloured YMCA is at the International Labour Office in Geneva.

Though the attempts of the bosses to separate the workers have been long and continuous they are no longer so successful. During the past several years Negro women have fought side by side with their white sisters in many industrial battles. The number of coloured women who took part in the miners' strikes in West Virginia, Pennsylvania, Ohio and Illinois, in the textile strike in Passaic, in the needle trades and paper box strikes in New York, show a growing solidarity of the workers. Struggles such as those of the cigar makers in Philadelphia and the date and fig workers in Chicago, which involved coloured girls exclusively show a fighting spirit with which the bosses must reckon. That they are aware of the new temper of the workers is shown by the belated effort of the AF of L to draw the coloured needle trades workers into the union.

It is plain that a small section of these workers have developed a clear cut class-consciousness. Their increasing participation in recent economic and political struggles of the revolutionary groups proves this. The number that have lately joined the Communist Party is further evidence of their awakening. This advance guard is determined to fight under the militant programme of the TUUL for the slogans of equal pay, 7-hour day and social insurance.

SECTION II

Organizing, Labor, and Militancy

The chapters in the second section comprise the years 1932 to 1940, the period of worldwide economic depression. In addition to a set of short articles written by Williana Burroughs for the *Negro Liberator*, the organ for the League of Struggle for Negro Rights (LSNR), this section includes work from Maude White Katz, Thyra Edwards, Ella Baker and Marvel Cooke, Louise Thompson Patterson, and Esther Cooper Jackson. Their writings echo and expand on Burroughs's early call to organize Black women workers economically and politically.

Maude White's 1932 and Thyra Edwards's 1935 articles on unionization efforts highlight how capitalist owners deploy racialized difference to prevent workers from organizing. The first African American Communist woman to attend the Communist University of the Toilers of the East (KUTV) in Moscow, White studied in the Soviet Union for three years before she returned to the US to work as a labor organizer and journalist.[1] Edwards also worked as a labor organizer and traveled to the Soviet Union in the mid-1930s. Even as Edwards explicitly admired the freedom and equality of women in the USSR, and even as she worked actively within the activist milieu of the CPUSA, there is no record of her officially becoming a member.[2]

White's "Special Negro Demands" reports on lessons learned from her assignment with the Needle Trades Workers Industrial Union (NTWIU). General demands, no matter how revolutionary, she contends, are not enough to bring over Black workers. The demands must be applied to the particular form oppression and exploitation take in a given factory. In her analysis, White puts to work the party's understanding of the national oppression of Black workers. She emphasizes: "If need be the whole union must be involved in attending to the everyday needs of one Negro worker."[3] It is the duty of organizers to explain the policy to white workers with the expectation that they must fight in defense of Black workers. Anything less is white chauvinism.

Thyra Edwards describes how Black workers are caught between their employers' compulsion to reduce costs and "uninformed and unscrupulous race leaders."[4] Organizing in a union together with white workers is the only way Black workers will improve their conditions. Edwards details the successful strike of the Black and white NTWIU, noting the brutality of the police assault on the picketing women and the many demands their collective courage won. Edwards supports the party's "dual union" tactic of organizing revolutionary unions rather than work with the more conservative and racist American Federation of Labor (AFL)—a tactic through which the party drew in more unskilled workers and Black workers. She observes that the highly disciplined and well-organized strike was not carried out by the AFL, and as such there were no sell-outs, thugs, or corrupt leaders.[5]

Chapters by Ella Baker and Marvel Cooke, Louise Thompson Patterson, and Esther Cooper Jackson focus on the condition of Black women domestic workers. Baker and Cooke recount conversations with Black women in the "Bronx slave market," that is, women looking for day jobs cooking and cleaning in the houses of middle- and working-class white people in the throes of the Great Depression. Thompson reiterates the point that Black women work in conditions similar to those of enslaved domestic laborers in the antebellum South. Blocked from better-paying jobs, they are confined to work in white people's homes and subjected to their unreasonable demands, wage theft, and disrespect. At times, Black domestic workers must even endure white men's sexual harassment. Here, Thompson presents her theory of Black women's triple exploitation—that is, their exploitation as Blacks, as workers, and as women. Baker and Cooke and Thompson all emphasize the imperative of organizing Black women into domestic workers' unions. This focus on Black women workers challenges unions and the party to expand their narrow emphasis on industry and thereby deepen their presence among Black people. Also noteworthy is Thompson's proposal to organize domestic workers into AFL trade unions specifically. This reflects the party's shift away from militant dual unionism and toward building a "Popular Front."

Thyra Edwards and Esther Cooper Jackson also present empirically rigorous analyses that demonstrate knowledge production as a political tactic. Both combat discrimination by illuminating the structures that generate and reinforce inequality. Edwards's critique of negative characterizations of Negro families receiving unemployment relief as "maligners, chiselers and indolent and hopeless parasites" confronts the racialization of poverty with a slew of statistics on unemployment: she documents real and undeniable effects of racist discrimination in hiring, employment, and the distribution of relief.[6] Edwards hammers home the impact of the Depression on Black businesses, farmers, and skilled and unskilled labor, and the resulting degeneration and disrepair of Black neighborhoods. These are facts any social worker should know, facts that indict the political economy creating these conditions. Cooper's master's thesis provides a powerful knowledge base for the work of organizing domestic workers. She points to the continuation of the "slave market" in Black women's working conditions. She also details the positive outlook for organizing Black women laboring in private households, in part because of their Depression-induced immiseration and in part because of their extant militancy, skills, and progressive orientation.

Cooper joined the CPUSA while a graduate student at Fisk University, having been radicalized by her admiration of Dolores "La Pasionaria" Ibárruri, a Communist leader in the Spanish Civil War.[7] She was not, however, the only Black woman in the Communist milieu inspired by the antifascist struggle in Spain. Thompson and Edwards both traveled to Spain and worked actively to build support for the Republican effort when they returned to the United States. Thompson raised money for the Negro Ambulance Fund for Republican Spain.[8] Edwards went on a speaking tour, representing the American Medical Bureau to Aid Spanish Democracy and the North American Committee to Aid Spanish Democracy.[9] Marvel Cooke's "She Was in Paris and Forgot Chanel" describes Edwards's experiences in Europe, bringing out the passion Edwards brought to her antifascist work.

Section II also includes two accounts of political organizing by Thompson: her appeal to the party to concentrate on recruiting, training, and promoting Black women (discussed above), and an excerpt from her memoir that details her work mobilizing the "Negro masses" for a march on Washington, DC, in connection with the campaign to free the Scottsboro Boys. She emphasizes that the goal of the march wasn't to involve intellectuals and the left, but rather to reach working people. At the time, she recalls, big marches and street demonstrations were novel "communist methods." Thompson also reflects on aspects of the campaign that helped to break down barriers to class unity, telling a story about Ruby Bates, one of the two white women sex workers who initially alleged she had been raped by the young men in the Scottsboro case but who eventually came forward to tell the truth of the young men's innocence. Thompson's analysis shifts blame for Black oppression from poor white people to the structural and institutional forces of the state; when poor and working-class women and men are willing to come together with, and to defend, Black people, their collective power can explode it all. It can make history.

6

Special Negro Demands
Maude White

Labor Unity 7, no. 5 (May 1932), pp. 10–11

There are some burning problems which face us in our Negro work in the needle trades at present. These are not simply problems in the needle trades, but of the whole Red union movement. Our experiences here (successes and shortcomings) are invaluable lessons for the development of the Negro work in the entire movement. More than this, our successes are more significant and our weaknesses express themselves more in a glaring form because of the characteristics of the industry—light, skilled, privileged (better paid and highly skilled), and unprivileged (low paid, unskilled and unorganized) categories of workers, which in itself breeds opportunism and antagonism.

Concrete Demands for the Negro Workers

The recent dress strike showed clearly the need of, first, concretizing the demands of the Negro workers; secondly, a correct understanding and settlement of the complaints and grievances; thirdly, conducting activities among the Negro workers primarily in the shops; fourthly, to begin immediately work among the Negro workers in the International Ladies' Garment Workers Union; fifthly, to fight persistently against white chauvinism.

In this article, we will deal with the first two points, namely, demands and complaints and grievances.

Our revolutionary needle trades union has general demands for Negro workers, based upon their special position in industry as a whole. The various revolutionary unions and leagues in industries where large numbers of Negroes are employed have the same. Industries, trades, crafts and shops where Negroes are not employed have no demands for Negro workers at all.

But general demands will not assure the carrying out of our revolutionary policy among Negro workers. Only by applying them to the specific conditions under which they work will we assure this. It means to take our general demands and apply them to the particular form which their exploitation and oppression takes in a given shop, mill or factory.

It may be sufficient to cite the case of the Schwartz and Dorfman shop (unorganized). In this shop we had a case of sub-contracting. Four Negro women pressers were hired at week work by a white presser. (The white presser was their boss.) Our tasks in this shop were first to explain the policy of our union in regard to sub-contracting, to explain our policy in regard to the Negro workers to all the workers, and to apply our general demands to the specific conditions of the Negro workers in this shop.

The comrade dealing with this shop felt that to explain to the white workers our policy in regard to the Negro workers and sub-contracting would antagonize them. So they spoke about general oppression and exploitation in an abstract way. The comrades also said that they did not want to antagonize the sub-contractor because he had influence over the white workers. They wanted to take the Negro workers aside and explain our policy but not so the white workers could hear it.

This showed a lack of faith in the willingness of the white workers to fight for the Negro workers. Behind this is also lurking something else more dangerous. How did these comrades know that the white workers would not fight for the Negro workers? They did not even ask them. So they were trying to put into these workers' minds the thing that is lurking in theirs — A LITTLE WHITE CHAUVINISM.

We corrected this mistake. Even after pointing out the mistakes made in dealing with this shop, some of the comrades accepted the correction reluctantly. This accounts for the presence of the sub-contractor (boss) on the shop strike and settlement committees. This concrete case shows that to speak about general demands without applying them to the specific conditions in the shop results in not carrying out our policy in practice.

Just a word about sub-contracting as it affects the Negro workers in the pressers' craft. These workers are mostly women and were formerly employed in laundries and cleaning establishments where more efficiency is required than in the dress trade. In the dress trade until recently Negro pressers were not employed. Now they are entering the dress trade as pressers, first, because they are efficient; secondly, they work for very low wages, $12 to $15 per week (the union scale is $50 per week minimum.)

This will give you an idea of the degree of their exploitation.

AS SOON AS THE SHOP IS ORGANIZED THE WHITE PRESSER TRIES TO GET RID OF THE NEGRO PRESSERS by intimidation and in some cases openly telling them to go. WHY? Because in an organized shop all workers (Negro and white) are to work on the same basis, one worker can not exploit the other. He then wants a white presser to work with him. He suddenly finds that the Negro presser's work is unsatisfactory. With little effort the boss will agree to send the Negro presser away. In many cases the Negro pressers leave the shop because they feel that the union will not fight for them, and if they remain their lives will be hard (dress will be scorched, etc., and the boss will always hold the Negro responsible). We had many cases where the Negro workers left the shop when it was about to be organized. (The question of sub-contracting requires a special article.)

In certain industries, trades, crafts where Negroes are not allowed we must raise the demand for their admission. Their exclusion is in itself discrimination.

A sure test of our understanding of the Negro question in our trade union movement is the manner in which we handle the complaints and grievances of the Negro workers. These reflect not only their economic exploitation, but their social and political oppression as well—their oppression as a national minority.

Some leading comrades in trade union work fail to understand this. Comrade Rose Wortis of the NTWIU states: "We handle the complaints of the Negro workers in the same manner as those of the white workers." (This is the prime reason why we can't keep them.) What does this indicate and where does it lead us?—that the Negro workers are not members of an oppressed group, suffer no special oppression and discrimination, need no special approach, Negro demands, and leads to neglect and indifference to their every-day needs. Likewise a denial of the national question. This is contrary to the I.P.C. resolution which states the following: "Pushing forward the fight for the realization of our revolutionary class line, the union should take special note of the national question in its policy, our activities among the workers of different nationalities, the Negroes, Poles, Jewish workers, Italians and so forth, are carried out in accordance with the specific peculiarities of the conditions."

If we handle the complaints of the Negro workers in the same manner as those of the white workers, we would proceed to the logical conclusion. An example—two workers, one white and one Negro, have complaints that the boss refuses to pay them the union scale. The organizer goes up to settle the complaints "in the same manner." The boss agrees without any ceremony to pay the white worker. He flatly refuses to pay the Negro worker. "In the same manner" fails to convince the boss why he should pay the Negro the same wage as the white worker. This results in the Negro worker remaining underpaid, the union capitulating before the white chauvinism of the boss—opportunism in practice.

Not only the organizer, but the whole shop must be mobilized to settle every complaint of the Negro worker. Bearing in mind—that in every complaint of a Negro worker is also involved his social and political oppression as well—no vacillations must be made in carrying out our revolutionary policy. If need be the whole union must be involved in attending to the every-day needs of one Negro worker. Only when this becomes the rule will [unions] be the real champions of the rights of the Negro workers.

Closely connected with the complaints and grievances is the victimization of Negro workers by the bosses. This is done in a very subtle way and in order for our comrades to understand this, they must bear in mind the very elementary fact — that Negro workers must show more efficiency in the performance of labor than the white workers. This is true not only in the economic sense, but in the social and political as well. This is one of the unwritten laws of the white ruling class in regard to the Negro workers.

7

Organizing the Unorganized: Two Articles on Unionization Efforts in Chicago
Thyra J. Edwards

"Let Us Have More Like Mr. Sopkins"

Crisis 42, no. 3 (March 1935), pp. 72, 82

This article is a picture of the plight of unorganized Negro workers and of the forces seeking to keep them unorganized.

> "Be Loyal to Your Family.
> Be Loyal to Your Friends.
> Be Loyal to Your Community.
> Be Loyal to Your Government.
> Be Loyal to Your Church.
>   But Most of All
> BE LOYAL TO YOUR JOB!"

Restaurants and shops on Chicago's South Side had their window displays heightened by these black lettered white placards when the Ben J. Sopkins Apron factories took advantage of President Roosevelt's "National Loyalty Week" to intensify the drive for corralling their Negro employees into the company's union.

Then word got abroad that a bona fide trade union organizer was in the district and that cotton goods workers, white and black, were to be organized. Most of the Sopkins employees are black. Last year they went out on strike—and stayed long enough to win their demands. So Mr.

Sopkins knows something about the power of labor when organized. When the strike was over and he had them back into the shops he spared neither pains nor money to see that they were not again exposed to any organization save his own. He employed an able Assyrian, Joseph Nahas, as a sort of personnel director, and, bringing Ex-Congressman Oscar De Priest into conference, secured the services of a seasoned ward politician, Miss Jennie Lawrence, who is dubiously titled "social worker." According to Miss Lawrence, her job is to collect dues of ten cents a week from each girl with which to arrange parties for the girls at the South Side headquarters of the Republican party donated through the good offices of the former congressman. She must also buy flowers for the sick and check attendance of the girls at the company union's parties and demonstrations.

Loyalty week might have passed with only the above described placards and the little imitation leather covered brochures "Gestures in Good Will" inclosing testimonials of prominent Negro South-Siders, aldermen, the Y.M.C.A., all bearing witness to Ben J. Sopkins—who has risen from obscure poverty to wealth on the labor of Negro women at sweat shop wages—as a sort of St. Francis of Chicago's South Side. It might all have ended with the placards and the little leatherette brochures but the International Ladies' Garment Workers Union announced its drive to organized cotton goods workers, skilled and unskilled, black and white.

Example for New Deal

Immediately Mr. Sopkins intensified his counter-union drive. He employed Nahum D. Brascher, able publicist. Mr. Brascher also served Sam Insull whose slogan was "the best stimulus for efficient labor is a long line of men waiting at the gate for jobs." With this publicist and company union organizer, Ben Sopkins launched a campaign in the name of Loyalty that could point directions in technique to the New Deal.

More placards were printed. This time mounted on poles and thrust into the hands of Negro women employees who paced back and forth before the plants each day picketing for the company's union and bearing high the legend:

"We Are Satisfied With Our Jobs."
"We Are Satisfied With Our Wages."

"We Are Satisfied With Our Hours."
"We Are Satisfied With Our Working Conditions."
"We Are Satisfied With Our Employer."
"AGITATORS, KEEP AWAY!"

And to supplement this, armlets—wide white cardboard bands, inscribed "I am a loyal employee of MR. BEN J. SOPKINS"—were attached to the right forearm of each Negro employee. Mr. Sopkins employs white men and white women in these shops also but they were overlooked in the Loyalty campaign. Evening and morning a white foreman stood at the door to see that each Negro girl left and returned wearing the badge of her master. Late at night these girls could be seen on the streets with a "date" or in the cinema still adorned with the arm band. She might run into Miss Jennie Lawrence, the social worker, or meet some girl from the shop who would "report." She had to "play safe" during all her waking hours.

For the noon hours Negro preachers were brought into the shops to preach to the Negro workers on their lunch period—white workers might go outside to enjoy the sunlight or puff at a cigarette. And the text was "Loyalty to Mr. Sopkins, who for 25 years has been like a father to the Negro women on the South Side letting them work in his factories on his machines." Well, so did "ole Massa" in slavery. What of it?

From day to day the campaign heightened . . . Daily picketing at the shops by the employees for the employer. On Thursday, the Chicago *World*, five hundred copies of which are distributed each week in the shops to Sopkins employees, displayed on five of its eight pages photographs of Sopkins girls in a "city wide" beauty contest for the coronation of the "Queen of Queens." (This coronation culminated at the Eighth Regiment Armory November 2 when Sopkins girls paid twenty-five cents admission to crown Miss Jennie Lawrence "Queen of Queens.") Incidentally they are a fine looking lot of girls. But the crowning feature in the Chicago *World*'s pro-Sopkinism was a three-fourth column length article headed "Sopkins, Our Last Stronghold" and ending on the note "We want more like Mr. Sopkins and less labor organizers."

And what is the meaning of all this?

Drive for Company Unions

Since the World War when organized labor in the skilled trades made considerable gains two forces have tended to undermine labor's position. The skilled crafts were inclined to ignore the unskilled, opposing industrial unionism which would embrace all the workers in an industry and would include the hitherto unorganized unskilled workers. In this latter class the bulk of Negro labor falls.

Employers were quick to grasp the advantage of this dual rift in Labor's ranks—skilled labor opposing unskilled labor, white labor opposing Negro labor. And so with the increasingly recurrent periods of depression during the post-war years we have the birth of that peculiar and exclusively American phenomena, the company union. European workers are politically too mature ever to be taken in by the false premise that employer and employee have a common rather than a contra-interest. Company unions built up a bulwark so formidable that bona fide trade unions have been effectively excluded from American capital industry—steel and automobiles. Employers and industry have further fortified themselves with extensive welfare programs, subsidies to social agencies, to churches and to community centers.

Now that the threatened collapse of our economic order has stimulated labor toward industrial unionization which must include unskilled Negro labor, we find the Negro, through misguided leadership still clinging to the frayed skirts of the employer. "Let us have more like Mr. Sopkins—." While Mr. Sopkins, tongue in cheek, conferring with his colleagues down in Chicago's loop, admits that unionization is inevitable.

"But," he adds, "when it comes I shall merely clear my shop of Negro help and employ an all white crew."

Not because Negroes are inefficient—for in twenty years they have made Ben Sopkins very wealthy. But because they are unorganized and have no bargaining power.

The recent Chicago *Defender* case is a brilliant example of the power of organized workers and the importance of collective bargaining power as protection. A Negro woman employed there for sixteen years claims to have been discharged on an hour's notice. Belonging to no workers' organization—the Negro employees of the Chicago *Defender* are not organized—she had no recourse. But when the Chicago *Defender* recently discharged its highly organized lino-typists replacing them with unorganized Negro operators at lower wage rates the employer learned very quickly that the employee has certain rights on his job that may or may not be jeopardized at the whim or convenience of the employer—provided the employee is organized and has collective power.

Mr. Sopkins is merely a symbol, not of black and white conflicts but of employers whose objective is reduced costs of production at the expense of the employee. The women in Sopkins' shops represent the great uninformed mass of unskilled labor caught between the nether stones of unscrupulous employers and uninformed and unscrupulous race leadership.

And what is to be the end of all this?

Either the Negro worker must organize, casting his strength and taking his chances with the forces of labor or, when organized labor has become strongly entrenched throughout industry the Negro will be shunted by the employer on the one hand and, on the other hand will have no moral claim on organized labor.

"Who Is Disinterested?"

Crisis 42, no. 6 (June 1935), pp. 173–4

In the April Crisis *Mr. Evans had an article, "Thumbs Down on Unions!" in which he took Miss Edwards sharply to task for her previous article on the company union in a garment factory in Chicago and its treatment of colored women workers. This is Miss Edwards's rebuttal.*

J. Wellington Evans lives in Chicago.

J. Wellington Evans is a cutter in the employ of the Ben J. Sopkins shops.

In private life J. Wellington Evans is the son of the Reverend Joseph W. Evans.

The Reverend Joseph W. Evans, pastor of the Metropolitan Community Church at 4100 South Parkway, was chairman of the Citizen's Committee selected by Ben J. Sopkin to "arbitrate" the strike of June, 1933.

It was in the Reverend Joseph W. Evans' Metropolitan Community Church that the Sopkin's Loyalty mass meeting was staged on the evening of Friday, October 5, 1934. At which mass meeting Negro employees of Mr. Sopkin, wearing the arm bands described in a previous article, were brought in to hear South Side leaders testify to the noble paternalism of the Sopkin institution. It is the established custom that rental fees are paid to churches for such use.

It is therefore gross effrontery to the intelligence of the Negro community that Mr. Sopkin should select the father of an employee to head his "arbitration" committee and to promote his interests. A greater finesse is used by most firms who do not permit employees or members of an old employee's family to enter even such non-controversial situations as competing for prizes.

No attempt is being made here to challenge the personal integrity of Miss Jennie Lawrence. Her professional status as a social worker is another matter. It is most certainly dubious and questionable. For social work today is a standardized and regulated profession just as teaching, nursing and the practice of medicine. Definite qualification and training are required. Mr. Evans failed to point out any such equipment on the part of Miss Lawrence. Nor did he show that she had ever been employed by any recognized social agency.

Incidentally the contest which Mr. Evans states occurred April 2 (1934) was advertised in the Chicago *World* issue of October 6, 1934. Obviously we are discussing the same contest.

As for the ten cents weekly due—I have that information from Miss Lawrence herself. I should like, therefore, that the promised "fifty sound American dollars" be used at the nucleus for a defense fund to be raised for the Moslems who were recently sentenced to imprisonment from a Chicago Court in a meleé in which the unarmed Moslems were held in the shooting of an armed bailiff. And because of their successful carrying on of the Scottsboro case I should like the fund to be turned over the International Labor Defense.

Public Relations Director

Nahum D. Brascher is an outstanding publicist and journalist of great ability and wide influence. In the present life and death struggle of Labor, black and white, to survive, it is expedient that the interests of so important and influential a person be thoughtfully examined.

According to Mr. Brascher, he served the United States Steel Corporation under the late Judge Elbert H. Gary, using his eloquence and his influence against the unionization of the approximately 40,000 Negroes then employed in the steel industry. To those familiar with the steel industry it is a well known fact that the Negro was brought in to force down the wage scale; that he was kept at the poorly paid, unskilled jobs, and was very shortly superseded by machines, supplemented by Mexican labor which was found to be available at even cheaper rates than Negro labor. And it has been said that Judge Gary seriously considered the importation of Chinese coolies to undercut the depressed wages of the Mexican. Immigration restrictions against Orientals forestalled this.

For a number of years now Mr. Brascher has been attached to the L. Fish Furniture Company, a large and extensive "installment plan" furniture house located at the entrance of Chicago's Loop. The greater percentage of the L. Fish Furniture Company's customers are Negroes on Chicago's South Side. A recent Trade Commission report called special attention to the exorbitant prices furniture dealers generally have extorted from the consumer. It is a regularly established policy in cities generally that all goods are sold highest to Negroes because their consumers, like their workers, are unorganized.

More recently, according to printed announcements sent out by that company, Mr. Brascher has been retained by the Schulze Baking company, wholesale bakeries, 40 East Garfield Boulevard, as an emissary of good will among the Negro population. His retention followed closely upon the heels of the Morgan Park school strike in which white children, supported by their parents, walked out demanding that Negro children be restricted to a Jim Crow school. It is complained on the South Side that a truck of the Schulze Baking company was used to display banners against the Negroes and for the Jim Crow issue in the Morgan Park controversy. There were probably repercussions in the sale of bread to Negroes and an agent of "good will" became expedient. "Director of Public Relations in behalf of (our) Business and Civic-Extension Program:" the official announcement sets out.

So much for men! Let's have a look at measures.

At 9:30 on the morning on June 19, 1933, 1,500 employees, Negro and white, of the Ben J. Sopkin's shops, led by the Needle Trades Industrial Union, downed tools and walked out on strike. The Needle Trades Industrial Union is not an American Federation of Labor union. The strike was one of the best organized and disciplined in Chicago labor history. To this day there has been no whisper of corrupt leadership, of hired thugs, of sell outs.

At 9:30 A.M. 1,500 workers, Negro and white, walked out of the several shops of Ben J. Sopkin and quietly and peacefully picketed the factories. At 9:45 A.M. Mr. Sopkin, "who for 25 years has been like a father to the Negro women on the South Side," called the police. Negro and white police were sent. The police kicked, mauled and slugged and cracked the heads of the women. Many were seriously injured and had to be taken to the hospital (although the Wabash Avenue police station failed to record any accidents). Twenty-five were jailed at one time, 65 at another. The treasury of the union was depleted bailing them out. But still they held out. In an editorial of July 1, 1933, on the Sopkin case the Chicago *Defender* points out, "It is not the duty of the police to settle strikes; they are to preserve law and order. Many of them seem to think they are to take sides with sweat shop keepers. At the time these women were assaulted by the police they were only peacefully walking the streets. There is no crime in peacefully walking on the street. Yet these women were brutally clubbed by the police."

Five Cents an Hour

And what were the conditions that provoked such heroic resistance to hunger, to brutality and to jail? What were the causes for the strike which Mr. J. Wellington Evans describes as "groundless"?

A check of the pay rolls and time keepers' records of the Sopkin shops disclosed that many of the girls were receiving 5 cents an hour for their work; that they worked 52 hours a week; that they received from $1.90 to $7.70 for a full week's work; that Negro cutters, a skilled technique, received $5.00 and $6.00 a week while white cutters received $18.00 a week for the same work; that the company made a charge for cashing checks; that inadequate rest rooms were furnished and that white foremen entered the women's rest rooms at will.

These charges were pretty unanimously confirmed by the investigations of the various committees. Aside from the Citizen's Committee called together by Mr. Sopkins, investigation was made by Mr. Marchand, a conciliator of the U.S. Department of Labor, Mr. Gabriel Allmond, of the Department of Political Science at the University of Chicago, Mr. Robert Morse Lovett, Professor of English at the University of Chicago and one of the editors of the *New Republic*, and the late James Mullenbach of the Steel Labor Relations Board. The consensus of their findings was that the practices existing at that time in the Sopkin's shops were vicious, unscrupulous and degrading.

After two heroic weeks—weeks that challenge anyone who presumes to say that Negro labor, once aroused, is not militant, class conscious and courageous—the strikers won 15 of their 17 demands and returned to work.

A 47 hour week.

A 17½% wage increase.

Reemployment of all strikers without discrimination.

Equal division of work.

Equal pay for equal work to colored and white workers.

No charge for checks.

And so on.

The fact that conditions in those shops is improved is due entirely to the struggle and sacrifice of the workers themselves, Negro and white, united under the leadership of the Needle Trades Industrial Union. With the major portion of their demands won, hunger, an exhausted treasury, police onslaughts that by this time had most of their leaders either in jail or in the hospitals the strike was forced to end without the Union securing contractual recognition. And thus it is that the present situation is foisted upon these workers.

"Uncle Tom" did not originate in fiction. Nor did he die with the Emancipation proclamation. He is perpetuated and immortalized in the type of leadership that sells the Negro for a few "sound American dollars." The girls in the Sopkin shops did not wear Mr. Sopkin's "loyalty bands" because they love Mr. Sopkin any more than Negroes down South love to ride in Jim Crow cars. It is compulsion and fear born of lack of organized power.

Against All Unions

Interestingly enough at the time of the strike Mr. Sopkin is quoted as saying that he objected to the N.I.T.U. but that he would be glad to deal with an American Federation of Labor union. Yet immediately this latter seems probable he employs the ablest talent available to start a whispering campaign against unionism and trade unions.

While calling attention to all the blessings of the unorganized shop he fails to point out that in Chicago today there are about 400 Negro women, members of the International Ladies' Garment Workers Union, employed in the silk dress good industry at weekly wages from a minimum of $19.34 for finishers, to $39.40 a week for pressers. And they work 35 hours a week. That they are scattered indiscriminately in shops employing white workers. That among these are Negro floor ladies, shop committee chairladies and head cutters. That in New York City there are 5000 Negro girls, members of the I.L.G.W.U., employed in the dress goods industry working side by side with white workers and receiving equal pay for equal work. That similar advantages and conditions exist in the Furriers' Industrial Union in Chicago and in New York today.

Moreover, no intelligent person, however sympathetic to organized labor, will maintain that the unions are perfect any more than he maintains that the Jim Crow policies of the schools, churches, business organizations and the United States government are without fault. This position is not necessary even for the most extreme partisan. All that we claim is that in a period where employers are organized in Chambers of Commerce, and Boards of Trade it is essential for the employees, regardless of race, to be likewise organized. It would seem to be almost axiomatic, and is to competent minds. Among the whites even those who oppose unionism know better. The necessity for labor organization is admitted and adopted by every white race and nationality in the industrialized world. Can Negros be an exception? This is maintained only by those persons who lack the fundamental interpretation of history with its uniformity of human nature whereby like causes produce like effects as well in the social as in the physical world.

8

Women's Department
Williana Burroughs

Negro Liberator 3, no. 32 (March 15, 1935), p. 7

In 1908, at the suggestion of the American delegates, a Socialist Women's Congress set aside March 8—as a day of special action for women's rights. The struggle at that time was for the vote. Acting on the motion of Clara Zetkin, a later congress, that of 1912, voted to stress also on International Women's Day the solidarity of women of every race and land. During the World War the day was not celebrated.

On March 8, 1917, however, the Russian women roused the working class by marching out of the factories, through the streets, demanding bread—and an end to imperialist war. Ever since, Women's Day has been celebrated by militant women everywhere in larger and larger numbers.

This year, the sixth of the crisis, the atrocities of war and fascism loom much nearer. The misery, suffering and degree of exploitation under capitalism and in the colonies is very great. In spite of this the women fight.

In our own country, during the past year, women have been active in every strike, demonstration, conference, and struggle for better wages, better living conditions, security and relief. The list of struggles is long. Seabrook farm, National Biscuit, Imperial Valley, Sharecroppers Union, Scottsboro, the textile, steel and coal strikes are only a few.

The Anti-War Fight

Negro Liberator 5, nos. 1–2 (July 1, 1935), p. 7

By August, the Women's Committee of the American League Against War and Fascism must have a million signers of its protest against a new war. On August 4, the anniversary of the beginning of the World War, a delegation will present the petitions to President Roosevelt. You can see for yourself that this means work.

We Remember

Least of all can Negro women have any doubts about the evils of war and fascism. Who among us has forgotten that courageous, expectant mother lynched so monstrously by a fiendish Georgia mob; the attempts to force women into the kitchens of the South under slave conditions; the sad return of brothers, sons and husbands, broken and maimed; the long list of our war dead; the insults heaped on Negro soldiers; and most contemptible of all, the studied degradation of Negro Gold Star mothers . . .

Fighting War

No, Negro women are among the first in the ever growing army of women who are daily fighting the brutal war mongers.

Petitions may be secured from the NEGRO LIBERATOR, 308 W. 141 St., N. Y. C. Send all your questions to this column, c/o Williana Burroughs.

Clean Food

Negro Liberator 4, nos. 3–4 (August 1, 1935), p. 7

A correspondent writes us: "While waiting for a friend to buy some food at a vegetable stand, I noticed some corn offered for sale, too old and worm-eaten to be thrown to the pigs or chickens. It was priced at three ears for ten cents. When I told the owner he should be reported for daring to sell such stuff, he turned the price tag down.

"Don't you think we need an active committee to go around and check up on the kind of food that is being sold to colored people, I do."

Every woman knows how important good, wholesome food is for the safety of her family and especially for that of the children. The doctor has often warned her on this manner. She spends much time getting the best food values possible for her few pennies.

Inspection Committees

All of our clubs should have its food committee, whose job it should be to see that only wholesome food is offered for sale, that food is covered and not exposed to the flies, dust, dirt and prowling cats.

Jobs for Women

Negro Liberator 4, nos. 5–6 (September 2, 1935), p. 7

So great is unemployment among women houseworkers in particular, that at many points in New York City women can be seen waiting patiently in the street, hour after hour, for some housewife to come out and hire them for a few hours or a day. It is rare luck if the jobs are for a week or two. I have been told that so terrible is the plight of these persons that some girls and women have been forced even lower. Many of them have given up the task of looking for a job as hopeless, and in desperation have gone into the street to get money for bread for their children and to keep body and soul together.

What does the widespread unemployment of the Negro women mean to the colored people? We must organize the women into the L.S.N.R., trade unions, etc., of our trade for a fight for work. Those of us who are union members should raise the question of a campaign for jobs for women in our locals. Let's begin at once.

Several folks have offered suggestions to me for this column. Some of them were good. In order that I can use proposals to the best advantage please send them by letter to this department % *Negro Liberator*. All ideas are thankfully received.

We are anxious to hear of your successes and difficulties in your work. This is the way we help one another.

9

The Bronx Slave Market

Ella Baker and Marvel Cooke

Crisis 42, no. 11 (November 1935), pp. 330–31, 340

In the Bronx, northern borough of New York City known for its heavy Jewish population, exists a street corner market for domestic servants where Negro women are "rented" at unbelievably low rates for house work.

The Bronx Slave Market! What is it? Who are its dealers? Who are its victims? What are its causes? How far does its stench spread? What forces are at work to counteract it?

Any corner in the congested sections of New York City's Bronx is fertile soil for mushroom "slave marts." The two where the traffic is heaviest and where the bidding is highest are located at 167th street and Jerome avenue and at Simpson and Westchester avenues.

Symbolic of the more humane slave block is the Jerome avenue "market." There, on benches surrounding a green square, the victims wait, grateful, at least, for some place to sit. In direct contrast is the Simpson avenue "mart," where they pose wearily against buildings and lamp posts, or scuttle about in an attempt to retrieve discarded boxes upon which to rest.

Again, the Simpson avenue block exudes the stench of the slave market at its worst. Not only is human labor battered and sold for slave wage, but human love also is a marketable commodity. But whether it is labor or love that is sold, economic necessity compels the sale. As early as 8 a.m. they come; as late as 1 p.m. they remain.

Rain or shine, cold or hot, you will find them there—Negro women, old and young—sometimes bedraggled, sometimes neatly dressed—but with the invariable paper bundle, waiting expectantly for Bronx housewives to buy their strength and energy for an hour, two hours, or even a day at the munificent rate of fifteen, twenty, twenty-five, or if luck be with them, thirty cents an hour. If not the wives themselves, maybe their husbands, their sons, or their brothers, under the subterfuge of work, offer worldly-wise girls higher bids for their time.

Who are these women? What brings them here? Why do they stay? In the boom days before the onslaught of the depression in 1929, many of these women who are now forced to bargain for day's work on street corners, were employed in grand homes in the rich Eighties, or in wealthier homes in Long Island and Westchester, at more than adequate wages. Some are former marginal industrial workers, forced by the slack in industry to seek other means of sustenance. In many instances there had been no necessity for work at all. But whatever their standing prior to the depression, none sought employment where they now seek it. They come to the Bronx, not because of what it promises, but largely in desperation.

Paradoxically, the crash of 1929 brought to the domestic labor market a new employer class. The lower middle-class housewife, who, having dreamed of the luxury of a maid, found opportunity staring her in the face in the form of Negro women pressed to the wall by poverty, starvation, and discrimination.

Where once color was the "gilt edged" security for obtaining domestic and personal service jobs, here, even, Negro women found themselves being displaced by whites. Hours of futile waiting in employment agencies, the fee that must be paid despite the lack of income, fraudulent agencies that sprung up during the depression, all forced the day worker to fend for herself or try the dubious and circuitous road to public relief.

As inadequate as emergency relief has been, it has proved somewhat of a boon to many of these women, for with its advent, actual starvation is no longer their ever-present slave driver and they have been able to demand twenty-five and even thirty cents an hour as against the old fifteen and twenty cent rate. In an effort to supplement the inadequate relief received, many seek this open market.

And what a market! She who is fortunate (?) enough to please Mrs. Simon Legree's scrutinizing eye is led away to perform hours of multifarious household drudgeries. Under a rigid watch, she is permitted to scrub floors on her bended knees, to hang precariously from window sills, cleaning window after window, or to strain and sweat over steaming tubs of heavy blankets, spreads and furniture covers.

Fortunate, indeed, is she who gets the full hourly rate promised. Often, her day's slavery is rewarded with a single dollar bill or whatever her unscrupulous employer pleases to pay. More often, the clock is set back for an hour or more. Too often she is sent away without any pay at all.

How It Works

We invaded the "market" early on the morning of September 14. Disreputable bags under arm and conscientiously forlorn, we trailed the work entourage on the West side "slave train," disembarking with it at Simpson and Westchester avenues. Taking up our stand outside the corner flower shop whose show window offered gardenias, roses and the season's first chrysanthemums at moderate prices, we waited patiently to be "bought."

We got results in almost nothing flat. A squatty Jewish housewife, patently lower middle class, approached us, carefully taking stock of our "wares."

"You girls want work?"

"Yes." We were expectantly non-committal.

"How much you work for?"

We begged the question, noting that she was already convinced that we were not the "right sort." "How much do you pay?"

She was walking away from us. "I can't pay your price," she said and immediately started bargaining with a strong, seasoned girl leaning against the corner lamp post. After a few moments of animated conversation, she led the girl off with her. Curious we followed them two short blocks to a dingy apartment house on a side street.

We returned to our post. We didn't seem to be very popular with the other "slaves." They eyed us suspiciously. But, one by one, as they became convinced that we were one with them, they warmed up to friendly sallies and answered our discreet questions about the possibilities of employment in the neighborhood.

Suddenly it began to rain, and we, with a dozen or so others, scurried to shelter under the five-and-ten doorway midway the block. Enforced close communion brought about further sympathy and conversation from the others. We asked the brawny, neatly dressed girl pressed close to us about the extent of trade in the "oldest profession" among women.

"Well," she said, "there is quite a bit of it up here. Most of 'those' girls congregate at the other corner." She indicated the location with a jerk of her head.

"Do they get much work?" we queried.

"Oh, quite a bit," she answered with a finality which was probably designed to close the conversation. But we were curious and asked her how the other girls felt about it. She looked at us a moment doubtfully, probably wondering if we weren't seeking advice to go into the "trade" ourselves.

"Well, that's their own business. If they can do it and get away with it, it's all right with the others." Or probably she would welcome some "work" of that kind herself.

"Sh-h-h." The wizened West Indian woman whom we had noticed, prior to the rain, patrolling the street quite belligerently as if she were daring someone not to hire her, was cautioning us. She explained that if we kept up such a racket the store's manager would kick all of us out in the rain. And so we continued our conversation in whispered undertone.

"Gosh. I don't like this sort of thing at all." The slender brown girl whom we had seen turn down two jobs earlier in the morning, seemed anxious to talk. "This is my first time up here—and believe me, it is going to be my last. I don't like New York nohow. If I don't get a good job soon, I'm going back home to Kansas City." So she had enough money to travel, did she?

Cut Rate Competition

The rain stopped quite as suddenly as it started. We had decided to make a careful survey of the district to see whether or not there were any employment agencies in the section. Up one block and down another we tramped, but not one such institution did we encounter. Somehow the man who gave us a sly "Hello, babies" as he passed was strangely familiar. We realized two things about him—that he had been trailing us for some time and that he was manifestly, plain clothes notwithstanding, one of "New York's finest."

Trying to catch us to run us in for soliciting, was he? From that moment on, it was a three-cornered game. When we separated he was at sea. When we were together, he grinned and winked at us quite boldly . . .

We sidled up to a friendly soul seated comfortable on an upturned soap-box. Soon an old couple approached her and offered a day's work with their daughter way up on Jerome avenue. They were not in agreement as to how much the daughter would pay—the old man said twenty-five cents an hour—the old lady scowled and said twenty. The car fare, they agreed, would be paid after she reached her destination. The friendly soul refused the job. She could afford independence, for she had already bargained for a job for the following day. She said to us, after the couple started negotiations with another woman, that she wouldn't go way up on Jerome avenue on a wild goose chase for Mrs. Roosevelt, herself. We noted, with satisfaction, that the old couple had no luck with any of the five or six they contacted.

It struck us as singularly strange, since it was already 10:30, that the women still lingered, seemingly unabashed that they had not yet found employment for a day. We were debating whether or not we should leave the "mart" and try again another day, probably during the approaching Jewish holidays at which time business is particularly flourishing, when, suddenly, things looked up again. A new batch of "slaves" flowed down the elevated steps and took up their stands at advantageous points.

The friendly soul turned to us, a sneer marring the smooth roundness of her features. "Them's the girls who makes it bad for us. They get more jobs than us because they will work for anything. We runned them off the corner last week." One of the newcomers was quite near us and we couldn't help but overhear the following conversation with a neighborhood housewife.

"You looking for work?"

"Yes ma'am."

"How much you charge?"

"I'll take what you will give me." . . . What was this? Could the girl have needed work that badly? Probably. She did look run down at the heels . . .

"All right. Come on. I'll give you a dollar." Cupidity drove beauty from the arrogant features. The woman literally dragged her "spoil" to her "den." . . . But what of the girl? Could she possibly have known what she was letting herself in for? Did she know how long she would have to work for that dollar or what she would have to do? Did she know whether or not she would get lunch or car fare? Not any more than we did. Yet, there she was, trailing down the street behind her "mistress."

"You see," philosophized the friendly soul. "That's what makes it bad for the rest of us. We got to do something about these girls. Organize them or something." The friendly soul remained complacent on her up-turned box. Our guess was that if the girls were organized, the incentive would come from some place else.

Business in the "market" took on new life. Eight or ten girls made satisfactory contacts. Several women—and men approached us, but our price was too high or we refused to wash windows or scrub floors. We were beginning to have a rollicking good time when rain again dampened our heads and ardor. We again sought the friendly five-and-ten doorway.

"For Five Bucks a Week"

We became particularly friendly with a girl whose intelligent replies to our queries intrigued us. When we were finally convinced that there would be no more "slave" barter that day, we invited her to lunch with us at a near-by restaurant. After a little persuasion, there we were, Millie Jones between us, refreshing our spirits and appetites with hamburgers, fragrant with onions, and coffee. We found Millie an articulate person. It seems that, until recently, she had had a regular job in the neighborhood. But let her tell you about it.

"Did I have to work? And how! For five bucks and car fare a week. Mrs. Eisenstein had a six-room apartment lighted by fifteen windows. Each and every week, believe it or not, I had to wash every one of those windows. If that old hag found as much as the teeniest speck on any one of 'em, she'd make me do it over. I guess I would do anything rather than wash windows. On Mondays I washed and did as much of the ironing as I could. The rest waited over for Tuesday. There were two grown sons in the family and her husband. That meant that I would have at least twenty-one shirts to do every week. Yeah, and ten sheets and at least two blankets, besides. They all had to be done just so, too. Gosh, she was a particular woman.

"There wasn't a week either, that I didn't have to wash up every floor in the place and wax it on my hands and knees. And two or three times a week I'd have to beat the mattresses and take all the furniture covers off and shake 'em out. Why, when I finally went home nights, I could hardly move. One of the sons had "hand trouble" too, and I was just as tired fighting him off, I guess, as I was with the work.

"Say, did you ever wash dishes for an Orthodox Jewish family?" Millie took a long, sibilant breath. "Well, you've never really washed dishes, then. You know, they use a different dishcloth for everything they cook. For instance, they have one for "milk" pots in which dairy dishes are cooked, another for glasses, another for vegetable pots, another for meat pots, and so on. My memory wasn't very good and I was always getting the darn things mixed up. I used to make Mrs. Eisenstein just as mad. But I was the one who suffered. She would get other cloths and make me do all the dishes all over again.

"How did I happen to leave her? Well, after I had been working about five weeks, I asked for a Sunday off. My boy friend from Washington was coming up on an excursion to spend the day with me. She told me if I didn't come in on Sunday, I needn't come back at all. Well, I didn't go back. Ever since then I have been trying to find a job. The employment agencies are no good. All the white girls get the good jobs.

"My cousin told me about up here. The other day I didn't have a cent in my pocket and I just had to find work in order to get back home and so I took the first thing that turned up. I went to work about 11 o'clock and I stayed until 5:00—washing windows, scrubbing floors and washing out stinking baby things. I was surprised when she gave me lunch. You know, some of 'em don't even do that. What I got through, she gave me thirty-five cents. Said she took a quarter out for lunch. Figure it out for yourself. Ten cents an hour!"

Miniature Economic Battlefront

The real significance of the Bronx Slave Market lies not in a factual presentation of its activities; but in focusing attention upon its involved implications. The "mart" is but a miniature mirror of our economic battle front.

To many, the women who sell their labor thus cheaply have but themselves to blame. A head of a leading employment agency bemoans the fact that these women have not "chosen the decent course" and declares: "The well-meaning employment agencies endeavoring to obtain respectable salaries and suitable working conditions for deserving domestics are finding it increasingly difficult due to the menace and obstacles presented by the slavish performance of the lower types of domestic themselves, who, unlike the original slaves who recoiled from meeting their masters, rush to meet their mistresses."

The exploiters, judged from the districts where this abominable traffic flourishes, are the wives and mothers of artisans and tradesmen who militantly battle against being exploited themselves, but who apparently have no scruples against exploiting others.

The general public, though aroused by stories of these domestics, too often think of the problems of these women as something separate and apart and readily dismisses them with a sigh and the shrug of the shoulders.

The women, themselves present a study in contradictions. Largely unaware of their organized power, yet ready to band together for some immediate and personal gain either consciously or unconsciously, they still cling to that American illusion that any one who is determined and persistent can get ahead.

The roots, then of the Bronx Slave Market spring from: (1) the general ignorance of and apathy towards organized labor action; (2) the artificial barriers that separate the interest of the relief administrators and investigators from that of their "case loads," the white collar and professional worker from the laborer and the domestic; and (3) organized labor's limited concept of exploitation, which permits it to fight vigorously to secure itself against evil, yet passively or actively aids and abets the ruthless destruction of Negroes.

To abolish the market once and for all, these roots must be torn away from their sustaining soil. Certain palliative and corrective measures are not without benefit. Already are the seeds of discontent being sown.

The Women's Day Workers and Industrial League, organized sixteen years ago by Fannie Austin, has been, and still is, a force to abolish the existing evils in day labor. Legitimate employment agencies have banded together to curb the activities of the racketeer agencies and are demanding fixed minimum and maximum wages for all workers sent out. Articles and editorials recently carried by the New York Negro press have focused attention on the existing evils in the "slave market."

An embryonic labor union now exists in the Simpson avenue "mart." Girls who persist in working for less than thirty cents an hour have been literally run off the corner. For the recent Jewish holiday, habitues of the "mart" actually demanded and refused to work for less than thirty-five cents an hour.

10

Toward a Brighter Dawn

Louise Thompson

The Woman Today 1, no. 14 (April 1936), p. 30

Cramped and crushed by prejudice and discrimination, fingers worn to the bone by ceaseless labor at coolie wages, the Negro women are the most exploited group in America. But they have banded together for the fight for freedom, and will win.

Early dawn on any Southern road. Shadowy figures emerge from the little unpainted, wooden shacks alongside the road. There are Negro women trudging into town to the Big House to cook, to wash, to clean, to nurse children—all for two, three dollars for the whole week. Sunday comes—rest day. But what rest is there for a Negro mother who must crowd into one day the care of her own large family? Church of course, where for a few brief hours she may forget, listening to the sonorous voice of the pastor, the liquid harmony of the choir, the week's gossip of neighbors. But Monday is right after Sunday, and the week's grind begins all over.

Early dawn on the plantations of the South. Dim figures bend down in the fields, to plant, to chop, to pick the cotton from which the great wealth of the South has come. Sharecroppers, working year in, year out, for the big landlord, never to get out of debt. The sharecropper's wife—field worker by day, mother and housewife by night. Scrubbing the pine floors of the cabin until they shine white. Boiling clothes in the big black iron kettle in the yard. Cooking the fat-back and corn pone for hungry little mouths. She has never to worry about leisure-time problems.

The same dawn in Bronx Park, New York. There is yet no movement in the near-by apartment houses. From the subway come women, Negro women. They carefully arrange the *Daily News* or *Mirror* along the park bench still moist with dew, and sit down. Why do they sit so patiently? It's cold and damp in the early morning.

Here we are, for sale for the day. Take our labor. Give us what you will. We must feed our children and pay high rent in Harlem. Ten cents, fifteen cents an hour! That won't feed our families for a day, let alone pay rent. You won't pay more? Well, guess that's better than going back to Harlem after spending your last nickel for carfare . . .

So thrifty "housewives" drive sharper bargains. There are plenty of women to choose from. And every dollar saved leaves that much more for one's bridge game or theater party! The Bronx "slave market" is a graphic monument to the bitter exploitation of the most exploited section of the American working population—the Negro women.

Over the whole land, Negro women meet this triple exploitation—as workers, as women, and as Negroes. About 85 per cent of all Negro women workers are domestics, two-thirds of the two million domestic workers in the United States. In smaller numbers they are found in other forms of personal service. Other employment open to them is confined mainly to laundries and the tobacco factories of Virginia and the Carolinas, where working conditions are deplorable. The small fraction of Negro women in the professions is hampered by discriminatory practices and unequal wages.

The economic crisis has placed the severest test upon the Negro woman. Representing the greatest proportion of unemployed workers in the country, Negroes are discriminated against in relief and work relief. Negroes must pay high rents for the worst housing in the city. Segregated Negro neighborhoods are invariably deficient in nurseries, playgrounds, health centers, schools. And in the face of such adverse conditions, Negro women must maintain and rear their families.

It was against such a background that there assembled in Chicago on February 14, 15 and 16, 1936, Negro women from all sections of the country for the National Negro Congress. They made up about one-third of the eight hundred delegates, men and women, who came together from churches, trade unions, fraternal, political, women's, youth, civic, farm, professional, and educational organizations. Women club leaders from California greeted women trade unionists from New York. Women school teachers made friends with women domestic workers. Women from the relief agencies talked over relief problems with women relief clients. Women from mothers' clubs and housewives' leagues exchanged experiences in fighting against the high cost of living. Negro women welcomed the white women delegates who came to the Congress as an evidence of the growing sense of unity between them.

The Women's Sub-Session of the Congress dramatized the conditions facing Negro women everywhere. Neva Ryan, slight but dynamic, pictured the plight of the domestic workers of Chicago and the steps being taken to organize them. Rosa Rayside of New York told how they already had an A.F. of L. charter there for a domestic workers' union. Tarea Hall Pittman, state president of the Federation of Women's Clubs of California, emphasized the necessity of linking together the struggle of women workers with professional women. Marion Cutbert of the National Board of the Y.W.C.A. and National Treasurer of the National Negro Congress, greeted the delegates and urged the need for organization on all fronts. A white delegate from Detroit, Margaret Dean, told of the valiant fight made in her city by both Negro and white women against the high cost of living. Thyra Edwards, social worker of Chicago, and chairman of the Women's Committee for the National Negro Congress, emphasized the need for consumers' co-operatives. Rositas Talioferro, student at the University of Wisconsin, urged the mothers to begin early in their children's lives to educate them upon the pressing problems under discussion. Herbert Wheeldin, from Westchester County, New York, one of the several men delegates who listened attentively, spoke of the severe exploitation of women workers by the rich families of Westchester.

The session ended all too soon, with many delegates yet to be heard from. The facts they related told sad stories, but there was no sadness in these women delegates, many of whom were attending a congress for the first time in their lives. There was a ring of confidence in each report—a confidence, born in many instances right at the congress, that it was possible to change these unbearable conditions. Negro women from all walks of life, unskilled and professional, Negro and white women found themselves drawn together, found that they liked being together, found that there was hope for change in coming together.

Organization and unity were the keynote of the resolution on women passed by the Congress. The resolution embodied a three-point program: (1) Organization of women domestic workers into trade unions of the American Federation of Labor; (2) organization of housewives into housewives' leagues to combat the high cost of living, to win better housing, recreational, and educational facilities for their families; and (3) organization of professional women. All three to be joined together to work for adequate social legislation, for better relief, and against war and fascism. This resolution was presented to the general session of the Congress by Mrs. Nellie Hazell, representing the Negro Democratic League of Philadelphia, and was unanimously adopted.

The delegates have returned to their homes, but not as they came. These women now have a program around which they will rally their sisters at work and in the home. They have a year in which to carry through the declarations of their resolution, so that by May, 1937, when the National Negro Congress again convenes—this time in Philadelphia—they will come together once more in greater numbers and with a different story to tell, of accomplishment, of a struggle nearer the goal of the liberation of Negro women from bitter exploitation and oppression.

11

Attitudes of Negro Families on Relief—Another Opinion

Thyra J. Edwards

Opportunity 14 (July 1936), pp. 213–15

An analysis of the questions raised by Professor Newell D. Eason in an article—"Attitudes of Negro Families on Relief," December "Opportunity."

Several years ago a distinguished agriculturist from Tuskegee Institute was presented to the secretary of the Negro Branch Y.M.C.A. at Gary, Indiana. The secretary, recently migrated from Texas, looked up at his tall, broad shouldered visitor, acknowledged the introduction, and added facetiously, "Alabama, eh, where there are the meanest white folks in the world."

"The meanest white folks and the meanest Negroes," was the agriculturist's unperturbed rejoinder. "Throughout the States I have found that the Negro community is in every instance a parallel reflection of the local white community. The variation is in degree only. The essential social pattern is the same."

Briefly this simple incident points the untenability of the thesis posed rather generally by Negro students and students of the Negro in treating the Negro as an isolated phenomenon rather than an integral unit of the community and national life. Any premise that sets apart certain attitudes, reactions and behavior patterns as particularly and peculiar to any one racial or cultural group, be it Negro, Aryan or Jewish, is sociologically and anthropologically unsound. There are no particular Negro emotions, reactions, or rhythms patterned by race exclusively. Unemployed Negroes and their families do not suffer a particularized hunger and exposure, nor do they react to it in a particular Negro fashion.

Unemployment has become, except for the Soviet Union, universal in extent. For the past seven years a very considerable segment of the American population has been sustained by public funds administered as Direct Relief, or as Work Relief Projects. In December 1935 there were, according to the conservative estimates of the American Federation of Labor, 11,401,000 employable persons in the United States separated from gainful employment.[1] Mass unemployment of Negroes became acute by 1927 and by 1929 there were 300,000 employable Negroes separated from employment. A number which has continued to rise. The percentage of Negroes in this category usually exceeds the whites by from 30 per cent to 60 per cent. There is a similar disproportion in the relief population. Negroes constitute 9.4 per cent of the population while comprising 18.4 per cent of all relief cases, 17.8 per cent of all the Negroes in America being maintained by Public Relief funds.[2] At present the Negro Relief population is 3,864,000.

And what is the source of this desperate disproportion between the Negro population and the Negro Relief population in relation to the total American population and the total American Relief population? It is generally recognized that the Negro, as a marginal and a minority group, suffers intenser employment hazards through discrimination in wages, in work allotment and in the disbursement of Relief. There is a prevailing sentiment that Negroes should not be hired as long as there are white men without jobs. There are in addition other basic factors: the introduction of machinery into unskilled functions formerly predominantly performed by Negroes has displaced a mass of Negro workers; the reduction of production in the automotive and steel industries in which large numbers of Negroes were employed, has displaced other thousands; cessation of activity in building construction which previously absorbed a great bloc of Negro skilled and unskilled labor; the reduction of incomes of families employing numbers of servants and the widespread use of electrical household machinery has thrown domestic servants on the labor market. The disappearance of small business into which category all Negro business fell, has not only created unemployment but destroyed and blasted the hope of a separate "Negro economy." The destitution of the southern farm population affects some 2,000,000 Negro farmers, largely share croppers and tenant farmers. And the government's removal of acreage from cotton cultivation has increased the destitution and intensified the insecurity of this group.

Even in the more liberal urban centers there is discrimination and segregation in the assignment of Negroes to certain work projects and to camps. Chicago uses the Batavia Camp, exclusively for white men. There are exclusive "white" projects.

Now after seven years, Unemployment and Unemployment Relief can no longer be classified as emergencies. Yet Federal and local governments continue establishing temporary procedures, made work, and work programs of a few months' life span only. Such procedure is mere wishful thinking. For as distasteful as are unemployment and relief to the American temperament and to the American philosophy of individual thrift and industry and individual success the permanency of unemployment and the problem of caring for the unemployed population are now recognized and accepted by the American public.

If indeed then, the Negro, in the face of these preponderous odds, has recognized the potential permanence of sustained unemployment and has adjusted his attitudes to the enigma of want and suffering in the midst of an abundance ruthlessly destroyed under government authority, then he has displayed an astuteness that exceeds and anticipates that of the finance capitalists and the political administrators who continue tampering and pottering with half measures. For there is doubtful virtue in the gesture of pacing the sidewalks in a futile search for jobs that do not exist.

Despite this it is notable that men and women on relief beg for and accept jobs, project and work relief assignments—even when the wage offered is the mere equivalent of their relief budgets. It restores some of their self respect to handle cash and to purchase direct and be able to shop about without the stigma and discrimination attendant upon buying on disbursing orders.

With the establishment of the Works Progress Administration this job-eager attitude repeated itself. A few men have refused jobs under slight pretexts. But the great number have anxiously accepted jobs, any kind of jobs, most of them at the ridiculous wage of $55.00 a month for full time. In large families this amount was cruelly below even the relief budget and families suffered the delays attendant upon cases being reopened for supplementation. Men went to these jobs often so poorly clad that "unsocially minded" foremen sent them home off the outdoor jobs. Waiting rooms in some relief stations displayed a gruesome exhibit of crisping, cracked, frozen ears, bleeding hands and swollen, frost bitten feet.

These men, eagerly accepting any kind of work under any kind of circumstances, represent a trend, not a phenomenon. At the American Association of Social Workers' Delegate Conference in Washington, February 14th, Mrs. Roslyn Scrota, Junior Supervisor of the County Relief Board of Philadelphia, Pa., reported that an impartial study of four urban centers disclosed that a very small proportion of job refusal (by the unemployed) are without justification. Physical disability, inability to perform the job offered, current employment, substandard wages are revealed as the common reasons for job refusals. Philadelphia has used a Job Refusal committee to define a bona-fide work offer and a "justifiable" refusal, and to hear complaints.[3] Before presuming to indict the unemployed such boards of impartial hearing should be set up in every community dispensing to large units of the unemployed.

"They were on the whole," complains Mr. Newell Eason, referring to Negro families on Relief, "averse to any suggestion of self help."

Well, Watts, California is remote from the experience and knowledge of the bulk of the American population. But in Chicago—the second city in the world for Negro population—the self-help efforts among Negroes are bravely defiant.

Last year a congested strip of Chicago's Black Belt comprising approximately nine city blocks and containing 1,349 households, a total of 4,422 individual souls was intensively studied and analyzed. There was the accustomed run of ice cream and water melon venders and window washers and news hawkers. And in addition, up and down the walks were fish vendors, carrying long strings of perch hanging from their backs or pushing their "catch" in rude carts converted from discarded baby carriages. The "junk men" had the middle of the street. These latter have hitched themselves to carts which they have built out of wheels, usually found on dump heaps, and irregular scraps of board gotten from some building in the process of demolition.

A conversation with the fish vendor disclosed this: "Three pounds for two bits, Miss. But sometimes I walk all day to sell three pounds. They's so many o' us on the street, we jus' 'cuttin' each other's tho'ts. I works wid a partner. A white fellow from the West Side. He stays out to de Lake and sets the nets and catch 'em, an' I walk up an' down an' sells 'em. I get a quarter outta ev'y dollar I sells. But fish don' bite ev'y day, Miss. 'Pends on how de wind blowin. Ef it ain't blowin' yo' way it jus' sweep de fish out toward de middle o' de Lake an dey don' bite. Fish don' bite ev'y day."

Behind the stone facade of the building down the street a colony of unemployed men and women have drifted in and settled. The building appears gruesomely debauched. Outside doors have disappeared so that is stands open always. Window apertures are stuffed with rages, old clothes, cardboard, wire netting, wooden doors, anything at hand. A side entrance formerly protected by a door is now barricaded by rusted bed springs, stoves and scraps of iron. Throughout the floors are rotted and in places broken out. On the stairways windows have become only great gaps where the cold packs in. All electric wiring has been torn out, all gas piping stripped. Various styles and sizes of coal stoves are used in the different individual "quarters." In the absence of flues these are piped through holes cut through to the outer walls of the building. Passing on the outside when several "quarters" have fires the adjoining vacant lot is a series of smoke puffs at various heights and levels.

Mr. Eason bemoans the wane of parental authority and the loss of prestige by the father. He cites the miserable example of Mr. S clinging to the last vestige of medieval male dominance by arbitrarily denying the necessary milk to undernourished Billie even when the money has been especially provided for this. His sole explanation, "the visitor has allowed the money but your father refuses to buy the milk!" That is the strongest indictment of the contemporary family pattern. Parental rule by blind, unreasoning might of authority bulwarked by school, pulpit, press and by the mores, and ultimately conquered by Relief!

For in the past the complete economic dependence of women upon their husbands, children upon their parents, and in turn in sickness and old age, parents upon their children has tended to warp every fine, free impulse in familial relationships. It has created the nagging wife wheedling an underpaid husband for the little luxuries of life which his inadequate wage cannot provide. It has created the demand upon older sisters and brothers to sacrifice their own education to help support younger sisters and brothers.

And so instead of decrying this overthrow of the tyrant-parent the sociologist should rather hasten the day when in addition sickness and invalidity insurance, a comprehensive unemployment insurance act and adequate assistance for the aged will relieve the burden of poor relations on other poor relations.

The fact is that professional social workers have been in intimate daily contact with large segments of the unemployed population for more than five years now. They have had continual access to the case records of thousands of these families. They are thus in possession of the facts to expose and explode these hair trigger conclusions branding the unemployed as maligners, chiselers and indolent and hopeless parasites. Instead of the too ready indictment of the unemployed condemnation should, it would seem, be directed against the political economy that creates these conditions of mass unemployment and its attendant malnutrition, disease, overcrowding, immorality, delinquency and family disintegration.

12

She Was in Paris and Forgot Chanel
Marvel Cooke

New Amsterdam News (December 12, 1936), pp. 8, 11

Thyra Edwards Back from Five Months' Study of European Social Conditions

Thyra Edwards, vivacious and vital returned Monday on the SS. Normandie.

Yes. She's been to Paris. But if she brought any Chanel or Poiret models back home with her, she failed to mention it during a packed hour of conversation on the day of her arrival.

What she did bring home with her, money couldn't buy—exciting experiences with leaders of women's and youth movements; vivid pictures of life in the Soviet Union; sharp impressions of life under the several Fascist regimes.

Interested in Women

But most of all, she brought back with her a passionate desire to mobilize Negro women in this country and acquaint them with such burning problems as social legislation for women, the organization of domestic workers and the lowering of living costs.

Miss Edwards, who was in Europe for five months studying social conditions, will be the principal speaker at a banquet given in her honor by the Greater New York Federation of the National Negro Congress in the Y.M.C.A. Little Theater next Tuesday evening. Mrs. Elise McDouglad Ayer will serve as chairman on that occasion.

Others on the program will be Lester Granger, Benjamin McLauren and Frank H. Crosswaith. The honored guest will speak of her experiences in her own graphic style.

Germany, Poland Wretched

Of all the countries she visited—England, Denmark, Sweden, Finland, the Soviet Union, Germany, Austria, Poland, Switzerland, and France— Miss Edwards declares Germany and Poland are the most wretched degenerating rapidly under Fascist dictatorship.

"Life in England and America," she declared, "is Utopian in comparison."

She told of visiting some German friends in a quaint little Bavarian village. She had intended to spend some time with them. But what did she find?

The husband who met her at the station, was positively scared to death. Anyone, he explained to Miss Edwards, who dared to entertain foreigners was immediately suspected of being an internationalist. And to entertain a Negro? That was enough to put you in jail for six months.

Hitler's 4-Year Plan

And so Miss Edwards did not tarry long with her friends even though they were already sunk deep in misery; she didn't want further to jeopardize their position in the community. But before she left she learned many interesting things, among them that the only youth movement in Germany is the Hitler youth movement and that Hitler's "four-year plan" is designed to make Germany independent of the rest of the world in four years.

Carrying out the country's vitriolic propaganda, *L'Illustrie*, a German illustrated newspaper, displays once a week huge disparaging pictures of Negroes and Jews, with such captions as "less than men," thus subtly singing silent praise to the supremacy of the Aryan race.

Searching Party

Perhaps the most harrowing experience Miss Edwards had was when she was leaving Germany. Just before the train crossed the border she and a man were unceremoniously hauled off to be searched for gold or incriminating papers.

"And do they search you!" Miss Edwards shuddered.

"Why, they remove every stitch of your clothing and even search your toe nails!"

"It seems, just to strike fear in the hearts of the people and to keep them in hand, one man and one woman is picked at random from every train crossing the border and searched. Because you don't know whether or not you will be the one to be picked, the experience is doubly horrifying."

Russia a Contrast

"Russia is a sharp contrast to Germany," Miss Edwards averred. "Whatever there is in the Soviet Union that you do not like, you can't help but react enthusiastically to the feeling of absolute racial equality which permeates the country. There, especially in the south of Russia, you find Armenians, Georgians, Persians and Jews living together in complete harmony."

Analyzing and comparing Fascist and Communist programs as exemplified by Germany and the Soviet Union, Miss Edwards says that it is simply this: Both Mussolini and Hitler declare that a country can only thrive in war. Stalin's slogan is peace at all costs. Both Mussolini and Hitler relegate women to child-bearing, the church and the kitchen. In the Soviet Union women are persons, not simply child-bearing machines and they have every advantage a man has.

Interested in Ethiopia

"I was surprised, and gratified too," commented Miss Edwards, "that Russians are tremendously interested in the National Negro Congress. They are excited about Abyssinia—honestly more excited about the Italian rape of Ethiopia than are Negro Americans."

"But France. Ah, there is the country. Women are organizing on three fronts: First, they are interested in getting the right to vote; second, they are vitally interested in the Spanish situation—why, only Sunday in Paris an international committee of women met to mobilize relief for the Republican women and children of Spain; and third, they are interested in the organization of domestic servants."

How to capture the interest of Negro women in this country—how to activize them in united front movements? These are the problems now worrying Miss Edwards.

But Thyra Edwards, vivacious and vital, will have no trouble in capturing the interest of the American woman or in mobilizing them, either.

All she has to do is talk simply directly, from the amazing wealth of her experience. They will be hypnotized into action by the challenge she makes to them.

Thyra Edwards has been to Paris. She left Chanel and Poiret behind. But she brought back with her the richest materials of the mind.

13

Negro Women in Our Party
Louise Thompson

Party Organizer (August 1937), pp. 25–7

A conference on Negro women was held in New York City a few weeks ago. This conference was considered historic, because it was the first such conference held. It was an historic one also so far as the composition of its delegates and the quality of the discussion that ensued there were concerned. It was held on June 6; there were 92 official delegates and 75 visitors. Fifteen of these delegates were Negroes; two non-Party women were invited and both joined the Party at the conference. One was the sister of Alonzo Watson, the first Negro to die in Spain. The topics of the conference were:

A. The Negro women in industry.

B. Organizing the unorganized, and neighborhood and church work.

C. The role of the Negro woman in the Party.

Recruiting was discussed freely and during those seven and a half hours which the conference lasted, not a person left the hall until the conference was over, and it was one of those intensely hot days. There were 43 women and one or two men who participated in the discussion. They discussed very frankly and freely all the problems concerning Negro women.

The Promotion of Cadres

The main emphasis in the conference was on the promotion of cadres. It was proposed that special attention be given to Negro women on the basis of their special problems; that special classes be organized where necessary; that more women be brought into the trade unions, the peace movement, and the Party.

I want to speak about the sewing project, where some of our best Negro women comrades are working. There are some 3,700 women of all nationalities on this project, Negro and white. We found at the beginning that Negro women were not given leading positions, were not given promotions. Through the work of our council we now have a number of Negro women who have the respect and are the leaders of all of these nearly 4,000 women. It is not insignificant to note that among these thousands of women, many of them are Italian women. The relationship that has developed between the Italian and Negro women on the sewing project is a splendid demonstration of what can be done by correct work.

A few remarks on building the Party among the Negro women. I think that if we examine our work we will see the necessity of finding special ways of recruiting Negro women in the Party. I know from experience—not personal, so much, but by observation—many times Negro women, because of extra special conditions that have kept them up to now out of the labor movement entirely, feel quite strange when they come into our movement. Perhaps we recruit some of them into the Party. Many of them feel strange. When they come to our meetings or affairs, they do not feel that they fit in, they do not feel as much a part of it as even our Negro men comrades.

Perhaps this is not the basic point to consider when we talk about the recruiting of Negro women into the Party, but I think it is an important consideration in helping to keep them in the Party.

I think, too, that Negro men comrades should place emphasis upon bringing Negro women into the Party. It seems to me it should be in a sort of personal way. Our women have been so cut off from the labor movement; I know they feel strange. Many times we have to win them in different ways—with some sort of human approach.

How to Recruit Negro Women

For example, I think that often, when we have affairs, dances, etc., if we went around we would find young Negro girls who would be glad to attend. If they got there and found they were given consideration, danced with—not made wallflowers—we would find that these are the things that count. These are the things that hold a lot of Negro women back from the Party. They are not so political, but they do mean a great deal.

As Comrade Browder said, as Bolsheviks we have to transform our lives in every way. It is true that political life and personal life tie up together. We have won over young Negro girls by bringing them into our personal circles, showing them that we are just like everybody else. It does a great deal to break down their antagonism and makes them interested.

Then there is the question of education. It is my opinion that even if we take such an example as we have of the development of the Party in Harlem, where our movement is cited always as an example, there are far too few Negro women in positions of leadership.

I think it will be necessary to take up as a special problem the ways to develop women cadres. When it can be seen that we have Negro women in our Party capable as leaders, as speakers, it is going to do a great deal for the Party.

I think that until we have a representative and large group of Negro women in the Party, our work in the Negro territories is going to be seriously hampered. Getting large sections of Negro women is going to root the Party among the Negroes. I think it is true—get the Negro women into the party, and not only will the men follow, but we will see that we will have a Party among the Negro people that has its roots among them and is a very vital part of their lives. I think the important thing is for us to see that special attention is given to bring them in, hold them, train them. This is essential to our Negro work.

14

Food Gets Scarcer and Scarcer on Spanish Front, Says Writer

Miss Thyra Edwards Tells Dramatic Story of Experiences in the War-Torn Country; Winter Rushing On

Norfolk Journal and Guide (December 4, 1937), p. 5

(Miss Thrya Edwards, together with Miss Constance Kyle, a white social worker from Chicago, paid a visit to the Spanish Civil War Front where they were delegates to the Social Workers Committee to Aid Spanish Democracy. In this article she gives her impressions of the country.)

PUIGCERDA, Catalonia, Spain (ANP)—We made ready to leave Puigcerda early this morning in October, Constance and I. And so we sprung out of bed and lunged gaily at the running cold water in the basin in the corner of our quaint beamed room extorting on the virtues of an icy morning bath in the early autumn days. There are no men about the hotel. So getting transportation to the station is uncertain. Most able bodied men are off at the front or occupied in the civil guard.

We shall have to score the neighborhood for a willing "hombre" or carry our bags in relays down. It then being twenty minutes of train time we decided to take the afternoon train thus allowing a few hours for work on our sunlit balcony overlooking the snows of the Pyrenees. It will also allow an extra hour for locating the "hombre."

Feels at Home

After three days we feel quite settled and at home in this picturesque mountain village which overlooks France and is therefore a carefully watched frontier. Spies slipping in and enemies slipping out. But by now all the authorities have seen our papers and it is accepted and generally known that we are on official business for the Aid of Spanish children.

Three days have been time enough to see the day to day lessening of food and tightening of belts. Even since our arrival butter has disappeared from the table entirely and the little café across the square where we go for coffee can no longer furnish sugar. "There is no more sugar," the manager says simply. Tonight the coffee was quite cold.

Ordinarily one could send it back to be exchanged for fresh, hot coffee. Ordinarily, one knows the café serves it hot. But now one recognizes at once that fuel is scare, hardly to be obtained at all and that the winter is rushing on. And so one takes one's coffee cold realizing that perhaps tomorrow or the next day at most there may be no coffee in the village.

Work Stripped to Waist

Four hours work on our mountain covered, sunlit, wrought iron balcony—we have persuaded the Senora to hang her daily wash a balcony below. I work stripped to the waist hoping to bottle up enough Pyrenees sunshine to battle off the awful insidiousness of Chicago's winter. Then lunch—the portions of sliced tomatoes are visibly less today altho' the tongue braised in a rich Spanish sauce, is delicious. Wine and cheese are good and the famous Puigcerda pears are excellent.

Then there is the settling of accounts. On a corner of a table in the kitchen the handsomest of the half dozen women of the house attempts to compute the bill. She is perhaps 25 years old. 1,080 pesatos! We are a bit indignant thinking she is playing us for stupid foreigners to be cheated. She reviews her computations. This time it is only 100 pesatos. Equally ridiculous. Only this time we realize that she can only read and write. She cannot count.

This is what the Spanish Loyalists are fighting about now! Common schools for common people. Education. Well, that's the side we're fighting on too. And so we take pen and ink and refigure with her, 180 pesatos including the tax of one pesato which we gladly pay and receive the gay stamps of little Spanish children. The tax is for aid to refugee children and another tax of 20 pesatos for refugee transport. We can understand that too for in these three days we've watched 5,000 refugees from the Asturias pass through this village of hardly 1,000 inhabitants.

Find "Hombre"

And then we get our bags down to the street. I keep watch while Constance locates an "hombre." He loads our two suitcases onto his pack. We take our respective type-writers. A packet of cheese and wine—just in case—a load of films, photographic apparatus and stationery supplies and start down the steep climb to the station. At intervals we stop to rest seated for a moment on the typewriter cases. Even "el hombre," used to these steps, finds it a tiresome climb.

Part of the way he swings them on a strap across his back. Finally he stops and borrows a wheelbarrow from a sympathetic neighbor. Unhappily there is only one wheelbarrow and it is only large enough for two suitcases. "El hombre" now travels much faster with the wheelbarrow and by slow stages and frequent stops we finally overtake him at the railway station.

The huge square outside the station is crowded with some 1,500 refugees siting about on the bales that hold their remaining worldly goods. A curly haired lad of perhaps six years cradles in his thin lap a mite two years while their mother, two others clinging to each hand, stands in line for the canteen from which she can get food for the whole brood without trying to find seats in the crowded canteen. There is talk, movement. But only at ordinary tones at ordinary speed. Men with bandaged heads, men with arms splintered on broad wooden racks, men on canes and crutches, move along in the line to the canteen.

Stay in Theatres

Perhaps 500 or 600 of these will board the train with us this evening. The others will sit about the station until the night becomes too cold. Then they will be sheltered in the town theatre and bivouacked in families. Of course a town of hardly 1,000 souls will scarcely be able to provide 1,000 extra beds so there will be shelter but no beds.

We move on to the customs. This is war time and one is inspected going out as well as coming in. The whole process is done neatly, kindly, matter of factly. I leave Constance to get the bags through the customs while I go for third class tickets to Vich. Customs finished, tickets purchased, we climbed onto the train to await whatever hour it might move on.

15

Excerpt from Memoirs on Scottsboro Boys Organizing

Louise Thompson Patterson

We Shall Be Free!, edited by Walter T. Howard (Philadelphia: Temple University Press, 2013), pp. 96–108

My assignment was to get the black people involved in the struggle for freedom of the Scottsboro Boys. Now, the committee itself was made up primarily of white intellectuals, and taking the office to Harlem was an effort to reach out and touch the common people, the working class people. Not that there was any ban on also getting intellectuals interested, but we wanted to get the masses of people involved. Perhaps it seems strange today when it is normal for the NAACP to call on people to mobilize and March in Washington. At that time these were considered communist methods. Taking the issue to the streets was not considered to be the way to carry on struggle. The Sixties, of course, changed all that. But in 1933, that was not the message that the NAACP and like organizations were putting down. It's true that all during the struggle for the Scottsboro Boys, especially many of the black churches and the ministers had been involved. There had been Father Bishop of St. Episcopal Church in Harlem on 133rd Street. Adam Clayton Powell had had mass meetings at Abyssinian. But still, taking it to the streets in organizing a march on Washington was unheard of.

The first thing I did was get an office up in Harlem. At that time 135th St., and not 125th St., was the center of black activity. There was a library on 135th Street; the YMCA was on 135th Street. St. Phillips Church had a housing development on 133rd St. Abyssinia Church was on 138th St.

The YWCA was on 137th St. All of these community organizations were pretty much between Lenox Avenue and Seventh or Eighth Avenues. So we wanted to center our activities right in the center of life in Harlem. The next thing was to staff the office. We had about two to three young black women who worked with us in the office. And then, of course, we had to get a committee in Harlem to sponsor and to help mobilize the people. And that was my first activity. I had never been involved in organizing any mass movement. But there were many who helped me, and so that began the work. It was very interesting. We had a storefront, so people could come in and find out all the information. We also had to raise funds because the people we were mobilizing didn't have any money. We solicited contributions so that we could get charter buses for the march to Washington.

Of course, we had to be in touch with other cities, particularly Philadelphia and Baltimore and Washington, because our effort was to mobilize the Eastern Seaboard; it was not at that point a national effort. We did not try to organize the march only for left people. We were getting the masses of people and the churches. Remember that at the same time the Depression was in full effect, so there were the unemployment councils and other organizations of people who were struggling to better their conditions who joined in willingly.

When the day finally came, the block between Lenox and Seventh, which was the main thoroughfare, was blocked off. There was no traffic on that block. The buses came, and the people came. Where they came from, I don't even know, but the buses that had been ordered were so promptly filled up that we had to get many more buses. The streets, the whole block was just like a huge mass gathering itself. And people of every category were there: old people, young people, mothers with babies in their arms, children. It was something else. I think it actually frightened me when I saw what was happening. We started mobilizing early in the morning, maybe around 7:00 [A.M.] or so, and we weren't able to pull away, to start for Washington, until about 1:00 o'clock in the afternoon. I didn't ride in the bus because I wanted to be able to travel back and forth and see what was going on, so I traveled by car. I don't remember whether we picked up people en route between Harlem and Philadelphia or not. I think we left solidly packed from Harlem. But by the time we got to Philadelphia, and that's only 90 miles, it was already dark. I can't recall the names of the churches, but a large Baptist Church had prepared food, and people slept on the pews and on the benches in the church. There were not enough beds.

Then we had to get up the next morning and start out. And the second day we made Baltimore, which was probably 100 miles. And we stayed in Baltimore all night, under similar circumstances. And the third morning, we got up and made the 45 miles to Washington, D.C. Just imagine, all these people, of all ages, all sizes, in various degrees of capacity to mobility.

We had huge meetings, and as Scottsboro caught on the people began to respond to our efforts. Then the politicians started trying to get a piece of the pie. And I can recall a tremendous meeting that was held in Brooklyn, in the Brooklyn Academy of Music, and all of the wards, all of the politicians, black and white, turned out for that meeting. William L. Patterson was on the platform. They had a white woman, political committee woman or something like that, the kind of people who would never have anything to do with Scottsboro, out there speaking. And I can remember William Patterson was so mad, angry, [and] cried, because when the time came for him, the leader of the ILD, to speak, all of the people had left the hall—because it was after midnight. So the next mass big meeting was held in Abyssinia Baptist Church in Harlem, and the church was packed to the rafters. Well, that same woman, white woman politician, was there. Pat got up and wiped the floor with her. He was quite an orator, you know, and he got the floor that night, and he got it early, he whipped it, talking about the Johnny-come-lately's and the people who were trying to do this to advance their own political careers. He had her in tears. The General Secretary of the International Labor Defense did a spectacular job—to the point that he lost his health and collapsed with Tuberculosis in 1934. He had to go to the Soviet Union for three years, to recuperate and regain his health.

The International Labor Defense began to work with the families and to get the families to directly participate in the struggle to free their children. The two mothers that I got to know quite well were Mrs. Ada Wright and Mrs. Patterson (I think her first name was Jennie). Mrs. Wright was a very alert person, and very determined to fight for the lives of her two boys, Roy, the youngest, and his brother.

When they first came to New York, I was living at 409 Edgecombe, and had enough room so that they stayed with me, and I got to know both of these women quite well. Mrs. Patterson used to sit very quietly for a long time, looking out the window. I don't know that I ever knew what she was thinking about. I remember she used to chew snuff. And she'd have a can, tin can, and she'd sit by the window for hours, spitting into that improvised spittoon and thinking. But when it came time to go to the meeting or whatever they had to do, they did it.

Two things I'd like to say about Mrs. Wright. When we think about slavery, we remember the role that Frederick Douglass played in going to England and France in gaining the support of the British working class people. I had occasion to see when I was there in 1972 or 1973, that there were monuments up in industrial towns of London of workers who had come out in defense of, in support of the Union during the Civil War and where Frederick Douglass spoke. I think of Mrs. Wright in that way. Here was this simple country woman who was taken to Europe and addressed masses of people in many different countries. The man who took her was Secretary at that time of the International Labor Defense, which was the organization that had been set up by the left-wing forces to fight for civil rights and for both black and white. They were very active in the fight to save Sacco and Vanzetti. And the Scottsboro case, I think, was the first major case the International Labor Defense took up to struggle against the oppression of black people.

At a later point in the defense of the civil rights, of the Scottsboro Boys, there came a cleavage between the forces that supported the NAACP, which originally had come in but had not done much about the defense of the boys, but later on as the struggle got broader, came back into the case, but yet did not support the policies that the International Labor Defense was taking, of making it as a mass struggle, of making demonstrations as we had in Washington of picketing. Their policy at that point was to leave it as a legal fight. So at one point there was the struggle to get the families and the victims in Scottsboro to end their participation with the International Labor Defense and come under the NAACP. So when the break took place, I happened to be in the South then. By that time, I had left the National Committee and was working for the International Workers Order (IWO).

In the midst of the split, carrying on the campaign and getting organizations, the funds grew low. Now we didn't get paid very much in the ILD in the National Committee. But that was the only income I had at that point. I think I was making $25 a week, which enabled me to pay my rent and buy my food. But there was a lull in the campaign, and the sources of contributions rather died out. And, of course, the expenses of carrying on the campaign itself were great. So I found that there were no funds, and I had nobody to fall back on. For the first time in my life, I began to fall back in my rent payments and didn't have any money to live on. But I felt that I had to do something about the situation—not that my interest was dimmed in the Scottsboro [case], but at least I had to have some money to live on. So I inquired among friends of mine whom I had made on the left, and a suggestion was made that maybe I could go to work for the International Workers Order, because it was a business, not a charitable organization. The International Workers Order was a fraternal insurance society made up of 16 different national groups, ethnic groups. The base of the organization was its insurance. Therefore, it did not depend upon voluntary contributions. They had a business to run. So you got paid.

So I went to work for them as a clerical worker, to begin with. But I didn't stay very long as a clerical worker because I was sitting there writing these policies, and seeing people paying and getting a policy for thousand dollars or two thousand dollars or three thousand dollars, and I began to think, well, that is something the black people should be interested in. Because black people, I got to know, as I was around working in the South on Scottsboro, even around in the black community, and down in Birmingham, could never afford adequate insurance. And what little they could manage was doled out in demeaning ways. I remember that in every black neighborhood, one day a week you would see these white insurance agencies weaving their way through the black community, coming to the door, never taking off their hats: "Is Maggie in?" Standing there in all of their arrogance and white supremacy and collecting the nickels, dimes, quarters or fifty cent pieces from black folk that netted them a policy anywhere from $100–$150. So they never had a kind of insurance that would be adequate even to bury them, to leave something for the families. It was a scandal. When I went to New York and saw that Metropolitan Life building down on 23rd and Madison, I thought, "This is the building that black workers built." The industrial policies were practically the only insurance that any of them ever had.

So I spoke to some of the leaders of the IWO. I was just there as a clerical worker at my $25 a week and paying my rent. At that time you could get a fairly decent apartment in Harlem for $50–$60 a month. So I began to look at these things, and I saw that there were certainly no blacks in there. I spoke to some of the organizers, the leaders of the organization. I said, "You know, I'd like to see black people get into this organization." I didn't sit at a desk and write policies very long before I was made an organizer, and my first track was down South.

Now, Samuel Leibowitz had been brought into the case before the new trial, by William Patterson. Pat felt that Leibowitz was the best man for the case because he was one of the best trial lawyers in the country. And he knew that when the new trial took place, down in the South, they would have to have a strong lawyer who, first of all, would dare to go down there and secondly, would dare to make a fight in the courtroom. This move on the part of the ILD and William Patterson split the National Committee for the Defense of Political Prisoners, with which I was identified. I was the assistant director. But the director and many friends, including people like Lionel and Diana Trilling, who were among the very bitter anti-Communist and anti-Soviet forces in the intellectual world at that time, withdrew from the National Committee with the defense of political prisoners because they felt it was wrong to take a lawyer who had been the foremost gangster's lawyer, known as such, and bring him into the fight. Pat's answer was, . . . "I don't give a heck what his background is, if he can win the court room in Decatur, Alabama."

Leibowitz, after all, was an opportunist. He was trying to make his name, and I think what he felt here was legitimate, accepted, respected in the NAACP, and maybe I'll have better luck than I did with the ILD. So he jumped ship to go with the NAACP. My job was to counter his influence.

So I jumped in my car, and it was a young black man, I don't even remember his name at this point, a hitchhiker, whom I picked up along the way and helped me with my driving. We left one night and went from Atlanta to Memphis. I remember that drive, because we had to go through a lot of valleys, and fog. He was driving almost blind. We drove all night to get to Memphis. Well, the first home I went to was the home of Ada Wright, the next day. I guess I went to their house and stayed with them. And I went out to where Ada was working to fetch her after her work day was over. Ada was working there for $5 a week. Cooking, cleaning that big house, taking care of the children, doing the washing and ironing, $5 a week. And I don't think they paid her car fare. So you can see the conditions under which people were living there. She was working in the white neighborhood. It was a huge house. I can remember it was a big old white house in the white neighborhood. I guess I went to the front door. I'm sure I didn't go round to the kitchen as most had to. And Ada came out, and her boss came out. He was going somewhere, and I asked him would he want a ride. So Ada got in the car, and he got in the car, and we started to go to the black community to her house. And he started talking to me. He said, "You know, I don't mind if Ada teams up with you, you folks, I've no objection about it." "But," he said, "the thing is you gotta tell her not to be sassy." He said "not to talk back" and to "stay in her place." He said, "If she does that, I don't have no objection at all what you are all doing because those boys should be free." Now, that was a liberal!

I went back to her house, and I spent the night. I went to bed, and suddenly I woke up. I didn't know what was happening. I was sleeping in the living room with one of the children. I looked up, and turned on the light to see what was happening, and the bed bugs were walking up and down the walls like an army. I got out of that bed and sat up for the rest of the night, and the child I was sleeping with never woke up. You know, I had been poor all my life, but I was seeing conditions that I had never, never, never seen in my life.

Well, I had no trouble with Ada. I arrived in time. Terry was there. And I went over to the Pattersons. There were two families, the Pattersons and the Wrights. And I saw Mrs. Patterson. Well, she said, "I can't go cuz [sic] I got to stay here to take care of my granddaughter, Louise," her name was. (They said "*Lou*-ise.") I begged her, got down on my knees to beg her to go. She wouldn't go. Terry had gotten the father, the Patterson father, to agree to go with him. And they were at the train. I jumped in the car and went down to the station, and there was Terry with Mr. Patterson, and the train was just about to pull out. As it tried to pull out, I tried to pull that man off the train. Oh, I was just heartbroken. The train went on out, and the only one Terry had was Mr. Patterson. Well, I think I went back and worked on Mrs. Patterson. I got on my knees, and I cried, and begged her to go with me, told her what it means. So finally I got her and Ada Wright to come to demonstrate, and we left out that night, to go down to Montgomery, where the boys were in Kilby prison.

Now, Terry had to go by train to Birmingham, and then change trains to go down to Montgomery. So me and my little company got in the car about midnight and drove all night long, racing against the train time, through all that fog and mist, and got to Montgomery the next morning, about 8:00 o'clock. We beat Terry there because he had to wait for the train. Ben Davis had been sent down by the ILD to counsel with the boys, and I took my party over to Ben Davis and turned them over to him, so that when Terry got there with Mr. Patterson, Ben Davis was there with the Scottsboro mothers.

I was no stranger to these women, because I wasn't just someone coming from the North. They had slept in my house, eaten my food, and I had traveled with them around to meetings. So I think they had confidence in me. And, of course, I knew them much better than the father, and it was the women who played the major role in the defense of their sons. And so it was. Terry was real surprised to see us there because the last thing he had seen of me was my trying to pull Mr. Patterson off the train.

While I was in the South, I found that this struggle became the symbol for any fighting for civil rights. The people down South kept saying "Yes, I'm a member of the ILD." And ILD became symbolic of the struggle.

What did this case symbolize? One thing I think was very important was the role of Ruby Bates, one of the so-called victims of the Scottsboro boys. We had always been taught, I mean black people, that the enemy was poor whites, and that they were poor white trash, and that the boss was the good white man. Ruby Bates and Victoria Price were known as prostitutes. This case, in a sense, exploded that myth about rape and exposed some of the forces that were behind it—that poor whites could be used as the agent to do the lynching, but behind it stood the state, its courts, its police, the whole government, in terms of oppression of the black people. Now I'm not saying that this came clearly out in every instance. But when Ruby Bates made that trip from the South and spoke at that first meeting of the 66th Street hall in New York City, the air was so electric that night, if you had scratched the match, I think it would have exploded to see this young white girl march up there and say that these black boys didn't do it. That was the first time that we know of in history. Some whites got to her to convince her to tell the truth. And there was enough decency in her heart that she had to be honest. She hadn't been completely corrupted. Victoria Price, the other woman, on the other hand, was a hussie, and she never repudiated her first testimony. Ruby, however, had stayed with me at times. I got to know her well. And she was a decent person who wasn't ready to kill nine black boys who didn't rape her. She finally left New York after the case was over and all; she had to stay out of the South, of course. The last I heard of her she was in Minnesota. She married someone. She had a lot of guts. And certainly Pat was right in saying that Leibowitz was good, because he had guts. I don't know that he had scruples, but he had guts. Finally, at the end, there was some kind of compromise made, the NAACP eventually came back into the case.

Amazingly, about a year later, in 1934, I found myself in the same jail with three of the Scottsboro Boys. And one of the girls in my cell block claimed to be the sweetheart of one of the Wright boys. She used to get notes from them. In those days, organizing in the South, amongst the rest of the activists, you would get involved at any facet of the struggle that happened to be current at the moment. It so happened at that point, when I was in Birmingham, the uppermost struggle at that point was a strike in the mines. Now Birmingham (and I've been in many Southern cities) was the meanest town I've ever seen in my life. Both the class and caste struggle were sharper there. I was there during May Day, and the tradition was, from a labor point of view, to have a rally of workers. I went down to the May Day rally to help hand out leaflets. Do you know, when you got downtown they didn't let two Negroes assemble together?! If blacks were on the street, they had to move. They did not permit anybody to stop. Do you know in the office buildings they had machine guns pointed down from the windows to where the rally was supposed to be held? Now, the main union there was the miners' union, and contrary to all the other unions that I know and to the credit of John L. Lewis, blacks and whites were organized in the same locals. It's the only union like that that I knew in the South, and they were out and steadfast in terms of the strike. The papers were full of the news of the strike. But of course, as with anything else, and kind of people's struggle, the newspapers claimed it was the Reds that were doing it and not the grievances of the miners. Well my work for the IWO was akin to the labor movement; we were interested in working with workers and giving them the benefits of our program. So I became interested in the strike. I had to. I went to strike meetings. And one night I went out, Endsley or some place, the Red Mountain, they used to call it, and attended one of these meetings, and there were important elements in the strike, some important knowledge that I wanted to get to some of my progressive friends. It had nothing to do with IWO, but it had to do with the workers, and their program and their struggle.

So the next day I tried to reach these friends, who were communists, and I couldn't find anybody. So I knew of a woman who was editing and publishing the *Southern Worker*, who was white, and I knew where she was, and I thought, "If I get hold of Elizabeth, she'll know where people are." She had done a great deal of writing about the South, and she wrote quite a bit. She was well acquainted and versed in Negro history. So I decided I'd go visit her, and see, and try to get the message across, and what I knew about where the strike was and some people I knew. Well, I was living with a middle class black family whose relatives I knew in Harlem. They used to worry about me. They'd say, "We don't like you going out by yourself." They'd never seen a young black woman doing this kind of activity. And they said, "We have a friend who has a lot of time, and he'd be glad to take you around, because we just don't like you going around like this. It's dangerous." I said, "All right," so that afternoon George came by, and I asked him would he drive me out to the white community, where this woman lived. He said, "Sure." Well, what I did was leave him, fortunately, several blocks away, and told him to wait for me. And I got out and walked, and I walked into this middle class neighborhood to an apartment building, and knocked on the door. It was opened by a policeman. There was a raid going on! Elizabeth, the woman I was trying to contact, quickly said, "We don't have any sewing for you today." The policeman said, "That don't hold." He said, "We know you're one of them Goddamn Yankee bitches from New York. Come on in here." So I walked into a raid. And when they came to take us away, they took all the whites and they put them in a paddy wagon, and they put me in a car. When this old white policeman took me out to the car, he said, "Daughter, what are you doing getting mixed up in a mess like this?" He said, "You know, [the] only thing wrong with these communists is they just like niggers too well. You shouldn't be involved in it." He just couldn't imagine a young black woman walking into a raid. So that's how I got jailed, and that's all it needed.

I WAS DETERMINED that I was not going to expose the people I lived with to anything, because, as I told them later, I said, "You have to live here." One was in the Post Office, one was a school teacher, one was a social worker—it was that kind of family. So I was determined that, no matter what it took, I would never let them know. I gave a false name, a false address, and I guess the word got spread around on the grapevine that I was in jail. It was even in the newspaper. There were about 50 of us black women in this very primitive wooden county jail the first night. Cots on each side. I had never seen a jail.

The next night they put me in this modern prison downtown, with the electric locked doors and the clicking of the steel as the door shut on your cell block. You had a cell block with about six individual cells where you slept. In the daytime you could come out to the general room, and that's where you ate, and socialized. They brought people up there to look at me like I was an animal on display. The white jailers did everything they could to insult me. They pretended they didn't know what I was saying when I spoke, and they couldn't understand my language. They had one of the Negro flunkies: when I turned around and stooped over for something, he hit me on my behind so they could laugh and sneer. When they were taking me to do the ID, I found myself in the elevator with the Sheriff, Bull Connor, who would become infamous in the 1960s. He pointed to me and said, "That's one of them goddamn Reds. They oughta do her like Mussolini does—take her out and shoot her against the wall."

I remember one of the girls in the first jail. She was a pickpocket. That night I spent my time finding out what crimes they were in for. All were black because, of course, it was a segregated jail. One was a pickpocket, one was a prostitute, one girl said she killed a man. I said, "What did you do? Shoot him?" She said, "No, Honey. I just put a knife right through his heart." The next morning when they came to get me to take me downtown to ID, Pinky, this big fat pickpocket, said to me, "Honey Jean" (I had given my name as "Jean"), "when you go down there, don't you be no goddamn fool. When that white man asks you a question, you say, 'yes sir; no, sir' . . . That won't cost you nothin', Honey, but it'll save you plenty of hard knocks." Well, I got down there, and that white man started asking me questions, and I got so mad, I forgot all about Pinky. And when he stopped at one point and put his finger in my face and said, "Look here, gal, you're in the South now, and when I talk to you, you say, 'Yes sir, no sir.'" I was ready to die before "Sir" would cross my lips. I could not say "yes sir, no sir." The next question he asked me, I looked at him and I said, "No!" Now, I think the only thing that saved me those hard knocks was, first of all, these prison employees had probably never encountered a black woman like me. Secondly, between Scottsboro and the strike, Birmingham had too much on its hands, it didn't want to have any more cases to fight or defend themselves. And I think that's the only thing that saved me. Because at that point nobody, nobody in the wide world, knew where I was.

Birmingham was the most segregated place I was ever in. The streetcars, the whole atmosphere, was like nothing I had ever known. New Orleans wasn't like that. And Atlanta was not like that. In many of the Southern cities, they'd have a little sign that you could take off and move, depending on the number of blacks and whites in the streetcar at any given moment. But in Birmingham you had permanent boards that went from ceiling to floor that separated the sections. On some of the streetcars you had to get to the front, and pay your fare, then get off and walk to the back and get to your seat. You could not even walk through. They had three kinds of streetcars. One blacks had to get on in the back, one they had to get on in the middle, and one they had to get on in the front to pay their fare. So one day I used to be so mad when they'd be standing there waiting to get on that I'd say, "At least I'm going to be the first person on that streetcar; I don't care what happens." And I'd get up and get on first. So I didn't always know which kind of a streetcar I was on. So one day I got on, went to pay my fare, and I looked up, and this old white conductor was sweating. And he looked at me and he said, "Please, ma'am, would you please tell me if you're colored or are you white?" I said, "I'm an American Negro." He said, "Well, will you please get off and go up to the front?" Tough days.

One night I was going to a left meeting. When you were down there, you know everybody that's progressive; whether you're in the Communist Party or you're ILD or you're in a labor organization or whatnot, you know people who are trying to bring about change in that area. So I was going to some meeting out in the industries on the outskirts of town. The guide who was supposed to tell me where to go was white. So we agreed that we'd go to this corner. I'd stand where I got on the streetcar, and he'd get on his where he was supposed to get off, and then when we got to where we were going, he would get off one block, and I would get off the next. We stood on that street corner for almost an hour waiting for the streetcar, and he never looked at me and I never looked at him. When we got on the streetcar, I sat in my section and he sat in his, and then we got off. We did it the same way coming back. One got on and at one corner, one at the next corner. Unfortunately, we had the same conductor. He looked at me as if he were saying, "This is no accident." That's the kind of attention that you got. You could never relax, you were conscious every moment. I was scared because he really looked at me. Birmingham was the meanest town.

Nobody was convicted in the Scottsboro appeal trial. The Supreme Court ordered a new trial based on the conclusion that the defendants had not had adequate counsel in the first trial. The boys were sentenced to 99 years in prison in the new trial, but, by 1950, the last of them had been released. Most of them were never the same. I believe only one was able to lead the semblance of a normal life.

16

The Negro Woman Domestic Worker in Relation to Trade Unionism

Esther V. Cooper

Excerpts from MA thesis, Fisk University, June 1940

Ch. 1: The Negro Woman Domestic Worker in the United States

The United States Census includes under domestic and personal service a wide range of occupations from laundresses and charwomen to hairdressers and manicurists. However, this study is limited to an investigation of Negro women employed in private homes, who perform general housework and who handle services for members of the household and their guests. In spite of the fact that there are many social and economic problems related to domestic work in private homes, there is little data available as to numbers, race, age and marital status of domestic workers.

Although the exact number of household workers at the present time is unknown, an estimate can be made from the 1930 census. More than 3,000,000 women were employed in domestic and personal service in 1930. There are no accurate figures as to how many women were engaged in domestic work in private homes, but from census figures, the Women's Bureau has indicated that well over 1,400,000 were in this group. Three of five Negro women workers reported their usual occupation as in domestic and personal service; included in this number, the Women's Bureau has estimated that over 600,000 Negro women were domestic workers in private homes in 1930. It is a striking fact that there is a high concentration of white women household workers in the age group under 20; 24.2% were in this class age, as contrasted with 15.6% of all white women gainful workers, 15.9% of all Negro women gainful workers, and 14.4% of Negro women in general housework.[1] There are, also, large numbers of older white women in domestic work, but for Negro women the age distribution is more scattered. It appears, then, that domestic work is predominantly an occupation for very young or relatively old white women and for Negro women of all ages.

Striking differences between white and Negro domestic workers with respect to marital status emerge from an analysis of census data on this subject. Among white domestic workers, the percentage married in 1930 did not exceed 25% for any age group. In the case of white women, domestic work is done characteristically by single, widowed, and divorced women. Among Negro domestic workers, however, the married woman is the rule. From 25 years on the percentage of single Negro women in domestic work is small. From census data, we find that in the 1930 population, 33% of Negro married women were gainfully occupied and 8% were in general housework, but of all married white women, only about 10% were gainfully occupied and less than 1% were in general housework.[2]

In order to understand more thoroughly the role of the Negro woman domestic worker in present society, and the problems which they face, we shall examine briefly the historical changes which have taken place in the number, problems, and conditions of work among these employees in the United States. As one commentator, writing at the turn of the century, put it: "In studying the question of domestic service, therefore, the fact cannot be overlooked that certain historical influences has affected its conditions: that political revolutions have changed its personnel, and industrial development its mobility."[3]

During the early history of our country, service of every kind was done by transported convicts, indentured white servants, Negroes and Indians. These servants often complained of long hours of work and ill treatment, while the housewives complained of "ungrateful servants and inefficient service." In the South, the large plantation developed with its big house and its economic self-sufficiency. Here the Negro slave was the house servant. With respect to this pattern one can see why Roscher, the German economist, discusses domestic service as an appendix to his treatment of slavery. The plantation owner and his wife looked on the Negro house servant with an air of benevolence and maternalism. The relationships between servant and mistress exhibited all the characteristics of the feudal relationships of master and serf. When slavery was abolished in 1863, many former slaves who had been domestic servants continued in this capacity, receiving a small sum of money for the work.

The number of Negro women domestic workers in the period just following the Civil War is not known. It was not known until 1890, when the first separate occupational statistics of Negroes was taken by the Census Bureau, that one could get reasonably exact information on the number of Negro women domestic workers in the country. In 1890 the total Negro population was 7,488,676 or 11.9% of the total population. Agricultural and domestic workers comprised the bulk of the Negro population at this time. Almost one-third of all the Negroes gainfully employed were classified as domestic workers, although the number employed as household workers in private homes is not available.[4] By 1900 there was an increase of 361,105 domestic workers in the Negro group, an increase of 37.7% over the number in 1890.

Migration of Negroes to both Northern and Southern towns in search of better wages, hours, and conditions of work and other urban attractions may account for some of this increase. Negro girls and women, especially, migrated to the city from rural areas in search of domestic work. In the South, many white women went into the cotton and steel plants, and in so doing employed Negro girls to look after their homes and take care of their children. For this the Negro domestic received wages ranging from 50 cents to $3.50 a week.[5] In the North, wages for domestic work were higher, and thus provided an attraction to those seeking better conditions of work. However, in the North the Negro faced much competition in domestic work in addition to the fact that he was refused work altogether in lines of industry monopolised by white persons. Thus, Greene and Woodson say in *The Negro Wage Earner*: "However, the keen competition for jobs in the North, the fact that domestic service carried with it no social stigma as in the South, and the higher wages paid, all served to weaken the Negroes in this field." These authors also point out that even though there was a numerical increase in the number of servants in 1900 over 1890, the proportion of Negro women in domestic service showed a decline in 1900 which was due to the keen competition for jobs and to the increased effort of the Negro husband and father to prevent his wife and daughters from "working out."

From 1900 to 1914, the proportion of all Negro women employed in domestic and personal service continued to decline. In the North some employers preferred whites and immigrants to Negro domestic workers. Added to this problem, was the tendency toward smaller homes so that housewives could perform household duties alone or with one domestic worker. The bakeries, the clothing stores, laundries, dairies, etc., began to do work which was traditionally the role of the domestic worker. In the south, the domestic servants began to tire of the feudal relationship and tie to the household; they had for so long been made to feel and acknowledge their social and racial lowliness. Thus migrations to the North continued. Even though there was a decrease in the proportion of Negro women in domestic work, this field remained one of the main occupations in which Negroes were employed.

By 1920, there was a further decrease in the proportion of all Negro women who were in domestic work. Here again we see various factors entering into the situation; not only does the decrease indicate that Negro women entered into some of the industries and other occupations at this time, but indicates also the whole trend in modern housekeeping. That is, the urban housewife began to use modern mechanical appliances and time-saving devices. She also resorted to the use of birth control mechanisms, so that there were few or no children, and thus there was a decrease in the number of mothers' helpers and other domestic workers whose duty it was to help care for the young. In spite of this decrease in the proportion of Negro women employed in domestic service which has continued to the present, there was an absolute increase in the number from 1920 to 1930. It seems highly probable that the Negro women will continue for some time to be employed in domestic service because of the keen competition which she meets in all types of industrial work. Thus, it is fitting to examine at this time the conditions under which domestic employees must work, and the problems which they face today.

From the few recent studies of domestic workers which are available one concludes that low wages, long hours, and poor working conditions are characteristic of this occupation. Negro women domestic workers have been discriminated against and exploited with double harshness. The high turnover among Negro women domestics is thereby partly explainable. From various available reports we may conclude that the major problems of domestic workers are lack of employment standards, long hours and low wages, exclusion from the benefits of social insurance and other protective legislation, and the social stigma attached to domestic work.

Lack of Employment Standards

Because household workers are scattered in many private homes, thousands of individuals bargain for work. To some extent competitive forces bring about an equalisation of wages. That is, domestic workers move from job to job in search of high standards, at the same time that employers are on watch for workers who will accept lower wages and longer hours. These competitive forces, however, are fully as likely to drive down the level of compensation received by domestic workers as to maintain or raise that level. Hazel Kyrk, Associate Professor of Home Economics at the University of Chicago, states on this point:

> The services of household workers are but one of many desirable goods for which personal income may be spent. Those with incomes sufficiently high can pay high wages as they can buy expensive clothes, and pay higher rentals. Those with lower incomes struggle to balance their budgets by searching more and more intensively for cheaper help. One of the most difficult points in the household employment situation arises from these two circumstances—a relatively low income and a standard of living that calls for one, possibly two hired workers, and two or more younger children. Every element in the situation makes for long hours, heavy work, low wages and limited accommodations.[6]

The household employee has no wage scale based on skill, amount of work required, or experience. She is usually untrained and unskilled. The demand for efficient and trained workers is much larger than the supply. Little efficiency can be expected when an employment office brings country girls to cities by the truck loads to work at "starvation wages," and when employment bureaus regard the payment of an application fee as the only requirement for placement. In a study made in Chicago by the Women's Bureau, Department of Labor (1933), it was discovered that of 246 domestic workers reporting on their training, just over one-fourth, whether white or Negro, had attended such classes, but less than 3% of the total had received there all the preparation for their work. More than one-fourth of the total had secured all their training in their own homes; about one-eighth had received all in the homes in which they had worked; and one-third had had their training in both these places. Employers reporting in this same study in Chicago indicated inadequacy of training and experience of domestic workers in their employment. More employers found training inadequate in cooking and serving than in any kind of housework; almost one-third had found it necessary to give training in these branches. Others reported that employees needed training in "my way of doing things." Other kinds of work in which employers had found it necessary to train their employees were planning, care of children, dishwashing, orderliness, and use of equipment, particularly electrical equipment.

Long Hours and Low Wages

Today employers of domestic workers work their million and half employees an average of seventy-two hours a week and pay them lower wages than are paid in any other occupation.[7] Knowledge of wages paid and hours required of domestic workers in various sections of the country are revealed in a number of special studies. In 1936, *Fortune* magazine sent to more than 17,000 *Fortune* subscribers, to 500 editors of women's pages of newspapers, and to 3,000 women's clubs, a questionnaire on the servant problem. The following conclusions on wages and hours were included in the results of the survey.

Wages were highest in the Northeast, lowest in the South. Thus, 73% of general houseworkers in the New England, Middle-Atlantic section earn $40 and over a month; 60% in the western half of the South earn under $40 a month.

Wages were highest in cities of over a million. Thus, 82% of general houseworkers in cities of more than a million earned $40 and over a month; 56% in communities of less than 5,000 earned under $40.

Wages of white and Negro houseworkers ran almost parallel up to $30 a month; thereafter, they favor the whites moderately. But in specialized jobs, wages over $50 favor the whites overwhelmingly.

Five out of every six domestic workers worked more than 8 hours a day; two out of every six worked more than 10 hours; one out of six work more than 12. Short hours were most frequent in the west and in small communities; long hours in the South and in the big cities.[8]

In Lynchburg, Virginia (1936–1937), a study was sponsored by a Joint Colored-White Committee of the YWCA and an Inter-Racial

Commission. A total of 141 questionnaires were filled out by 64 employers and 77 employees. The following conclusions on wages and hours
were included in the results of the study.

> The typical wage of the group covered by the study was $5 or $6 per
> week, as represented by the two largest classes of approximately the
> same number of cases. Two cases were reported at $1.50 and one at
> $10 and there was one report of payment in the form of a house "on
> the lot" rent free, and one payment made only in clothing.
>
> There were 63 employees who received pay during sickness as
> against 40 who did not; 58 were paid for vacations and 31 were not.
> There were 19 employers who stated that they gave a raise in wages
> after a period of time, while 55 employees said they had received no
> raise on their present job.
>
> There was one report of a working week of 91 hours and 16 of 80 to
> 90, the typical number being 72 hours per week.[9]

Another study was conducted in Philadelphia in 1932 by the Women's
Bureau of the United States Department of Labor. Of the 74 domestic
workers who answered questionnaires, only one-fifth were white, and
the majority of those were foreign born; this fact is significant for our
purpose. The following conclusions on wages and hours are included in
the results obtained in this study.

> About two-thirds of the women living in who reported the length of
> their usual day worked as much as 12 hours. Of the women living out,
> two-fifths had a day of 12 hours or more. Two-fifths of all reporting
> went on duty between 7 and 8 o'clock in the morning. Nearly one-half
> of those by whom the time of quitting work was given, went off duty
> between 7 and 8 o'clock in the evening
>
> The median of the week's wage of the 72 women reporting is $14.60;
> for those living out the median is lower than for those living in, the
> amounts are $12.70 and $15.25 respectively. The white women had a
> median somewhat higher than that of the Negro women—$15.35 in
> contrast to $14.50.[10]

A more recent Government investigation is that of the Bureau of
Research and Statistics of the Social Security Board. An analysis was
made of 3,846 registration cards providing a random sample of the

active and inactive files for domestic workers registered with the State Employment Offices in four cities—Cincinnati and Lakewood, Ohio; Wilmington, Delaware; and the District of Columbia. Data on wages were obtained for 1,734 workers registered in 1936, 1937, and 1938. The following results seemed significant.

> In all of the cities covered and in each year most frequent weekly cash wage was from $5 to $7. In Cincinnati, Wilmington, and the District of Columbia, a larger proportion of Negroes than of white workers received from $7 to $9, but larger proportions of white workers received $11 and over.
>
> In Cincinnati, Wilmington, and the District of Columbia, daily wage rates varied from 50 cents to $3.50; the largest number of workers, 164 our of the total 450 received between $2 to $2.50 a day. In each of these cities 90% of the workers reported to have been working on an hourly basis received from 25 to 30 cents an hour.
>
> In the records covered by this field study it was found that there was little difference, as a rule, in the wage rates of those who live in the homes of their employers and those who live out, and, in a few instances, wages were lower for those living out.[11]

In all of these studies presented here and in other scattered studies it was discovered that overtime is rarely paid for, that a regular 8-hour work day such as thousands of other workers now take for granted is only an ideal to domestic workers. Thus, in Rochester, New York, a domestic worker recently begged for a code setting hours of household labor at 84 a week, twice that of most factory regulations.

Exclusion from Social Insurance and Legislation

Legislation in the field of domestic work has been slow, partly due to the lack of standardization of domestic work, and the lack of a united front of either employers or employees to set up standards in wages, hours, and conditions of work upon which favorable legislation might secure a foothold. Only three states, New York, New Jersey, and Connecticut, place household employment under workmen's compensation laws, and Connecticut only if there are four employees working for one employer. New York places domestic workers in line for unemployment insurance only if there are four employees working for one employer.

Today only one state, Washington, has a law which regulates hours of work in household employment. This law was passed in 1937 and establishes a 60 hour work week for all employees in private households but permits longer working hours in emergencies.[12] The original draft of the bill included a six-day week, double pay for overtime, and provision for $50 fine for violation. In order to get the bill through the legislature, its proponents were forced to drop these provisions. The results of the passage of the bill have not been what its proponents had hoped for; employers have been non-cooperative in many instances and employees are hesitant to report violations of the act for fear of losing their jobs.

Only one state, Wisconsin, has set minimum wage rates for women and minors in domestic work. This legislation, the Oppressive Wage Law, passed in 1925, is quite flexible in that it is interpreted and administered by the State Industrial Commission.[13] However, the officials who administer the Wisconsin Law find it difficult to see that the laws are being upheld because of the many and isolated places of employment, because of public opinion, which resents investigation of private homes, and because the employees are reluctant to file complaints.[14]

In the Social Security Act, passed in August, 1938, household employers were exempted from Federal old-age and unemployment insurance. The Social Security Board, however, has pointed out the sound policy of extending old-age insurance to as many of the nations' workers as possible and has recommended that the exception of domestic service be eliminated with allowance of a reasonable time before the effective date.

Social Stigma Attached to Domestic Work

Domestic workers have been made to feel and admit their social inferiority. They are called by their first name, both by strangers and friends, children and adults. What one commentator said in 1897 often holds in 1940:

> The domestic employee receives and gives no word or look of recognition on the street, except in meeting those of her own class; she is seldom introduced to the guests of the house, whom she may faithfully serve during a prolonged visit. The common daily courtesies exchanged between members of the household are not always shown her; she takes no part in the general conversation about her; she speaks only when addressed, obeys without murmur orders which her judgment tells her are absurd, is not expected to smile under any

circumstances, and minsters without protest to the whims and obeys implicitly the commands of children from whom deference is never expected.[15]

The owner-slave, lord-vassal, master-servant tradition remains, as *Fortune* points out, the chief reason on the one hand, "why housewives have failed to be realistic in their handling of servants . . . and on the other, why domestic work is unpopular and domestic workers difficult to obtain." Again, the Public Informant Assistant of the Women's Bureau, Department of Labor, points out quite vividly: "Household employment generally is viewed as unskilled work and persons so engaged are looked down upon socially. This belief holds despite the fact that household tasks are varied and when they are done efficiently demand intelligence and a considerable variety of skills." Finally, the domestic worker may be given a room off the laundry, or even in the garage; she has no security of any kind, and is treated in such a way by members of the family that a social stigma is attached to her.

Worker conditions faced by domestic workers constitute a serious problem for the thousands of individuals directly affected, as well as for society as a whole. Individuals and organizations, in attempting to shape a program for improving conditions of domestic workers have come to the conclusion that organization of domestic work is one of the bases upon which higher standards might be maintained. In the efforts to unionize domestic workers, leaders have followed closely the experiences of other workers who have organized trade unions and have focused public opinion on their problems.

Ch. 6: Gropings Toward Unionism Elsewhere

The various attempts to establish trade unions among domestic workers which have been described have all been successful, at least to the extent that a beginning has been made and that the Union is still functioning. There is still to be recorded the story of a number of attempts which have ended in failure, as well as certain other ventures which appear to represent partial steps along the road to unionism.

A Union was started in San Diego, California, in 1933.[16] The organizer was a young woman in her early twenties who went into domestic work after withdrawing from college because of lack of funds. After several positions in homes where she experienced long hours, poor living conditions, and low wages, she decided that it was time to do something to improve the situation of girls and women in household employment. Accordingly, she started the San Diego Domestic Employees' Union. The Union had a sincere leader, attractive rooms where members gathered for meetings, classes, and a social time. It became affiliated with the AF of L as a local of the Building Service Employees International Union. Any one would have predicted that the Union would continue to grow, and still be in existence today. Yet the Union has given up its charter. It has failed in its attempts at organizing household workers, although it did, in the course of its existence, accomplish a good deal in arousing public opinion to the need of better standards and legislation for domestic workers.

The organizer of the San Diego Union feels that the problems which led to its disintegration were many. These problems include poor leadership, lack of concerted drives for one objective, insufficient funds, and ignorance on the part of domestic workers concerning conduct of meetings and unions generally. Furthermore, there was strong opposition on the part of employers toward the Union, an opposition with which the weak Union was unable to cope. The organizer is now working with the Y.W.C.A. domestic employees' club and finds that "this is a more sensible course of action to follow because of the support of many influential persons and organizations which may be secured by way of the Y.W.C.A. and because of the recreational and social activities which it has and which are certainly needed for domestic workers." The organizer, however, emphasizes that one disadvantage in working with the Y.W.C.A. on this matter is the fact that "the employers on the board must themselves be educated and won over to support the household worker."

Another effort at unionization of domestics is one which was organized in Philadelphia in 1935 called "The Domestic Workers of America." This organization hoped to unite all household workers in Philadelphia and then to establish a national group. At the Philadelphia headquarters, there was published for some time *The Domestic Worker*, a small bulletin which printed information on conditions of household workers, on special problems of Negro women workers, on legislative procedures, and other pertinent topics. In 1936, the organization promoted a series of mass meetings and published mimeographed bulletins calling attention to the miserable pay, over-work and general exploitation suffered by domestic workers in the Philadelphia area. The program set forth by the Domestic Workers of America included (1) a legislative program for laws to benefit domestic workers (2) a program for better relationship between the employer and the employee (3) an employment program to obtain jobs for domestic workers (the employment service to be free for members of the Union) and (4) an educational program for domestic workers to include special training in domestic art, domestic science, domestic hygiene, and trade unionism.

That the intention of this Philadelphia Union to organize nationally has not been carried out may be ascribed to inadequate funds, insufficient leadership, and to the fact that in several cities similar movements were developed with national ambitions. To all appearances, the Domestic Workers of America is hardly more than a paper organization, organized and led by people who are not domestic workers and who do not give sustained attention to the work of the Union. Finally, the Philadelphia organization has failed to catch the imagination of domestic workers, themselves, and until it does so, its success as a Union will be meager.

Efforts at unionization of domestic workers in the South have been least successful of all. The attempts have been few, and have received little enthusiasm and support. In the South the belief still exists to some extent that the relationship between housewife and domestic worker is personal rather than contractual. Often housewives cling to the old benevolent attitude toward Negro domestics which was the accepted attitude during slavery. The Negro domestic in turn often feels dependent upon the white employer for his wants. This type of Negro domestic is often docile or full of flattery for his employer. To such Negroes, unionism offers no inducements, and to such housewives, unionism is "preposterous." The failure of unionization of household workers in the South can be explained in terms of the attitudes of both Negroes and whites toward this occupation.

However, there are some employers of domestic workers and some domestic workers in the South who have become conscious of the household employee. Where the Negro domestic worker begins to see her relationship to her employer in a different light than formerly, she asks for higher standards as to wages, hours, and conditions of work. Some have turned to organization as a possible solution to their problems. Thus, in 1935, a group of Southern Negro women organized the National Association of Domestic Workers which had headquarters at Jackson,

Mississippi, and which had hopes of establishing branches at St. Louis, Mo., Knoxville, Tenn., and Baltimore, Maryland.[17] The National Association of Domestic Workers had possibilities of becoming a strong organization at its inception, since it grew out of the tremendous hardships which household employees suffered during the depression when some were forced to work for as low as $1.50 a week for an 80-hour week. The leaders hoped that this southern organization might grow into a bonafide trade union, but it lacked experienced organizers and trade union contacts. Today it is merely a paper organization, even though it has done some educational work in a few Southern cities.

In Nashville, Tennessee, a very interesting club of domestic workers has been organized. In November, 1933, I. L. Dungee, a Negro chauffeur, called together a dozen or more Negro domestics, both men and women, and organized the Faithful Workers League. The purpose of the club was at first recreational. However, its organizer began to think of the club in terms of a placement bureau for efficient domestic workers. Because the organizer had insufficient time for making the contacts necessary to increase membership this club was merely a paper organization from 1934 until October, 1939, when it was reorganized. Under the new title, the South Nashville Civic League, the membership has increased to 100 members. The joining fee is $1.00, but there is no set sum for dues; members pay what dues they can. The club proposed to the City Council of Nashville that the latter establish a Domestic Service Commission consisting of three housewives who employ regularly domestic workers, and three domestic workers. The purpose of such a Commission will be to promote cooperation between domestic workers and employers in the city of Nashville. A resolution embodying this proposal failed by one vote to be passed by the City Council.

Attendance at the weekly meetings of the South Nashville Civic League varies from a dozen to 50 or more. Here, the members, about half of whom are women, discuss their problems and plan benefit programs or recreational evenings. The officers of the club have plans for reaching domestic workers through the churches in Nashville where Negroes attend in large numbers. So far, however, this program has not been carried out due to lack of time of the organizers, and insufficient numbers of domestic workers who are willing to undertake the task of visiting the many Negro churches in the city. Nashville domestic workers in general appear reluctant to join the organization for fear that they might lose their jobs or that their employers might hear of the club.

Those who are afraid of an organization that has purposes similar to those of labor union must be assured that the group is merely fraternal before they will join.

Another club of domestic workers, known as the Pink Carnation Club, has been organized in Nashville, Tennessee. This club is composed of 17 Negro women who earn no less than $8.00 a week. Members learn how to sew, embroider and crochet at their club meetings. Experiments in cooking are a part of the program although there are no cooking classes. The problems of domestic workers in Nashville provide topics of discussion. The president of the club states as its purpose: "To improve the service of workers, to secure jobs for unemployed members and to provide social contact."

Either one of these clubs in Nashville has the possibility of becoming an organization for collective bargaining if it can secure the cooperation of a large number of domestic workers and win the support of some of the outstanding social and civic organizations in the city.

In other cities we find clubs of domestic workers which seem to emphasize the training and efficiency of employees rather than adequate wages. Y.W.C.A. groups in a number of cities invite domestic workers to social evenings, motion pictures and other recreation; in some cases they promote training classes and placement services. For example, the Colored Working Women's Club of Englewood, New Jersey, is composed of employed women, most of whom are domestic workers. The aim of the club is to improve the efficiency of its members and to raise the standard of living in the Negro community as a whole. It has established training classes for its members; it has attempted to place the members; through benefit programs, movies, and plays, it has established a fund which is used for "worthy causes" in the Negro community. In addition to these activities, the Colored Working Women's Club has established a minimum wage, a standard below which it refuses to place its members. The National Urban League which has kept in contact with this organization and is well-informed about its activities, makes the following statement:

> The club has done a great deal to build respect among its members for the occupation they follow, and to impress Englewood employers with a respect for the qualified domestic worker. It furnishes a civic contact for its members which is helpful to the workers themselves as well as to the community.

Well known among domestic workers' clubs is the Domestic Employees Club of Milwaukee, Wisconsin, organized by a woman civic leader. This club has emphasized legislative activity. From February, 1938, to the present, the club has concentrated its attention on a bill for an 8-hour day, a minimum wage, and a 24-hour rest period in every 7 days. A more recent bill which the club has proposed provides for wage collection by the Industrial Commission in cases of non-payment of wages. Because the organization regards itself strictly as a club, it has never considered seriously affiliating with the AF of L or the CIO. Its organizer stated in September, 1939: "We are not yet affiliated with the unions or the AF of L because we first must have a State law to protect wages and hours." For this reason, a legislative program has been emphasized in this club.

Recent developments in the Milwaukee Club reveal a feeling of discouragement. One of the leaders has stated: "In this last state legislature we had a very bad showing. We have been before the legislature three times concerning standard wages and hours." This same leader said: "It's very hard here to get colored women to organize. And in fact all houseworkers are hard to organize. They all want better working conditions but just don't seem to realize that it is they who must support the organization."

Another type of club which grew out of the depression is the Big Sister Organization of Scranton, Pennsylvania. This organization has set up a code which employers must follow if they want employees who are guaranteed to do efficient work. The code was set up in 1936 with the following provisions: (1) a clear understanding between the employer and employee of the requirements of the position, before the position is accepted (2) a written copy of the day's program, with duties clearly defined and provision for emergencies (3) total actual working hours not to exceed 66 a week; a 24 hour leave to be granted weekly, including Sunday afternoon and evening and one or two other evenings; an hour's free time to be provided every afternoon (4) four out of 8 holidays and one week of annual leave with pay (5) overtime to be compensated by extra time off within a month (6) minimum wage of $5.00 a week with board and room, payment to be weekly or monthly (7) opportunity to attend the church of the employee's choice (8) one week's notice of termination of services or a week's pay (9) living accommodations to include a room of the employee's own, furnished simply but attractively; access to bath facilities; a room where she may entertain her guests;

adequate heat, light and food (10) compensation for injury to be covered by accident insurance carried by the employer, preferably in the form of a blanket policy protecting the holder of the position rather than the individual.

The Big Sister Organization has met with small success in achieving these high standards. It has encountered strong opposition from employers, and has received little cooperation either from employers or form other organizations. Today, the organization is not very active, and it reaches few workers.

Thus, we see that there have been many gropings towards unions among domestic workers, some of which have ended in failure while others have the possibilities of developing into bonafide trade unions.

Ch. 8: Conclusion

This study has examined the conditions and problems of Negro women domestic workers in the United States today and has emphasized particularly their participation in trade union activity.

The fact that Negroes have often been the founders and organizers of domestic workers' unions in the United States is of significance for our study. More Negro women are in domestic and personal service than in any other occupation. Negro women have not only suffered from lack of employment standards, long hours and low wages, exclusion from social insurance and legislation, and social stigma attached to the occupation, but they have also been forced to receive lower pay and to work under lower standards than white employees. Housewives, knowing they can get domestic workers at almost starvation wages, have played employee against employee. One of the worst types of human exploitation is the "slave market" found in New York City, and one of the ugliest aspects is the way in which girls are shipped up in carloads from the South to stand on corners waiting for work at 25 to 35 cents an hour. These workers have formed the nucleus of the Union in New York.

In looking over the four Unions considered in this study, we see that the bulk of unionized domestic workers are those who have suffered most from economic exploitation and racial discrimination. In the main it is these workers who have taken the first step toward unionization, rather than the workers who have served faithfully in one family for years, or those workers who are paid comparatively well by wealthy employers. Domestic employees who work by the day or night, who are hired and fired often, and who receive far below a living wage are the ones from whom an active union program may be expected.

Of the 600,000 Negro women domestic workers in private homes in the United States today, less than 2,000 are organized. These 2,000 are concentrated in four cities: New York, Newark, the District of Columbia, and Chicago. We find that domestic workers' Unions have set up wage and hour standards and have established union contracts to enforce these standards.

The Domestic Workers' Union of the District of Columbia has set up a contract which not only includes wage-and-hour standards but indicates just what the work is to include, such as general housework, ironing, sewing, cooking, etc., has set up standards as to uniforms, breakage, living arrangements, vacations, insurance, holidays, and provision for entertainment of friends when the worker is living in the home. Both employer and employee sign the contract, both agreeing to one week notice by either party if the contract is broken. Housewives are often willing to sign contracts if they are assured of efficient service in doing so. Although training classes have been started by the District of Columbia Union with the cooperation of the WPA classes, the Union has not yet been able to guarantee well trained workers for all the calls which come through the Union office.

The Washington Union is facing other problems, too. The total membership of the Union, 500, is an insufficient number for effective collective bargaining. Leadership among the domestic workers has been slow in developing, and Union members often do not cooperate fully with the Union's employment office and placement bureau. Domestic workers in the District as yet have little feeling of unity; they have been accustomed for generations to work in isolation. Negro domestic workers often have more loyalty to the class which they serve than to other domestic workers. Thus we find a number of serious problems facing the Washington Union. The Union has proved, however, that a domestic workers' Union is not impossible in the District, that wage scales and classification of domestic workers by type of work is important for effective unionization, and that work can be found for members of the Union at standard wages, hours, and conditions.

The New York Domestic Workers' Union, with a membership of over 1,000, is the largest of its kind in the United States, and the only domestic workers' union affiliated with the AF of L. It has emphasized a legislative program, centering about a drive for a 60-hour week, inclusion of domestic workers in workmen's compensation benefits and minimum-wage laws. In attempting to carry out this program, the Union has been handicapped by insufficient funds and lack of cooperation on the part of domestic workers and the public in general. However, the Union, with the aid of the International Labor Defense has had some success in dealing with grievances between employee and employer. Its members, nearly all Negro women from Harlem, report to interviewers the improvements which they have achieved since joining the Union, although they are reticent at first in talking with outsiders. The New York Union will perhaps be the nucleus for unionization of domestic workers on a nation-wide scale. In New York may be found domestic workers already union-conscious with a program, with leadership, and knowledge of union tactics. Here, too, are the headquarters for many other unions in the country, powerful unions which started out with small memberships and with many obstacles to overcome.

The Newark, N.J., Domestic Workers' Union is perhaps the least active of the four Unions investigated for this study. Organized in 1935, the Union now has 250 members, some of whom never come to union meetings or participate in any of its activities. Perhaps the development of the Union in Newark has been slow because of tremendous opposition which members have met on all sides. Negro women themselves have looked on the Union as an impossibility and have cynically waited for its failure. White housewives upon being interviewed have expressed opposition to the Union, and have predicted that it can never include in its scope all domestic workers and therefore cannot be effective. Housewives have carried this opinion to domestic workers in their employment; these workers in turn have often been impervious to any pleas which the organizers and members of the Union have made to them. The future of the Union cannot be predicted. Perhaps the fact that over 200 women are receiving wages and working hours according to union standards may be an incentive for building the Union.

The Chicago Domestic Workers' Union, as far as can be ascertained, has roots which extend further back than any of the other domestic workers' unions. As early as 1930, some investigation of conditions of work among domestic workers in Chicago had been accomplished, with the aid of the National Committee on Household Employment and the Women's Trade Union League. The work took on a fresh start in 1935 when the Domestic Workers' Association was organized. This Union has been characterized by waves of optimism followed by waves of pessimism. After the defeat of the 8-hour bill for women in domestic work in 1939, the Union entered its most bitter days. The Chicago Union seems to be holding its membership but not increasing in numbers. Its newly defined program is modest; it includes opening training classes for domestic workers, and continuing a program of education through newspaper articles, church contacts and union-sponsored programs. The future of the Chicago Union depends on its ability to find leaders among its members who will devote full time to developing and carrying out the program of the Union, and on an expansion of its program so as to include much more than a legislative drive.

There are possibilities that the Milwaukee Domestic Employees' Club and the Englewood, N.J., Working Women's Club, among other organizations, may develop into bonafide unions. Many of these clubs are of recent origin and have not yet gained a foothold or have been confused as to program and policies. They may, however, be able to derive guidance and some degree of encouragement from the experiences of the four active unions.

The many difficulties of organizations are not the only problems which domestic workers face. They must deal with deep rooted opinions and attitudes hostile to unionization, such as those expressed by women's clubs, by employers, by employment agencies, by certain domestic workers who identify themselves with their employers, by newspapers and magazines. The domestic workers' unions have realized that such attitudes have been counteracted at least partially by active support given to the Unions by such prominent organizations and agencies as the Women's Trade Union League, the National Urban League, the National Negro Congress and the Women's Bureau. Other support has come from progressive employers and women's clubs, and certain Negro newspapers. Finally, the CIO has supported the various attempts of unionization and has expressed its intention of taking organizational steps in this field in the future. The conviction of the CIO that unionization is possible for domestic workers is of significance for the domestic workers' Unions already organized and for any which may be attempted in the future. Such support tends to stimulate organization.

We have seen in this study that unionization among domestic workers is a fairly recent phenomenon in the United States, and hence, a very small percentage of the total number of organizable domestic workers is unionized. In examining the history of some of the large labor organizations of today, such as the United Mine Workers, the Amalgamated Clothing Workers, and the Newspaper Guild, etc., we have discovered that membership was very small in the first years of organization. It is true also that when the CIO was first organized, it gave its attention to helping small Unions of rubber and automobile workers, which were the forerunners of the many affiliated CIO Unions of today. Hence, the small beginnings made in unionizing domestic workers are no indication that they are unorganizable.

It has been stated elsewhere that domestic workers are unorganizable for a number of alleged reasons including especially the point that they work in isolation. However, it has been shown in this study that similar statements have been made concerning agricultural, white collar, technical and professional workers, and yet these workers have organized themselves to an appreciable extent and have sought to standardize their work conditions. We have seen also that domestic workers in England, in the Scandinavian countries, in Russia, and pre-fascist Italy have proved that domestic workers can effectively bargain for higher wages, fewer hours, favorable legislation, and more humane living conditions. While the future of unionization among domestic workers in the United States cannot be predicted, nevertheless, it can be concluded that the problems faced by Negro women domestic workers are responsive to amelioration through trade union organizations even when we recognize the many difficulties which are involved in unionizing this occupation.

SECTION III
Fighting Fascism

The five chapters in the third section were published during and after World War II. Together they trace a shift from the opening the war provided for Black people to access better jobs and training to the rapid rollback of those opportunities once the war came to an end. They also demonstrate how fierce advocacy for democracy and basic rights could be mobilized as a critique of the United States. Black soldiers had died as part of the Allied military effort to fight fascism only to continue facing white supremacist violence and oppression when they returned home.

Esther Cooper Jackson's stirring speech at the fifth All-Southern Negro Youth Conference presented German, Japanese, and Italian fascism as a threat to democracy, to civilization and progress, and to "the right of our people for human existence." A linked threat to the survival of the nation was the denial of basic rights to Black people in that police brutality and discrimination played "into the hands of the Axis forces." To defeat fascism, it was necessary to end lynching, abolish the poll tax, and unify the American people. Cooper also held up Black women as "strong fighters for freedom"; indeed, "the difference between victory and defeat may well depend on how effectively the nation's womanhood is mobilized."[1]

The first two chapters from Thelma Dale and Claudia Jones track an intensification of race hatred as "Big Business" sought to divide the working class by pushing Black people out of industry. Relegated to low-wage service jobs or the insecurity of the "reserve army of the unemployed," Black people could be used as strike-breakers to weaken unions

and drive down wages. Dale describes how union seniority requirements led to Black workers, especially Black women, being the first
fired. She argues that Communists must do more than embrace modifications to seniority requirements. They must "lead and always be in the
vanguard of the struggle for Negro rights."[2] She criticizes the party for its
practical and theoretical failures with respect to Negro work, arguing for
the necessity of strengthening Black leadership in the party.

Relatedly, Jones criticizes the party for its revisionist turn away from
the analysis of Black oppression as national oppression and argues for a
recommitment to the call for Black self-determination in the southern
"Black Belt" as central to the Black–labor alliance. This analysis of the
special condition of the "Negro question" in the United States had put
Communists at the forefront of the struggle against white supremacy
because it enabled them to teach white workers that it is in their interest
to fight for Black rights. It also aided the party in encouraging Black
workers to go beyond narrow bourgeois nationalism to see their
common cause with white workers against exploiting bosses. Dale's and
Jones's chapters were initially published in *Political Affairs*, the CPUSA's
leading journal of political analysis.

Dale and Jones also draw out the impact of rising reactionary forces
on women. In February 1947 Dale documented the status of Black
women in the United States in a report given at an International Council
Meeting in preparation for an upcoming convention of the Women's
International Democratic Federation (WIDF).[3] The WIDF was an international peace organization that had formed two years earlier at a gathering in Paris that Dale had attended.[4] Convened by French women
associated with the resistance movement and the Communist Party, the
initial gathering brought together over 800 women from left, labor, and
antifascist groups working in forty countries, including the USSR and
colonized countries. Dale's report describes the specific effects of anti-
Black discrimination on Black women, not least that the majority of
Black women are forced to seek waged labor outside the home because
their husbands don't earn money to support their families. With an eye
to bringing international attention to the horrors of segregation, Dale
also details the disenfranchisement of Black people in the US South.
White supremacists were escalating the violence against and lynching of
Black people, trying to terrorize them into not voting. Jones challenges
the CPUSA directly to amplify its organizational work with women. The
party was failing to make the "woman question" a matter of central

concern to all party members. It was failing to root out "male chauvinism" and activate, involve, and train women in the party. Until it does, she warns, it will fail in its efforts to fight fascism and organize the working class.

One of the most significant contributions of Dale's and Jones's chapters is the emerging theorization of the US as the primary source of the fascist threat. No longer does the US lead the struggle for democracy and peace. The concentration of imperial power, cultivation of white supremacy, aggression of big business, and reactionary confinement of women to the domestic realm was becoming a force as dangerous and oppressive as that which the Allied powers united to defeat. Arising out of monopoly capital and the semifeudal economy of the US South, the growing reaction of the late 1940s attests to the fact that fascism had not been wiped out. It is an ongoing threat to peace and progress everywhere.

17

Negro Youth Organizing for Victory

Esther V. Cooper

19 April 1942, draft speech delivered at the Fifth All-Southern Negro Youth Conference (April 18, 1942). Manuscript Department, Moorland-Spingarn Research Center, Howard University

[Note: words stricken out in this chapter were crossed out in the original speech draft document. The italicized words in this chapter were handwritten into the original speech draft document.]

We who are meeting today in this 5th All-Southern Negro Youth Conference are the representatives of Southern youth. We are from the ~~factories~~, churches, schools, *Y.W.C.A.'s, Y.M.C.A.'s,* mines, mills, government agencies, farms—from every walk of life. Among us are youth of the north and west representing many interests and special problems, all of which are part of and related to the one great common problem of all America—how to contribute most effectively to the winning of the War.

We have come together because we are patriotic Americans to discuss ways of implementing our efforts to the resolute persecution of the war for a speedy victory. We ever recognize and we are agreed that only through the destruction of the German, Japanese, and Italian *fascist aggressors'* powers which threaten the right of our people for human existence and threaten at the same time all civilization and progress, can democracy remain or be built anywhere on the face of the earth. The nation, ourselves and all civilizations are under attack by the Axis forces. We know that without their destruction, our striving for a peaceful world of brotherly respect and cooperation among men cannot be consummated in our time.

Our organization was founded at a Conference of youth, meeting in Richmond, Virginia in 1937. This was a year when Negro youth were a generation of the depression to whom main avenues of living were closed. Our organization was formed on the initiative of a representative number of serious minded youth who were determined to lend themselves to the task of organizing the youth to find opportunities necessary for useful living. Consistently we have centered our program around job opportunities, recreation, education, health service, protection of our person from mob violence, police brutality, and cultural expression for our generation.

Our struggle has historically been one to place the talents, and resources of our generation in creative channels for the service and enrichment of our country.

In the critical years of the past, our program has helped save from frustration and despondency many of the best representatives of the youth of the South and to strengthen their character and enlarge their vision in the process.

~~In 1935 in the lower depths of the depression, the American Youth Commission was established by the American Council on Education to study the special problems facing the youth of the South with an adequate budget of several thousand dollars.~~

In 1937, the Southern Negro Youth Congress was established out of the determination of a group of courageous young people to determine to give their strength and lives if need be to help solve the problems of youth. ~~They had neither money or the sponsorship and encouragement of great national personalities.~~

A young man, a native of Texarkana, Texas, Edward Strong, accepted the responsibilities of Secretary of this dream. There was no money for salaries or even for stamps and stationery. But with consecrated devotion to the task, great personal sacrifices and loyal support of such ~~excellent~~ youth as Thelma Dale, James Jackson, Louis Burnham, an organization was built. By the following year, the 2nd All Southern Negro Youth Conference was called in Chattanooga, Tennessee and the Southern Negro Youth Congress was already a lusty, healthy, growing infant.

In 1939, in Birmingham, Alabama, the 3rd All Southern Negro Youth Conference had recorded considerable growth of the organization. It met with considerable experience in the struggle for rights of Negroes.

It could record victories in the field of employment of Negro youth. Its mass campaigns had resulted in enlarged N.Y.A. opportunities for Negro students. It had organized Negro community theaters as social weapons and means of cultural expression in Richmond, Nashville, and New Orleans. It had won a victory for Negro labor in the tobacco factories of Virginia, in a labor struggle which remains a classic model until this day.

In April 1940, the 4th All Southern Negro Youth Conference met in New Orleans attracting 580 delegates representing 400,000 youth and attracting the active and sympathetic support of outstanding Southern leaders such as Dr. F. D. Patterson, Mr. Forrester B. Washington, Dr. Rayford Logan, Dean Ralf O. Hara Lanier and many others.

Since the early beginning in 1937 when the Southern Negro Youth Conference was still a figment in the imagination and dreams of a few courageous youth, we record an individual membership today of 7,000 and with 112 affiliated organizations. Through the distribution of 90,000 pieces of literature in the past 9 months period, including our publication, *Cavalcade*, the *Rural Bulletin*, Southern summary special bulletins, speeches and action folders, we have conducted an educational job on the issues of the War as they affect the interest of the nation in the cause of justice and advancement of the Negro people.

We who are assembled in this great Conference of Southern people represent many organizations in the South. The Councils of the S.N.Y.C. and other groups who have sent delegates have done so because they are deeply concerned with how Negro youth can more fully share in the nation's war tasks and in larger measure contribute to the winning of the War.

The following program of activity is addressed, therefore, to the organizations represented here today and to the councils and city wide federations of the Southern Negro Youth Conference. Delegates, in this period of great crisis for America, we should like to see each body of Negro youth organize its program around 2 concrete issues, first, to educate and train youth for effective community leadership and, second, to stimulate youth to social action for defense of the Negro people and the nation. This can only be done through unity of activities and programs.

How can we train youth for effective community leadership? This can only be done through the education of our membership. Through community forums, library projects, through current event discussion classes. The National Office of the Southern Negro Youth Conference will pledge a steady stream of printed material during the next year to be distributed throughout the South. It is our recommendation that the National Office make as one of its major tasks—supplying teachers outlines, study outlines, and other pertinent material to the Councils, affiliated organizations and other interested groups. It is important to know the government agencies and what they are doing, to be familiar with such material on youth as that published by the American Youth Commission, to read the Negro press, the labor press, to be familiar with city governments, to know where the youth congregate and what they like to do.

Secondly, we would like to see this Conference stimulate youth to social action for defense of our nation and the Negro people. For action in service of our country there is much to be done. Negro youth will strive to win increased opportunity for training in defense industries. We support whole-heartedly Donald Nelson's plea for all out defense production. We ask for increased opportunities in the nation's war program. In the South, we should like to push forward for more jobs and a wider range of jobs in all industries. In September 1941, federal government agencies had approved of thousands of defense industrial projects in the government's program of defense plant expansion. Of this amount, 13 Southern states were represented by 20% of the national total.

Let us look at our Southern communities. Where are the Negro youth employed? Miners, steel workers, students, all of you—what jobs are there for Negroes in your town and city. Delegates, we are many. Let us work together to see that Negro youth do receive training and contribute to the winning of the War. Let us work out together a plan of action for jobs. President Franklin D. Roosevelt in his letter to the 5th All Southern Conference of Youth has said, "Your strength, your courage and your loyalty to your country help assure this victory." We need jobs training to do this task well. In the South, what part are Negro women taking in the nation's defense program? According to Mary Anderson, Director of the Women's Bureau, the skills of women of all races will be needed by the nation to meet the demands of maximum war production. She points out clearly that Negro women are an important part of the total woman labor supply needed in this crisis. Women's organizations have been outspoken in asking for job opportunities in the defense industries—Alpha, Kappa, Alpha Sorority, The National Council of

Negro Women, the Colored Women's Methodist Episcopal Convention and many others.

Organized labor has readjusted itself to the emergency of the hour. With such a beginning, let us organize Negro women to contribute their maximum to the winning of the War. Trade unions are of particular value in taking the leadership in such a program because they will be more readily able to assure equal pay for equal work. We should like to see Negro women as nurses, machinists, ~~welders~~, electricians, experts in radio communication. ~~We propose, therefore, that we as youth endorse a plan to send a delegation to Production Chief Donald Nelson calling for his support in our efforts to win jobs.~~ Let us work our state training plans. ~~Women, too, especially should be included in such a presentation.~~ ~~for~~ The role of Negro women in the war program is particularly important today when the armed forces and the nations production centers are making such great demands upon the nation's manpower.

The Women's Bureau has pointed out there is an increased need for nurses both on the civilian and military front. Trained Negro women nurses should be able to seek such positions on the home front and in the army training centers. As industrial nurses, women can play an important part in reducing the loss of accidents in the new industries which are increasingly to employ women workers.

In order that we may serve more fully in the war effort we will find the means to strengthen our efforts in support of the continuation of N.Y.A. and C.C.C. Training. In many Southern states, N.Y.A. Training is the only opportunity which Negro youth have to increase their skill. Scrapping these projects on the grounds that they are non-essentials at the time of national crisis is to do disservice to the nation's total war effort. It is worthy to note that many Southern people and organizations are opposed to the abolition of N.Y.A. Training. Recently the Alabama State Principals Association and the Alabama Parent Teachers Association petitioned Congress for the continuation of youth training projects. Fellow delegates, you who are from the schools, the colleges, the workshops—all of which will be greatly affected if the NYA is dropped—go back to your communities and schools and solicit petitions to be sent into Congress. The NYA hearings are next week. Get to your phones— send telegrams to your Senators and Congressmen. Let them know how you *and our nation's war program* will be affected if ~~the~~ NYA closes down.

Negro schools and colleges can become centers for defense training. At Howard University, at Hampton Institute campus wide programs for integrating every student and faculty member into the nation's war efforts are well underway. High schools too may be placed on a 24 hour basis for the duration of the War. The high school carpenter shop can become a "defense center" for all the boys and girls in the neighborhood to *train for producing* ~~produce~~ vital war needs. Negro students might well form voluntary defense training corps—sending in their names to government agencies and asking for teachers.

The Negro farm youth is a large and increasingly important group in the War against fascism. Farmers have been the most impoverished in the South's millions. After the attack on Pearl Harbor, Secretary of Agriculture Claude R. Wickard revised the farm production goals of 1942 calling for the greatest [production] in the history of American agriculture in order to assume a maximum supply of food and fiber for those fighting the "world battle of democracy and civilization." The fact that over one half of the Southern rural youth examined were rejected by the army because of poor health is living evidence to the fact that diet corrections *& increase of garden acreage* are part of the nation's war program. Secretary Wickard says that thousands of additional acres of crops and pasturage are necessary to supply rural people in the Southern states with a minimum adequate diet.

In October 1941, the Southern Negro Youth Congress sent identical letters to President Roosevelt and Secretary Wickard urging them to establish a government agency which would investigate and penalize all acts which limit full participation of Negro farmers in benefits of the government agricultural program. We asked that a bi-racial body similar to the Fair Employment Practices Committee be set up to act in the field of Agriculture so that Negro farmers might have the same assurance for the Negro industrial worker. Since that time, Dr. Patterson and Mr. Claude Barnett have been appointed assistants to the Secretary of Agriculture. We would like to see Rural Youth initiate a program for southwide cooperation with the Department of Agriculture, at the same time pointing out to Secretary Wickard that the farm worker who has no income at the end of the year can be expected to contribute little to the stores of food material needed for our civilian population and armed forces and pointing out secondly that the power of the large landlords to withhold the benefits of the various agricultural programs from Negro farmers will have to be broken.

Rural youth, you who are assembled here—let us return to our homes and organize our communities to *increase food production and to oppose* protest any cuts in the Farm Security Administration Loans and see that Negroes receive a full share in these loans. Recently, Southern Senators and Congressmen have been attacking the F.S.A. on the grounds that it is not necessary to national defense and has wasted federal funds. Yet the F.S.A. has directed its entire program toward support of the War program. President Roosevelt has realized the importance of F.S.A. to increasing production and declared this agency essential to the success of the Food for Freedom Campaign. Mr. President, listen to the voices of the South's rural youth. Answer their calls for fuller participation in the nation's war production efforts.

We should like to see farm youth follow in the foot steps of Negro youth of the F.S.A. in Arkansas who are taking night school defense training classes. This training has prepared Negro youth to make repairs in farm equipment at home and in the necessary war skills.

We as youth will act to end police brutality and other forms of attack upon the Negro people so prevalent in the Southern states. It is clear that those who deny the principles laid down in the Bill of Rights to Negro Americans do a disservice to the cause of the democracies. The continuation of discrimination against the Negro is threatening our nation's very survival, and playing into the hands of the Axis forces. Negro youth—fellow delegates—friends—let us take the leadership in striking our against every instance of attack upon the Negro people. We shall view such cases as attacks upon the nation. We are asking for severe penalties for those who commit such crimes. Let us see that there are no more Sikestons. Now is the time to renew our campaign on a southwide and nationwide scale for *action by the Department of Justice and executive action to end* lynching as a powerful blow to the Axis nations.

Police brutality which has recently been on the [increase] in many southern communities is one of the worse crimes against National Unity. We Southern youth will take the leadership *among* in making demands of the Negro and white citizens *in urging* training courses for the police force, for Negro policemen, for severe penalties to the full extent of the law for policemen who attack citizens of the South.

The right to vote has been traditionally denied Southerners. Many of us in this assembly of youth and adults have never cast a ballot. The campaign of the Southern Negro Youth Congress and other organizations for the abolition of the poll tax and other suffrage restrictions has become part and parcel of progressive organizations all over the country. In the past year, we have conducted an historic campaign, National

Anti-Poll Tax Week, involving all major national organizations. Recognizing that "the right to vote is the pearl of liberty," we would find the means to revitalize our right to vote activities as an important step in helping to win the war. In Washington ~~where~~ a current drive is on hand to abolish the poll tax, ~~citizens feel that~~ it is more than movement to restore democracy to the citizens of the poll tax states ~~but~~ it *also contributes* ~~is viewed by many as an effort~~ to *heightening* ~~bolster~~ the morale of the Southern people. Poll tax senators and congressmen are again and again sabotaging acts before Congress necessary for winning the war and unifying the American people. The hearings on the Pepper Bill (S. 1280*) to abolish the poll tax have shown clearly the widespread support throughout the country for abolition of this most undemocratic practice. *Now this fight must be won.*

What can we as youth do to further our Right To Vote Campaign? We would like to see hundreds and thousands of organizations in the South pass resolutions to be sent to our Congressmen and Representatives asking them to support the Pepper Bill. We would like to see from this Conference a Southwide campaign for the abolition of the poll tax and all other restrictions upon the right to vote in the South which will be as broad in representation as the sponsorship of the 5th All Southern Negro Youth Congress.

~~Our Honorable President, F.D. Roosevelt agrees with us that to act in the service of the nation is fundamental to the winning of the War. Yet in the army the government has projected a policy of Jim-Crow. In every other field, the government has made steps toward integration of the Negro people in the nation's total defense. It is not difficult to see that where there is Jim-Crow, in the armed forces, there the problems are most acute. Mr. President Negro youth want to be fully integrated into every phases of army life.~~

~~Already such leading youth in the Southern Negro Youth Congress as Peter Price of Nashville, Tennessee; Frances Grandison of Richmond, Virginia; Laurence Jones of New Orleans are making rapid strides in our nation's armed forces. They can do more if they were able to advance more rapidly, and secure an increased opportunity for training.~~ [censored: Jim Crow in armed forces]

In this War as in the past, Negro heroes like Private Robert H. Brooks, first American soldier killed in far east fighting for whom the main parade ground at Fort Knox, Kentucky has been named, like Julius Ellsberry of Birmingham Alabama, like Dorie Miller of Waco Texas whose parents are with us today, are again examples of the participation of the Negro people in the nation's war effort. President Roosevelt, you have recognized the important part that Negro youth are taking in this war when you cited William M. Brooks of St. Louis (Mo.) for heroism who saved the lives of 20 of his comrades. *We await our government to take further [action] for our full integration into the nation's armed forces so that we may serve more and better.*

The experiences of the Citizens Committee for Army Welfare organized by the Southern Negro Youth Congress in Birmingham, Alabama show what can be done in the field of Army Welfare today. In September 1941, we called a mass meeting, a salute to "Our Soldiers" at one of the large churches in the city. In this meeting, other organizations participated—the NAACP, the United Mine Workers of America, Labor's Non-Partisan League, Alabama State Teachers College and others. Louis Burnham in making the main address said, "The struggle against fascism is a struggle which Negro youth understand and support. The splendid morale which Negro soldiers have exhibited in the face of continued abuse is a token of their resolve to contribute to the fullest to the defeat of Hitlerism." After this meeting, a permanent Citizens Committee for Army Welfare was organized—with 30 organizations of the city participating. On January 8th, it held a Memorial Meeting for Julius Ellsberry by which time the Committee had become an established organization in the city. Carrying the campaign for a U.S.O. Center for Negro troops from the local organization to the national office of the U.S.O.—the committee won a fine Center in the center of the city. And now appearing under the U.S.O. sign is the following title, "auspices of Citizens Committee for Army Welfare."

Our soldiers want to, like to read. They need books and periodicals by the thousands. Let us initiate a southwide "Books for Soldiers Drive," the books being collected to be sent to nearby camps and to U.S.O. centers. Do we have a group here who would like to work on the details of such a drive?

Southern Negro youth will take the initiative in going to white communities, getting the mayor and outstanding figures to show full courtesy and warmth to incoming Negro soldiers. We would like to see new and bold steps taken in army welfare such as getting city bodies to sign petitions welcoming Negro soldiers.

~~We should like to see advancement made in the promotion of Negro officers and an increased number of Negro officers. only a few weeks~~

ago, the War Department announced its intention of calling back
ex-officers for service. In our Army Welfare Committees, we will be able
to petition for more Negro Officers, more than the now 337 in the
nation's army. We should like to see Negro military police in every army
camp. Delegates, investigate the camps in your state—are there Negro
military police. If not, you can easily secure the support of thousands of
people for winning such training for the Negro soldiers stationed there.

Let us urge the War Department and the local school systems to
include R.O.T.C. training and cadet training in our colleges and high
schools. Students, teachers, go back to your colleges, academies, high
schools—take the leadership in asking for pre-military training such as
that at Howard University where youth receive training in the latest
trends in military science and tactics.

What of Negro seamen? The latest action of the Secretary of Navy in
lowering the barriers of the admittance of Negroes into general service
on certain small battle craft such as motor torpedo boats, costal mine
sweepers, submarine chasers and submarine net-tenders can only be
viewed as but the nearest beginnings of the adoption in that branch of
service of the policy of full and complete integration of Negroes in all
departments and with full opportunities to advance in rank according
to merit and skill. This small beginning at a correct policy in respect to
the mobilization of the naval manpower in our country for winning the
war must be seen *not* as the *full* solution of the problem of ending Jim
Crow restrictive policies in the Navy, but only as a step in the right direction which in order to win the war must be accelerated. Nothing short
of full integration of Negroes in all departments of the armed forces can
ensure us of maximum utilization of our man power and machinery to
crush the enemy on land, on sea and in the air.

President Roosevelt has said to us, "We must work to fight with every
ounce of our strength to preserve the right to dream, organize and
build." Mr. President, Negro youth in the U.S. Navy are ready to *work
and fight to* so dream, organize, and build. *To do so we need to win* greater
opportunities to serve in every phase of the armed forces. Seamen, you
who are here from New Orleans, Mobile and other Southern ports—go
back to your cities—-make this of your greatest concern.

When 5 Negro pilots received their wings last month at Tuskegee—
Negroes all over American breathed deep and said, "We have 5 *army*
airmen at last." They pointed with pride especially to Captain Benjamin
O. Davis, Jr., Negro graduate of West Point and son of Brigadier General

Benjamin Davis. The training of America's Negro flying forces we will work to increase. *Integrate Negroes to disintegrate the axis.* Let us work for more training centers, larger schools and more teaching personnel so that Negro airmen may join their white comrades against the Axis and thereby contribute *evermore* greatly to the winning of the War.

We would find the means to see that Negro youth are speedily integrated into the civilian defense program in the South. Negro youth are anxious to enroll in the great army of civilian defense workers. In the South, many problems have occurred in the integration of Negro youth in the civilian defense program. In Birmingham, Alabama, for example, only when the initiative was taken by the Negro people themselves were air-raid wardens, first aid and other classes begun. For full integration of Negroes in the civilian defense program, there is yet much to be done. For example, in many neighborhoods there are white auxiliary police. We will find the means to increase the number of Negro military police in Negro neighborhoods. Homewood, Alabama, a community adjacent to Birmingham already has Negro auxiliary police. I understand there are delegates from that group at our Conference. They are, I am sure, convinced of the necessity of a southwide ~~movement~~ *action on similar lines* for Negro auxiliary police. ~~We address honorable F.D. Roosevelt when we say,~~ Negro youth will help protect the homes and families in our Southern communities. Delegates, go to your local O.D.D. headquarters—request Negro auxiliary police and write letters to the National Headquarters by the thousands requesting them. We must see that Negro women are rapidly drawn into civilian defense programs in the Southern cities and rural areas. Some steps have already been taken in a few Southern centers. In Birmingham, Alabama, for example, the demand of hundreds of Negro women for first aid classes was so great that there were insufficient teachers to cover them. As a result, members of a class for instructors first took the standard course and then the advanced courses. In the advanced course, Negro and white worked together. In Durham, North Carolina, we have received word that classes for Negro women sponsored by the American Women's Volunteer Services include home nursing, first aid, nutrition and civilian protection.

Our public schools and Sunday school classes may take as a part of their victory program, first aid classes, knitting classes, etc. It is our job to take the initiative that we may be included in every phase of the civilian defense program. Let us begin on such a program immediately when we return to our homes at the beginning of next week.

Recreation and entertainment are important functions of our organization. We will make these activities a part of our civic and political program. For instance, let us "Swing" for democracy. Give a "Play" for Freedom. Radio programs, theater parties, hikes in the summer are popular with our youth. In Birmingham, Alabama, the failure of our youth council was due in a large degree to the fact that the meetings and activities were so political and serious in nature that many young people soon tired of the meetings and the Council died. Today the Council has been revived. It is popular with the youth of the city for it has not only won a police brutality case, sent a large delegation to this meeting but has sponsored many successful social affairs.

In our organizations we would build fine character. We would educate leaders to dedicate their talents, their energies, yes, their life's blood to the practical jobs close at hand for the liberation of our people and defense of our country. Our generation of Negro youth will be a generation consecrated to the realization of total freedom for ourselves, for our people, for our country. We need young people in our organizations to stand up, to be morally strong and not succumb to war morality. ~~We need young people modeled in the patterns of such youth leaders as Edward Strong and Herman Long who are leaving us to take their place in the adult world.~~

In order to accomplish our aim, we would recommend that the members of the Youth Councils, city federations and other [organizations] begin now a major educational job in training individuals for leadership. We propose, therefore, that a Southern Negro Youth Congress leadership training school be held in July on some Southern campus—with special emphasis on preparing young women.

We cannot emphasize too much the importance of training young southern women today. Negro women have distinguished themselves over a period of years as strong fighters for freedom. In this war, Negro women are not bystanders in the War against the Axis. The difference between victory and defeat may well depend on how effectively the nation's womanhood is mobilized. The Southern Negro Youth Congress recognizes the importance of women in winning the war. A month ago, we issued a special appeal to the women of the South to attend our Fifth all Southern meeting of Southern Negro youth.

Let us look at the historic role Negro women have had in America. Phillis Wheatley was among the first Americans to write poetry to encourage the fighters for freedom in the American Revolution.

Elizabeth Freeman, Frances Ellen Watkins were other outstanding Negro women in our early history. Harriet Tubman is renowned today for her courageous career, whereafter securing freedom returned to the South during slavery, many times—bringing approximately 300 slaves to free soil. Sojourner Truth is known as a great anti-slavery orator. Today with the nation facing the greatest crisis in its history, Negro women join with the valiant Chinese, Russian and British women in an all out war effort. In England, over a million women have entered the war factories and at least a million more will soon enter the expanding war industries. Showing great initiative, women in England have organized shop conferences for increasing their production and for eliminating [bad] time keeping and absenteeism. Chinese women have proven their unconquerable strength from years of resistance to the enemy forces and as the War has developed their strength and power has continued to grow. The role of Soviet women in strengthening the people's resistance to the enemy is now known to most of the world. Dorothy Thompson, Newspaper columnist says of the Soviet women, "In this War, the Russian women have justified the freedom and education granted them by the Soviet Union. They have not been bystanders in the War; they have fought it on the assembly lines and in the ranks of the guerrillas." And who does not know the story of Tanya, the Soviet School Girl. A Joan of Ark in this global war in defense of civilization.

~~In the United States, during 1942 probably 2,000,000 more women will be added to those already employed in war production. Others will replace men in jobs not directly related to war production.~~

Negro women, we repeat again and again will have their heroines of this War for the preservation of democracy in the world. May I say a few words about domestic workers who constitute 3 out of every 5 Negro women employed in the country. We would like to see all organizations support legislation for inclusion of domestic workers in the Social Security Act to provide these women with old age insurance. ~~President Roosevelt has stated that inclusion of domestic workers in the old age survivors clause of the Social Security Act will help prevent inflation after the War. Mr. President, how much would we like to see this come to pass in cities such as Birmingham, Alabama where household workers make as little as $1.50 a week. In the Kentucky State Legislature a Bill has already been introduced to include within the scope of the present wage and hour law for women, the domestic workers.~~

Domestic workers will be able to play an important part in winning the War. They are the logical air-raid wardens protecting as they do the family's welfare. Working in hotels and apartments, their hours of labor should be staggered so that they may enter into civilian training classes.

Now a word about the organizational problems of the Southern Negro Youth Congress. The City federations of the Congress are the most important part of our organization. We cannot make any headway in understanding the ideas, habits, needs, desires of youth without knowing the young people with whom we come in contact. Therefore Council Chairman and officers will do well to know the leading persons in their communities. It is desirable to establish a friendly cooperative relationship with organizations and people of the community-contribution to the success of their organizations.

These city federations work to affiliate and unify the existing youth organizations in the city community—trade unions, church, civic, and social groups. Our prospective is for each of these federations to have its own headquarters and city wide, country wide leadership. These groups are based on the national principles of our organization adapted to local needs. In some places, we have achieved close cooperation with the national office—Birmingham, Newport News, Virginia, Adamsville, Boothton, Alabama, the Tuskegee Student Chapter, but in most places we have not because our membership has failed to understand the significance of such close cooperation and unity necessary to insure maximum results.

We place individual memberships as imperative to building our organization. We expect to double or triple our membership by our next conference. This is the only effective method of control of the S.N.Y.C. Individual members may form S.N.Y.C. clubs in any name such as the Booker T. Washington Youth Club which would work to carry out the program of the national council.

The Southern Negro Youth Congress is an organization which attempts to unite the generations—not to divide them. We want improved relationships between the old and the young and therefore seek to educate our membership to an appreciation of the work and sacrifices of adults. We will build the Advisory Council of the Southern Negro Youth Congress. We recommend state and city Advisory Councils which will be, we believe, indispensable in the solution of many problems.

The Southern Negro Youth Congress is faced today with the most serious task in its history. We have much work to do. We have, therefore the problem of financing the organization and doing it well. Educational material, radio program, travel, salaries—all are necessary items today if we are to ride the tide of opportunity in its flood to its full ebb. This will entail an overall budget for the next year of $6,000.

At times of War, events we find move on the wings of airplanes. So must our activities move. The National Council recommends therefore that we enlarge our staff if we are to live up to the task of the hour. An Educational Director, Business Manager and financial secretary are "musts" today in the National Office of the Southern Negro Youth Congress. *Cavalcade*, our publication we hope to put on a regular and permanent basis.

The South is large. We have only the beginnings of a Southwide organization. Let us build the Southern Negro Youth Congress in all of the Southern states in the very near future. The Southern Negro Youth Congress, ~~the only independent youth organization in the South~~, can make a great contribution in building that unity needed to win the war. We will find a basis for common action for Negro and white youth of the South.

As long as we play a positive, a decisive and enthusiastic role in the South's history, we will emerge an organization with strength, with character, and with *an influence in the* determination of *an early* victory, ~~to an extent unknown in the history of America~~.

Delegates, let us go back to our homes and begin immediately on this program in our councils, schools, Y's, unions, Lodges, and other groups. July 4—we would like to set as Youth *War* Mobilization Day to be observed all over the South and to be participated in by thousands. This event would mark the climax of 3 months of activity in the service of the nation and the *advancement of the* Negro people.

As I look from here over the hall and see all of you—who have come from near and far to this important assembly of Southern people, I am sure that we will work together this year, we youth and adults of the South and contribute more than our share to the nation's war program.

Here at Tuskegee in the preparations for this Conference, we have already demonstrated the unity necessary for a successful program. We particularly wish to thank Dr. F. D. Patterson, Chairman of our Adult Advisory Board who has so graciously welcomed us to Tuskegee, Mr. Charles Gommillion, Advisor of the local council of the S.N.Y.C., Mr. T. Rupert Braday of the Dept. of Records and [Research] the faculty and students who have rearranged their schedules and made many sacrifices for us. There are only a few—

The Government Agencies and officials, and many other national groups who are cooperating with us to make this Conference a success— we wish to thank. President Roosevelt, in his greetings to the 5th All Southern Negro Youth Conference, said and I quote—in part, "Your strength and your courage and your loyalty to your country help assure this victory out of which must come a peace built on universal freedom such as men have not yet known and which all the youth of today shall enjoy as the men and women of tomorrow."

Our own unity, our determination to win this War, our confidence in ourselves is the guarantee that such a day for victory and peace will come to pass—we ourselves will guarantee the future.

18

Reconversion and the Negro People
Thelma Dale

Political Affairs 24, no. 10 (October 1945), pp. 894–901

Final victory in the Pacific and events on the home front since bring into bold focus the continued second class citizenship status of the Negro people. Whether the 13,000,000 Negroes in America will be able to realize the fruits of victory, for which they too fought, is a challenge to all Americans. It summons the Communists especially to the full exercise of their duty as vanguard in the struggle for Negro rights. The military victory over fascist racism and aggression has not yet been translated into terms of freedom and equality for Negro Americans. Instead, reaction is lighting a fire of race hatred in America against the Negro people which can destroy many of the important gains made by the entire working class movement during the war unless it is checked quickly and decisively.

In the succeeding pages is a statement on some of the most pressing problems confronting the Negro people, as well as on some of the ways in which Communists and other progressives can deal with these problems.

Negroes, like all workers, today face a critical situation with respect to jobs. However, Negro workers, precisely because of their continued insecure statues in American life, face the possibility of a return to pre-war economic instability more than any other section of our population. Already employers are beginning their age-old policy of utilizing Negroes as the unemployed reservoir to break labor organizations and depress wages.

The Struggle for Jobs

Of the million and a half Negroes employed in 1944 in war industries, reliable estimates indicate less than half are employed today. Employers have already begun the down-grading of Negro workers in those plants which have kept them. A good many other employers are using every possible means, including the alleged "inviolability of seniority rules," to exclude Negroes from their plants.

Reports indicate that the United States Employment Service even in the North and East is reverting to its pre-war policies of forcibly encouraging Negroes to return to domestic service and other low-paid fields of employment despite new skills learned during the war. What will happen in the South in this connection in the coming period, unless drastic steps are taken by the trade union movement and people's organizations is clear.

Negro women who were the very last to be hired in industrial employment, of course, have borne the major brunt of the lay-offs in the present period. Reports from Detroit as early as the spring of 1945 indicate wholesale lay-offs of Negro women in the automobile industry.

More than a year ago a few leading Communists called attention to the need for developing programs for maintaining and extending the wartime gains of the Negro people in industry. One of the means suggested was a flexible application of seniority, where necessary, to maintain in the plants during the reconversion period a fair proportion of Negroes in all occupational capacities.

Later a study of several plants in the New York area by the National Negro Congress substantiated this thesis,[1] as well as a more recent study by Dr. Robert C. Weaver.[2]

However, opinion was sharply divided over the issue in the country generally as well as in the labor movement. The lack of a unanimous, clear, and decisive position in our own Party on this issue deprived the labor movement of effective stimulus and assistance to meet this problem.

Opponents of seniority modification argued that any modification would break down the whole seniority system, and thus ultimately destroy the unions; that white workers would not accept it because it would be unfair to them and would turn them against the Negro people, and that, moreover, the Negroes themselves did not want it.

Those who argued for seniority adjustments contended that unless the labor movement was willing and able to find the means with which to keep a proportion of Negroes in the industries and in job classifications achieved during the war in the crucial reconversion period, employers would use the unemployed reservoir of Negro workers as a threat to weaken the labor movement and depress wages. Such weakening of the strength of the unions might spell the difference between success of labor's reconversion program and defeat for all workers.

Further, it was pointed out that the assertion that white workers would not accept seniority modifications was a time-worn argument used against every advance of the Negro people. Proponents of seniority adjustment did indicate that the vast majority of white trade unionists would have to be educated to accept the proposal for their own good and that of the union. The vast majority of trade union leadership became so engrossed in the quarrel over seniority modification that it failed, for the most part, to look for the necessary answers in terms of upgrading and the carrying out of day-to-day struggles to eliminate discrimination in employment.

Now, when thousands, perhaps millions, of workers have already been laid-off, even the Communists have just begun to agree on the validity of seniority modification as an important means of maintaining and extending wartime employment gains of Negroes.

What must we therefore as Communists do to safeguard the basic rights of the Negro people to work at jobs commensurate with their skills and abilities?

First, we must demand a program of full employment for the entire nation. President Truman and a score of Senators have already indicated their support for the Full Employment Bill. We must fight vigorously for the passage of this legislation immediately.

Second, it is necessary to wage an uncompromising fight for the immediate passage of the permanent F.E.P.C. Bill. All efforts to make this fight a partisan or limited one must be thwarted. The fight for a permanent F.E.P.C. must become the property of every progressive force in America.

Third, Communists in the trade union movement must carry on a struggle to clean out of its ranks all opportunism on the Negro question and in every way carry on a relentless fight to maintain and extend the unity of the Negro people with organized labor in support of jobs and all social benefits, without discrimination, for all.

Fourth, in plants where a rigid and formal application of seniority plays into the hands of employers by placing the brunt of lay-offs on Negro workers, seniority regulations must be flexibly applied so as to retain a proportionate number of Negro workers, or in the case of rehirings, efforts must be made to achieve the rehiring of a proportion of Negro workers at least commensurate with the wartime employment gains of Negroes.

It can be noted that despite the excellent record of most CIO and some AFL unions on the fight for Negro rights, the basic lack of understanding on the part of the trade union movement of the necessity of full integration of Negroes on the job and within their ranks has already cost a great deal. Unless we quickly rectify this situation the anti-union, anti-Negro, anti-democratic forces within the nation will ride rough-shod over the rights of all American workers by the simple process of division of the workers.

Negroes in the Armed Forces

The sorest spot among the Negro people today is the continuing discriminations and inequalities existing in the Armed Forces, both at home and abroad as well as the plight of returning Negro veterans. The brazen and false vilification of Negro servicemen by the Bilbo, Rankin, Eastland alliance is only one indication of the disastrous trend in our country to light a fire of race hatred which will pave the way for political reaction. In the win-the-war camp a false illusion existed that Negroes would *automatically* win their rights through all-out support of the war effort. Even the Communists, as part of the revisionist policies, to an extent were affected by this illusion which resulted at times in the soft-pedaling of the struggle to fight against the inferior status of Negroes in the armed forces. Our politically phlegmatic position on the fight for equality within the armed forces became so untenable that even before the Duclos article we had been forced to re-evaluate and adjust our position.

Despite some positive and constructive efforts to integrate Negroes in the armed forces, the result of America's dual Army policy has been a deterioration of Negro–white relations in the Army; a greater disrespect for American democracy on the part of Allied peoples throughout the world where our dual Armies have been stationed; and, perhaps most important, the frustration, the bitterness and lack of faith in American democracy on the part of the Negro people and Negro troops, among them, many of our finest Communist forces.

Let us pause long enough to hear what a young Negro soldier, with four years in the Army, two years overseas, two dependents, but still insufficient points for discharge, has to say about our ineffective struggle against Jim Crow in the Army as well as on the home front:

The Negro soldier doesn't appreciate shame, and of course he didn't talk much. He's had too much sympathy and too little fight on his behalf. When you're in a struggle you need allies, fighting, vigorous allies, and sympathizers make you sick at heart.

The Negro soldier comes home filled with misgivings and certain that his fight for freedom still must be fought in his own backyard. He was heart and mind and body in the struggle to liberate the French, Belgians, Italians. Despite Jim Crow and a hundred bitter abuses in his own army, abuses which never reached the public, he made his contribution to victory. Now, turning homeward, he looks for his fighting allies to win his freedom. Let's not feel sorry for him. A solider hates being patronized. He's stood on his own feet and asks that his friends show him respect, give him concrete aid to win his final battle.

The grievances of this Negro soldier are typical of the experiences of nearly one million Negroes who have served in the armed forces during this great war. Space does not permit a recital of the many varied and ingenious methods used to humiliate, persecute and rob the Negro serviceman of his rights, his honor, and his opportunities.

A leading white trade unionist recently returned from a tour of the battlefronts, is reported to have been far more disturbed by the virulent anti-Negro attitudes present among white serviceman than by the once felt anti-labor spirit previously reported. It is unfortunate that no apparent efforts were made to bring this situation to the attention of the American public. If it was reported to the War Department at all, it obviously was pigeon-holed for future reference or sent to the dead files.

Substantiating this general impression are a raft of court-martial cases, in many of which death penalties have been invoked, framed-up rape and mutiny cases, and scores of "incidents" now breaking in the Negro press as a result of the lifting of censorship.

Typical among such cases are the Fisher-Lowery case, the Army "Scottsboro" case, and the recent case in the E.T.O. in which twelve of the fifteen Negro servicemen were given death sentences on alleged charges of mutiny.

But perhaps, more insidious than these cases which have been brought to the public attention are the innumerable cases of Negro officers and men who are dishonorably discharged or discharged under Section VII Blue Discharge (without honor), (in both instances without benefit of G.I. Rights) as reprisals against their failure to adjust to discrimination and inequality in the Army.

One such Negro officer writes:

As far as E.T.O. is concerned the dismissal has stuck. I am on my way home to be separated from the service without benefit of a record, or the G.I. Bill of Rights.

As I stated, I don't intend to have a lousy deal like this go through without a stiff fight on the basis of the facts I outlined in my last letter. I have no intentions of having given up four and a half years of life, and gone through the bitter hell, stink and deprivations of war in vain.

The crux of the whole situation of Negro troops is the failure of the Army to accord equal treatment to Negroes. Negroes have not been given fair opportunities for advancement, even in the segregated set-up.

Of the nearly one-million Negroes now in the armed forces, there are only approximately 6,000 officers. Reliable information indicates that the vast majority of these are not in command of troops particularly in the overseas theaters.

Further reports indicate that generally not more than 1–2 per cent of any branch of the Army is Negro except in Ordnance where 92 per cent of those assigned to Ordnance Ammunition (essentially unskilled labor) and approximately 98 per cent in Quartermaster Trucking and Service are Negroes.

The assignment of Negro troops on the basis outlined above now seriously affects their release from the Army under the present point system which is weighted in favor of combat experience.

Since Negroes were not responsible for their assignments in the war, it is clearly necessary to demand the establishment of a separate point system for Negroes, so that they may have an equal opportunity for an early return to civilian life and all the benefits which this implies.

Negro Veterans

The recent situation of the refusal to allow a broadcast of a play written by Cpl. Arnold Perl on the question of Negro veterans, their welfare, etc., is a dramatic portrayal of the seeming crassness of approach on the part of the Army to deal realistically with its Negro members on a basis of equality with all other troops and to guarantee their speedy return and adjustment to civilian life.

Those Negro soldiers who are being released are finding it increasingly difficult to gain their rights under the G.I. Bill, since the Army thus far has operated under policies which mitigate against Negro veterans.

It is the general practice to return veterans to hospitals nearest their homes. This means for the vast majority of Negro men injured in line of duty they return to hospitals in the South. Likewise, definite pressures seem to operate to limit Negroes who seek further education under the G.I. Bill to attend schools in their home states, or in the South.

Generally, the G.I. when separated from the service is given the understanding that his local draft board will assist him in securing all benefits due him. It is not necessary to elaborate here on the ways in which white-supremacy-minded Southern officials will deny Negro veterans their rights.[3]

The safety and well-being of our entire nation hinges upon what we do now and in the immediate future to improve the status of Negroes in the armed forces as well as secure opportunities for returning Negro servicemen. There must be a greater awareness on the part of every Communist and white progressive to effect a positive and constructive program to deal with this highly explosive situation. It is high time the brass hats in the Army and Navy heard from, and responded to, progressive America on the demand for military equality for Negroes.

It is imperative that this whole situation be rectified now even after military victory has been won to insure the operation of a democratic policy both for the occupation forces and for peacetime military training. Practically, we should press for:

1. the early enactment of the Powell Bill, H.R. 2708, banning discrimination in the armed forces six months after victory;
2. the passage of the G.I. Assault Bill making it a Federal offense to assault a G.I., and for improvements in the G.I. Bill of Rights with particular emphasis on the need for uniform Federal application and control of all veteran facilities and services; and

3. the establishment of interracial veteran's organizations, particularly as exemplified in the Labor Legionnaires. In many instances, mass organizations will have to establish Veteran Information Centers to assist ex-service men in securing a fair deal.

The South

It is impossible to deal adequately here with the problems of the South, where the majority of the Negro people still live. This subject should be dealt with in an authoritative and comprehensive manner in an early issue of this magazine.

Much of what has been said above concerning the plight of the Negro people is due in the main to the continued domination of our American life by the poll-tax white supremacy doctrinaires of the South. Fundamental to elimination of Jim Crow in America must be the building and mobilization of democratic organizational expression on the part of the masses of white and Negro Southerners in support of full civil, political, and economic rights for all in the South. Indispensable to such a mobilization must be the re-establishment of the Communist Party in the South and making this area of our work a major point of concentration.

After World War I when Negro veterans still in uniform returned to many parts of the South there were vicious attacks upon them and their fellow citizens. There is the imminent danger of new frame-ups, Scottsboros, and lynchings in the coming period unless the labor movement and all progressives marshal their forces against the flames of reaction still burning throughout the South.

The organized labor movement has much at stake in this crisis. It will become a potent force in the liberation of the entire working class in the South only as it cleans out all white chauvinism in its own ranks and fights for equality of Negroes and all other minorities.

Even the C.I.O. in the South has some real house-cleaning to do if it is to maintain the record on non-discrimination of that section of labor.

As to the reactionary leadership of the A.F. of L. and, in regard to this issue, also the Railroad Brotherhoods, it is well known that, in the South as well as throughout the nation, they are the active purveyors of white supremacy policies in the labor movement, which must be combatted and rooted out.

Communist Responsibility

Communists obviously must lead and always be in the vanguard of the struggle for Negro rights. In order to play an effective role, we as Communists, will have to extricate ourselves completely from the revisionist way of thinking and acting, and move with dispatch to meet the immediate problems confronting us.

The lack of any fundamental theoretical analysis of the Negro question at the recent national and state conventions was a serious weakness. It is even more serious that, to date, very little if anything has happened to translate the good resolutions passed at these meetings into concrete policy and programs of action.

It is imperative that we cut through the red tape of any bureaucratic hangovers still existing within the Party and quickly set up the Commissions on Negro Work, both nationally and locally.

These Commissions should become part of the life-blood of our Party, continually adding new life and vigor to our struggle. The Convention resolutions proposed that these Commissions be staffed with some of the top leadership of our Party, both Negro and white, as well as shop workers, mass organization people, etc. It is felt by some that those decisions should be taken a step further by making a member of the National Secretariat the chairman, or at least co-chairman, of the National Commission (with like procedure in the State Commission), so as to provide a definite organizational tie between the Commissions and our entire Party organization.

The Commissions on Negro Work should not become mere debating societies or advisory committees, but should provide the necessary apparatus for research, theoretical analysis, and policy making.

Our theoretical understanding of the Negro question must be developed in practical day-to-day action, carefully planned and executed. Negro leadership within the Party must be strengthened and broadened, in the interests of a wholesome movement. We must continue the trend in training Negroes as Marxist-Leninist teachers, thinkers and workers within the Party. Negro Communists should function in every realm of Party life and not in any sense be restricted to work amongst Negroes only.

Mass organizations of the Negro people should be encouraged and helped to follow a correct political line with major emphasis on strengthening the role of Negro labor and cementing a closer tie between the

Negro people and the trade union movement, the Jewish people's movement and other progressive forces in our nation. Never again must we allow a situation to develop in which Social-Democrat and Trotskyite demagogues can assume leadership of important struggles in the Negro movement.

The Communists have always enjoyed the highest respect of the masses of Negroes. We must maintain the faith of the Negro masses in our movement through a conscious and virile program of action destined to achieve full citizenship status for the Negro people.

19

On the Right to Self-Determination for the Negro People in the Black Belt

Claudia Jones

Political Affairs 25, no. 1 (January 1946), pp. 67–77

The political attacks that are being directed against the Negro people by Big Business have once again placed serious questions before the American working class.

These attacks, reminiscent of post–World War I, are all the more serious because today the main danger of fascism to the world comes from the most colossal imperialist forces which are concentrated within the United States. The perpetrators of these attacks are the representatives of the most reactionary section of monopoly capital and of the semi-feudal economy of the Black Belt. This hook-up, expressed in Congress by the reactionary Republicans and the poll-taxers who draw their power from the oppression of the Negro people and the working class, makes it obvious that the two main forces for democracy are the working class allied with the Negro people.

In the short period since the war for national liberation, our nation has witnessed a revival of lynchings—three *known* lynchings in the space of three months. This blot of shame lies in America, while we proclaim to the world our "championship" of democracy for other nations!

The two-pronged drive of Big Business to decimate the war-time gains of the Negroes in industry and at the same time to destroy the alliance between labor and the Negro people, the fascist-inspired "race strikes" of American students, the recent attacks on Negro veterans in the South, and the closing of F.E.P.C. offices in city after city—all this necessitates the greatest political initiative and action by the trade unions and by our Party.

Coupled with this reactionary drive on the economic and political fronts, are the growing Hitler-like incitements of the Bilbos and Rankins. While popular indignation has been aroused by these events, it is obvious that labor must move more aggressively that it has so far on the vital issues affecting the Negro people.

If the alliance, crucial to progress, between the Negro people and labor is to be reinforced and extended, it is necessary to clarify the relationship between the struggle for national liberation of the Negro people and that of the working class against capitalist exploitation and oppression.

In opening this discussion, it must be made clear that the conclusions here arrived at should in no sense be regarded as a condition for the united struggle of the Negro people and the working class for Negro rights. What differences in outlook may be present as regards the thesis here presented must in no way hinder unity of all progressives in the struggle for the immediate needs of the Negro people.

The basis for this discussion article is the Political Resolution of our National Convention in July, which rejected Browder's revisionist position on the national character of the Negro question. A further basis is the preliminary exchange of opinion registered recently at an enlarged meeting of the newly-established National Negro Commission of our Party. At that meeting it must be stated, the views expressed revealed varying opinions on our fundamental theoretical approach to the political essence and ultimate aim of the Negro liberation movement in the United States. Similar differences of opinion are indicated in communications, club resolutions, and articles submitted to the National Office which discuss the issue of the right of self-determination for the Negro people in the Black Belt.

It is clear that a deep-going discussion of the subject is necessary. While this article will attempt to discuss some of these views, it is to be hoped that it will be followed by further discussion. The views presented here are my own.

The National Character of the Struggle for Negro Rights

Even the worst enemies of the Communist Party cannot fail to admit that we have been in the forefront of the struggle for equality of the Negro people. It was the Communist Party which fourteen years ago made the name of Scottsboro ring the world around. It was the Communist Party which was the first, since the overthrow of the Reconstruction governments, to raise in the heart of the South the issue of full Negro freedom.

What galvanized our Party to become the initiator and vanguard of these struggles? It was our understanding of the Negro question in the United States as a *special* question, as an issue whose solution requires *special* demands, in addition to the general demands of the American working class.

It was essentially this understanding that found Communists in the forefront of the struggle to combat the imperialist ideology of "white supremacy" which is today endangering the unity of the labor-democratic coalition and of the working class itself. It was essentially this knowledge that taught white American workers to fight for Negro rights in their own self-interest, to understand that to fight against white chauvinism is to fight against imperialist ideologies and practices of America's ruling class which serves to separate Negro and white workers. It was this understanding that taught Negro workers to fight against petty-bourgeois nationalism—a result of white chauvinist ideology—and to have both Negro and white workers form strong bonds of unity with each other.

It was our understanding of the Negro question as a *national* question, that is, as the question of a nation oppressed by American imperialism, in the ultimate sense as India is oppressed by British imperialism and Indonesia by Dutch imperialism. It was our knowledge, grounded in Lenin's teachings, that every aspect of Negro oppression in our country stems from the existence of an *oppressed nation*, in the heart of the South, the Black Belt.

We knew that the semi-slavery of the Southern sharecroppers; the inferior status of the Negro people in industry, North and South; the existence of Jim Crow in the armed forces; the Jim Crow practices of New York and Chicago, as well as of Birmingham and Tampa; the shooting two months ago of a Harlem child by a trigger-happy cop—all can be traced back step by step to the continued existence of an oppressed Negro nation within our borders.

Wherein do the Negro people in the Black Belt constitute an oppressed nation? To answer this question, we must first determine the characteristics of a nation. Marxist-Leninists hold that "a nation is a historically evolved, stable community of language, territory, economic life and psychological make-up manifested in a community of culture."[1]

The Black Belt, an area in which the Negro people form a majority, came into existence with the growth of cotton culture and plantation economy. As the area of cotton cultivation moved over Westward in the days before the Civil War, so did the area of the plantation that consisted of a white-master family with its slaves.

The Civil War, which abolished chattel slavery, failed either to break up this area of Negro majority or fully to liberate the Negro people within it. Retaining their plantation lands, the ex-slaveholders soon forced the return to these lands of their former slaves as sharecroppers. A series of laws passed by Southern states—the crop lien laws, the jumping contract laws, and so on—prevented and still prevent the free migration of the Negro people. Scarcely less than before the Civil War, is the Black Belt a prison-house of the Negroes; the chains which hold them now are the invisible chains of poverty, the legal chains of debt-slavery, and, when the landlords deem it necessary, the iron shackles of the chain gang.

The Civil War might have broken the bars of the Black Belt; it did not, for the Northern capitalists, who had gained a united market and field of exploitation throughout the nation as a result of the Civil War, were terrified by the simultaneous rise of Southern democracy, the Northern labor movement, and radical agrarian organizations. They betrayed the Negro people and the Southern white masses, and turned the South back to semi-slavery.

The migrations of the 1870's, of the First World War, and of the Second World War, did not appreciably diminish the proportion by which the Negroes find themselves a majority today in the Black Belt—these are virtually the same. It cannot be said that this majority is accidental, or that the Negro people continue as an oppressed people within the Black Belt by inertia or by choice. They continue so because the sheriff's posse of the twentieth century is carrying on, under new forms, the work of the slave-catchers of the nineteenth. The majority remains a majority by force.

This community in which the Negro people are a majority is neither racial nor tribal; it is composed of a significant minority of whites as well. The territory stretches contiguously westward from the Eastern shore of Maryland, and lies within Maryland, Virginia, North Carolina, South Carolina, Georgia, Florida, Alabama, Mississippi, Louisiana, Tennessee, Arkansas, and Texas.

Following the Civil War, boundary lines were definitely shaped by the defeated slaveholders to prohibit the full participation of the Negroes and poor whites in political life. If it is true in the North, where certain election districts are "gerry-mandered" to prohibit the full expression of the Negro vote (and of the white vote as well), it was no less true of the Black Belt, where the majority of the inhabitants were Negroes and represented its basic core.

As to the other characteristics of nationhood: Have the Negro people, for example, a common language? They have a common language—English. If it be argued that this is the language of the entire country, we say that this is true. A common language is necessary to nationhood; a different language is not. When the American colonies separated from Britain, they had a common language, which was the same as that of their oppressors. Surely no one will argue that our community of language with our British oppressors should have kept us indefinitely in the status of a colonial people.

Is there an American Negro culture? The peculiar oppression of the Negro people and their striving for freedom have been expressed in a native way, in spirituals, work-songs, literature, art, and dance. This does not mean that American Negro culture is not part of American culture generally. Negro culture is part of the general stream of American culture, but it is a distinct current in that stream; it arose out of the special historical development and unique status of the Negro people; no other people in America could have developed this particular culture.

Have the Negro people a stable community of economic life? First, let us discuss what is meant by a common economic life. It is sometimes said that people have a common economic life when they make their living in the same way—they are all sharecroppers, or they are all work-ers. Actually, a common economic life with reference to a nation or community under capitalism means that the nation or community has within it the class and social relations that characterize society; it has capitalists, workers, farmers, and intellectuals, ranged according to their position in the production relations. In this case it means that a Negro must be able to hire a Negro, buy from a Negro, sell to a Negro, service a Negro.

Such class stratification exists among the Negro people in the Black Belt. There is a Negro bourgeoisie. It is not an industrial bourgeoisie. It is not a big bourgeoisie; the bourgeoisie of an oppressed nation never is; it is one of the results of national oppression that the bourgeoisie of the oppressed nations is retarded by the oppressors. The market of the Negro bourgeoisie is founded upon Jim-Crowism; it functions chiefly in life insurance, banking, and real estate. Its leadership among the Negro people is reflected in an ideology—petty-bourgeois nationalism, whose main purpose is to mobilize the Negro masses under its own influence.

By these distinguishing features, therefore, the Negro people in the Black Belt constitute a nation. They are an historically developed community of people, with a common language, a common territory, and a common economic life, all of which are manifest in a common culture.

As far back as 1913, Lenin emphasized that the Negro people constitute an oppressed nation. In an unfinished essay on the national and colonial question he made a *direct* reference to the Negro people as an *oppressed nation*, stating:

> In the United States 11.1 per cent of the population consists of Negroes (and also mulattoes and Indians) who must be considered an oppressed nation, inasmuch as the equality, won in the Civil War of 1861–65 and guaranteed by the constitution of the Republic, has in reality been more and more restricted in many respects in the main centers of the Negro population (in the South) with the transition from the progressive, pre-monopolistic capitalism of 1860–1870 to the reactionary monopolistic capitalism (imperialism) of the latest epoch. (V.I. Lenin, *Miscellany*, in *Collected Works*, vol. XXX, Russian edition.)

Browder's Revision of Leninist Teachings

In discussing the right of self-determination for Negroes in the Black Belt, we surely cannot ignore the revisionist position taken by Earl Browder, as set forth in his article in *The Communist* for January, 1944, which was presented as a declaration of policy for American Communists. There Browder wrote:

It was in view of the gathering world crisis that we Communists at that time—in the early 30's—raised the issue of self-determination. At that time, we necessarily faced the possibility that the Negro people, disappointed in their aspirations for full integration into the American nation, might find their only alternative in separation and in the establishment of their own state in the Black Belt, in the territory in which they are a majority. We raised this as one of the rights of the Negro people, in case the Negro people found this was the only way to satisfy their aspirations.

Browder further wrote:

The crisis of history has taken a turn of such character that the Negro people in the United States have found it possible to make their decision once and for all. Their decision is for their complete integration into the American nation as a whole and not for separation.

Browder thus denied that the right of self-determination for Negroes in the Black Belt was any longer an issue, since, according to him, the Negro people had already made their choice!

What was the fallacy on which Browder's premise was based?

Browder's fallacy was inherently connected with a false estimate of the relationship of forces in our nation and the world. Clearly, if a rosy future was to be envisioned in which a "peaceful" capitalism would voluntarily relinquish its exploitations, solve its contradictions, etc., the Leninist program which showed that the very essence of imperialism was the distinction and conflict between oppressed and oppressing nations no longer applied to our country!

Moreover, Browder based his premise, not on evaluating the right of self-determination as it applies to the Negro people in the Black Belt, but on one of its aspects, separation. That he saw fit to discuss the whole question from the standpoint of a "practical political matter," confirms this. His treatment of these two demands as being identical needs examination.

Is separation identical with self-determination? The right to separation is inherent in the right to self-determination, whether that right is eventually exercised or not. It becomes a practical political matter only when the concrete objective conditions for that choice are at hand. Therefore, to identify self-determination with separation, or to substitute one for the other, is tantamount to forcing on the Negro people a choice, which they are clearly not in an objective position to make—which, in other words, though a right, is not necessarily a function of their exercise of self-determination!

It is obvious from this that the right of self-determination is not something one can dangle, withdraw, or put forward again as a sheerly objective factor. Either the objective historic conditions of nationhood exist, in which such a right remains inviolate, or they do not. Either the objective conditions exist for the choice to be made by the oppressed nation (either for separation, autonomy, amalgamation, etc.), or they do not. Thus, and only thus, can we approach the issue as a practical political matter.

How then, does the question of integration apply? Are the Negro people demanding integration in American political life? Most certainly they are! But this is no new phenomenon insofar as the Negro people are concerned. Negro Americans have been fighting for integration for over two hundred years. Every *partial* fight—whether expressed in the demands of the Reconstruction leaders, together with the white workers in the South for land, or in the present-day demand of Negroes in Atlanta to enforce the Supreme Court ruling against the "white primary" laws; whether it be the fight against lynching and poll-tax disfranchisement, or the recent successful campaign, conducted in Negro-white unity to re-elect Benjamin J. Davis, Jr., to the New York City Council—is a step towards integration.

But integration cannot be considered a substitute for the right of self-determination. National liberation is not synonymous with integration, neither are the two concepts mutually exclusive.

What does integration really mean? Integration, that is, *democratic* integration, means breaking down the fetters which prohibit the full economic, political and social participation of Negroes in all phases of American life. This does not mean that a merger, or an assimilative process necessarily takes place. In a general sense, the struggle for integration waged today by the Negro people is directed toward achieving *equal rights*—economic, political and social.

But the basic difference, in fact the touchstone of programmatic difference, between the liberals (as well as the Social-Democrats) and the Communists hinges on the application of the program of equal rights to the Black Belt, and, therefore, to the *source of Negro oppression* throughout the country—a difference based on diametrically opposed concepts of the nature of the question.

In the North, the struggle for equal rights for the Negro people is chiefly that of heightening the fight to secure equal participation in every sphere of American life. The problems of the Negro people in the North are akin to those of an oppressed national minority. Particularly here, the fight for equal rights as a whole is enhanced by the presence of a large and growing Negro proletariat, in the area of the most highly developed capitalism, as well as by the participation of the advanced workers throughout the country for equal rights for Negroes. In fact, it is the existence of a strong Negro proletariat—represented today by close to one million organized trade unionists—that provides the intimate link between the American working class as a whole and the struggle for emancipation and land for oppressed Negro people and white workers in the Black Belt.

In the Black Belt the problem is chiefly that of wiping out the economic, political, and social survivals of slavery, of the *enforcement* of equal rights. Without the necessary *enforcement* of equal rights for the Negro people in the Black Belt, including social equality, it is folly to speak of integration as being equal to the achievement of national liberation. Hence, equal rights for the Negro people in the Black Belt can be achieved only though enforcement, through their exercise of the right of self-determination.

The right of self-determination does not exclude the struggle for partial demands; it pre-supposes an energetic struggle for concrete partial demands, linked up with the daily needs and problems of the wide masses of the Negro people and the white workers in the Black belt. The fight for such partial demands, moreover, is a struggle for democracy. It does not divert or overshadow the working-class struggle against exploitation, it is an aid to it.

It is only by helping to interconnect the partial demands with the right of self-determination that we Communists, in concert with other progressive forces, can contribute guidance to the struggle for complete equality for the Negro people.

Certain Contentions Examined

We Communists adhere to the fundamental belief that complete and lasting equality of imperialist oppressed nations and peoples can be guaranteed only with the establishment of Socialism. The aim of Socialism is not only to abolish the present division of mankind into small states, not only to bring nations closer to each other, but ultimately to merge them. But we have never ignored the historical process necessary to the achievement of that goal. Nor can we "postpone" the question of national liberation until Socialism is established or speak solely in general nebulous phrases about national liberation. We must have a clear and precisely formulated political program to guide our work in the achievement of that goal. For we know that "mankind can achieve the inevitable merging of nations, only by passing through the transition period of complete liberation of all the oppressed nations, *i.e.*, their freedom to secede." (Lenin, *Selected Works,* vol. V. International Publishers, p. 271.)

As Leninists, we are distinguished from the reactionary Social-Democrats in that we reject, even if it is under the name of "internationalism," any denial of the right of national self-determination to the oppressed peoples. For true internationalism, that is, Marxism-Leninism, places the right of self-determination as a basic programmatic point. The "internationalism" of the reformists is nothing more or less than the nationalism of their own respective imperialist rulers, while the national program of Lenin is an essential part of internationalism. Any "internationalism" that denies the right of self-determination to the subject peoples is false, is a mere cover for imperialist chauvinism.

Our approach is based on proletarian internationalism, which recognizes that the workers of an oppressing nation best fight against national oppression—especially by their "own" bourgeoisie—once they understand that such is the road to their own freedom. It is based on the Marxist proposition that "no nation can be free if it oppresses other nations."

Clearly then, those who impute to the Negro people the main responsibility for "accepting" or "rejecting" the principle of self-determination ignore this tenet: they base their conclusions on the subjective factor, instead of the objective and historical conditions of oppression of the Negro people in the Black Belt.

But let us examine some of these arguments. Is it true that the Negro people do not want self-determination, that the Negro people shy away from this concept with abhorrence? Definitely not! It is, of course, quite a different matter if we speak of the Negro people as not being fully conscious of this concept in our terms. But to challenge the deepest desires of the Negro people for freedom and equality as being other than that of the fullest national self-affirmation is to fail to understand their fundamental aspirations!

What do the Negro people abhor? They abhor the continuation of their *actual* status in the Black Belt—that of forcible segregation. They abhor Jim Crow from which they suffer in many forms today. They abhor the freedom with which the poll-taxers and feudal landowners, by dividing Negro and white, continue their oppression of the Negro people. They abhor the ideology of "white supremacy" which flouts the basic tents of our Constitution, as the counterpart of Hitler's "aryan supremacy." They abhor any idea which holds out the perspective, not of full freedom and equality, but of something less than these things. And the slogan of self-determination expresses precisely these aspirations in the most complete sense.

To argue that the Negro people "don't want self-determination," is unwittingly to give sanction to the poll-taxers and feudal landowners in the South to continue exploiting the Negro people and poor whites on the basis that "this is what the Negroes want"; it is to argue against a conscious fight by white American workers to help achieve the objective conditions in which the Negro people can freely make their own choice. It is to blunt the struggle for national liberation, to have at best, a bourgeois-liberal approach.

Is it any wonder, then, that the most vehement voices against this principle are *not the mass* of the Negro people, but the enemies of the white workers and the Negro people? The Social-Democrats (and the reactionary mouthpieces of monopoly capital and semi-feudal economy), who advance the ridiculous charge that self-determination would "Jim Crow the Negro people," "Create a Black Ghetto," and other such arguments *ad nauseam,* are exposed in their full light when we examine their real motives. They seek to cover up their denial of the double oppression of the Negro people—as wage slaves and as Negroes. They seek to obscure the fundamental character of the status of the Negro people in the Black Belt—which is essentially *national* and rooted in economic and historic conditions of a pre-capitalist nature. Nor can all the piety and wit of Social-Democracy cancel out its real aim—which is to serve imperialism and therefore betray the Negro people and the working class.

Another view holds that the industrialization of the South and new migrations had fundamentally altered the relationship of the Negro people to the land. The proponents of this view maintain that such a development has radically changed the character of the Negro question in the Black Belt from that of oppressed nationhood, if such it was in the past, to that of a class question.

In discussing such views, we should, at the outset, distinguish between the effects of industrialization in the South as a whole and in the Black Belt. The continued existence of economic slave survivals in the Black Belt is a fundamental distinction that must be made in an examination of the characteristics of nationhood among the Negro people. Unless this is done, we shall not be able to understand the problems either of the South as a whole or of the Black Belt in particular.

There has unquestionably been some increase of industrial expansion in the South. The war requirements for victory necessitated the expansion of a number of basic Southern industries, such as steel, coal, textile, lumber and shipbuilding. In addition, new industries, such as aircraft and munitions, were built. Capital investments, however, came primarily from the Federal government. Over $7,000,000,000 were thus expended solely as a war necessity. It is obvious that such investment for expansion of existing plants and the building of new industries no longer exists. The reverse is true—that is, the closing down of plants and a drastic curtailment of industrial production. Thus, it is clear that no trend exists at present which would permit one to speak of the industrialization of the South. The trend that was evident during the war was a temporary phenomenon.

By 1944, Mr. D. B. Lasseter of the Atlanta, Georgia, Regional Office of the War Manpower Commission was able to warn us of this trend in summarizing what war orders meant to the South. Taking note of the more than seven billion dollars in prime contracts in six Southern states alone, Lasseter wrote in *Social Forces* for October, 1944:

At first glance, these factors appear as bright prospects, but there is ample cause for anxiety lest this war-inspired prosperity prove only temporary. For while industrial activity and facilities have increased tremendously, there will be great difficulty in maintaining these gains after the war. When the shooting is over the plants responsible for the current boom will shut down entirely, or production will be sharply curtailed. And a glance at the record shows that there is a heavy concentration of this type of industry and activity. The South is packed with Army camps, and shipbuilding, airplane and munitions plants further account for much of our industrial development. None of these offers a rosy future as a peacetime investment.

Lasseter added:

> The South faces a grave readjustment. Having had its first taste of prosperity resulting from increased industrial activity, it is slated to lose the source of this prosperity.

It goes without saying that expansion and building of new industries in the Black Belt would, of course, have its influence among the Negro people. Such a process would lead to the extension of the working-class base among the Negro people. Instead of de-limiting the national characteristics of the Negro people, it would help importantly to develop the national consciousness of the Negro people and thus accelerate the realization of the aim of self-determination. The extension of the working-class base in the oppressed Negro nation is fundamentally the guarantee of the successful forward movement of the national liberation cause of the entire Negro people.

Self-Determination—A Guiding Principle

It is my opinion that we again must raise the right of self-determination for the Negro people in the Black Belt, not as a slogan of immediate action, but essentially as a *programmatic demand*. It might perhaps be argued that, raised in this manner, the slogan is academic and should therefore not be raised at all. Such criticism fails to take into account the difference between a slogan advanced as an issue on the order of the day and a *guiding principle*.

We must place the question in terms of historical perspective, taking into account concretely the stage of the Negro liberation movement today and the present practical struggle for full Negro rights, in behalf of which there must be established both the broadest Negro unity and the broadest Negro and white alliance. Between the current struggles and the programmatic slogan here advanced there is no conflict, but a vital interconnection. The goal of national self-determination should serve as a beacon to the day-to-day struggles for Negro rights, and these struggles, in turn, should serve to hasten the realization of the right to self-determination.

20

The Status of Negro Women in the United States of America

Thelma Dale

February 3, 1947, New York City

Approximately six million Negro women in the U.S. face the double oppression of both racial and sex discrimination. All women in America have had to overcome the barriers set-up to limit their participation in our society as equals. Women were only given the right to vote by the 19th Amendment to our Constitution which was passed within our own generation after tremendous campaigns waged by the "Suffragettes." Today, all women in the U.S. are required to wage continuing struggles, even within the most progressive organizations, including some trade unions in order to make their best contributions to the growth and development of our country.

Negro women, brought to this country as chattel-slaves, and used for three hundred years of slavery as breeders and hard-laborers, have found it even more difficult to attain a position of equality either with white women or even with Negro men.

Because Negro men have always been relegated to the lowest paid and most unstable jobs Negro women have found it necessary to find employment out of the home in far greater proportions than other women. Primarily because of discrimination in employment and in education, Negro women have been forced into domestic service as the main source of employment. For example, in 1940 about four-fifths of all the Negro women employed in New York City (most liberal and progressive city in America) were in domestic service or other services, such as laundry, dry cleaning plants and the like. Of all Negro women employed, less than five percent were in professional fields and only eight per cent were in manufacturing industries.

This picture was somewhat changed during the Second World War, due to several important factors: (1) the imperative necessity to utilize every available worker in the country to produce the weapons of victory, (2) the Executive Order issued by the late President Franklin D. Roosevelt forbidding discrimination in employment in war industries. Through the efforts of the Fair Employment Practices Committee established under the Executive Order and the activity of some other State Agencies, recalcitrant employers, some of whom preferred to lose the war than disturb the "lily-white" composition of their factories, were coerced or persuaded to employ Negro workers for the first time.

Not alone was it necessary to wage struggles to get Negro women employed in war industries, but important struggles were also waged to secure employment of Negro women in the government services. Particularly important in this respect was the campaign waged to get the Army and the Public Health Services to take Negro women nurses. As late as 1944, the National Association of Colored Graduate Nurses was told by Surgeon General Kirk (U.S. Army): "The Army takes Negro nurses where we can use them, but we don't mix them— where we have Negro troops we use Negro nurses, but until now we haven't used them for white troops. We don't use Negroes and whites together."

The fight to get the opportunity for Negro nurses to serve their country in its most critical hour was taken all the way to the President of the United States, with the result that a few thousand Negro nurses were given the opportunity to get training and preparation to serve their country. It should be noted, however, that Negro women in the Women's Army as well as in the Nurses Corps continued, with few exceptions to serve their country, as did their men, in a second class, jim-crow status.

Although the percentage of Negro women in industry increased approximately three-fold between 1940 and 1944 (from 6.5% to 10%), since the close of the war, Negro women have steadily been relegated again to domestic and service occupations. No comprehensive government statistics are available at this time, but partial reports from the U.S. Employment Service and trade union reports indicate that the first out-backs in employment hit the Negro women first, since they were the last to be hired. In addition, the collapse of the Federal Fair Employment Practice Committee has been felt hardest by Negro women.

In New York City, the White Collar section of the United Office and Professional Workers of America, CIO, report that approximately 25 percent of its applicants for employment are Negro, despite the fact that Negroes comprise less than 10 percent of the total population and an even lesser percentage of the total employees covered by the Union. This same pattern is reflected throughout the country in the major industrial centers.

Because the trade union movement and other progressive forces in our country believed that the positive aspects of the Roosevelt program would be put into effect after the war, particularly, full employment, special steps were not taken to assure decent jobs for women and Negroes in industry. As a result Negro women who were the hardest hit find themselves today with little hope for attaining the economic position which they held during the war. And although all women are suffering to some extent from job discrimination at the present time, Negro women are at a decided disadvantage, because, the vast majority of Negro women work because their husbands do not make sufficient money to support their families, or because they must work in order to live.

All of this is not to say that there have not been tremendous gains in the economic status of Negro women during the war, for there have been. But the stability of these gains will have to be fought for continually. Organizations of Negro women and interracial women's organizations such as the Congress of American Women have an important role to play in helping to maintain and extend the war time employment gains and opportunities of Negro women. Just as the stability of the white worker is dependent upon the stability of the Negro worker, so it is, that the stability of all women in America will be dependent directly upon the economic stability of Negro women.

In addition to the Federal Fair Employment Practice Committee, some measure of credit should be given the Women's Bureau of the Department of Labor for its untiring efforts to secure equal wages for women, for its work in collecting the only available data on the economic status of women and for its general efforts to see that all women were integrated into our war set-up.

Economic discrimination is only one facet of the discrimination suffered by all women in America. A South Carolina Senator once said, "The Negro has no rights which a white man is bound to respect." So it has been with women, generally. Although our female forbears tilled the soil and worked alongside their menfolk in the building of our country, through the years, women have with few exceptions been relegated in the sheltered life of homemakers. Even when in the case of most Negro women, they have been main supporter of the family, the man still maintained a superior status to that of women. With such a background it is not difficult to understand how Negro women have been placed at the bottom of the ladder both politically and socially.

The advance of trade unionism and the fight of some women's organizations have resulted in some drastic changes for women generally, even though, Negro women are far behind their white sisters in this respect.

Women in America are very proud of the fact that in the last presidential election in 1944 when women constituted a majority of the electorate, that our late president Franklin D. Roosevelt, running against tremendous reactionary odds was reelected for a fourth term. Elected along with President Roosevelt, were perhaps, the largest number of women to the House of Representatives, and to State and Municipal legislative bodies.

Today, with reaction becoming increasingly entrenched in America, women are finding it more difficult to maintain their position in the political life of our country. This year, for example, only seven women were elected to the Congress of the United States. Four of these were elected by Republicans, and already some of these Republican ladies are showing that they are the tools of reactionaries, although they were elected on a presumed progressive platform. No Negro woman has ever been elected to the Congress of the United States. As far as we can determine, there are no Negro women in elected posts on either a State or Municipal level at the present time.

During the war Mrs. Mary McLeod Bethune, President of the National Council of Negro Women, held the highest post of any Negro women, that of Advisor on Race Relations in the National Youth Administration. She was appointed to this position by President Roosevelt. Judge Jan Bolin, Magistrate in the Children's Court in New York City is the only Negro women judge in the United States.

The almost total absence of Negro women from posts in the government is due in part to the fact that the majority of the 6 million Negro women in the United States live in the thirteen southern states where disfranchisement through "white supremacy" laws and other legal entanglements deny millions of American citizens the free exercise of the right to vote. The poll-tax which exists as a requirement for voting in seven southern states robs ten million citizens of the right to vote; six million whites and four million Negroes.

During the past summer, when primaries were being held in most States, the efforts of reactionary, "white supremacists" to keep Negroes from voting led to the lynching of a score or more Negroes. The Negro women lynched in Monroe, Georgia along with their husbands were among the many victims of the reign of terror designed to prevent Negroes from exercising their democratic right to vote. The Federal Constitution of the U.S. guarantees all citizens the right to vote, but all Southern states shortly after the Reconstruction period in the 1870's enacted laws denying Negroes basic rights of citizenship. Some of these laws have been declared unconstitutional by the Supreme Court of the U.S. However, in day to day practice, all Negroes in the South, including the Nation's capital, Washington, D.C., are denied full citizenship rights.

During the term of office of the liberal Governor Ellis Arnall, the poll tax law was repealed, thus making it possible for millions of poor Negroes and whites to vote. However, when the threat of a large Negro vote was seen, the rabid reactionary Eugene Talmadge campaigned and was elected on a platform of "white supremacy"—that is, of keeping Negroes from voting. Governor Elect Talmadge died before he could take his oath of office and his men, through illegal and fascist coup d'état took over the Governorship and was successful in getting the State Assembly to vote in favor of a white primary law which would deny Negroes the right to belong to and vote in the Democratic Party of Georgia.

When the President of the United States, Harry S. Truman, was asked by a delegation headed by Paul Robeson and comprising some outstanding Negro and white citizens of the country to speak out against the reign of terror in the South directed against Negroes, the President found it politically inexpedient to do so. Despite similar requests made recently with regard to the Georgia situation the President still has found it politically expedient to remain silent, while the rights and the lives of millions of American citizens are being held in jeopardy.

It is not possible in such a brief statement to give a comprehensive view of the status of Negro women in America. Nor is it possible to refer you to any one document which can give all the facts, for just as we suffer discrimination in our daily lives so we suffer the discrimination of not being treated as an important enough subject for research which would give all the facts.

The important fact to Negro women today, is that there is a growing concern with their plight. It is particularly important that organizations like the Congress of American Women and some of the progressive trade unions are beginning to deal with the problem, knowing full well that there can never be real equality for all women until Negro women are also given equality.

It is likewise most important that the Women's International Democratic Federation has seen fit to include this problem on its agenda for discussion and action at this International Council meeting. What, then are the specific suggestions for action on this problem? We believe the WIDF can help in the following ways:

1. Make the women of the Federation and of the world conscious of the plight of their Negro sisters in America. This can be done through articles in our bulletin discussing in detail many of the problems which were not dealt with at length in the present statement. In addition, some of the leading Negro women should be invited to tour various countries to speak on their problems.

2. Increased support should be secured for the Petition to the United Nations on behalf of 15 million Negroes in America submitted last June by the National Negro Congress. Already the WIDF and the Congress of American Women have indicated their support for this petition to the Secretary-General of the United Nations. However, in view of the fact that there are some one thousand similar positions now before the UN, special steps will have to be taken in order to get the Negro Congress petition on the agenda of the UN. Many of the members of the WIDF are in leading positions in their governments and trade unions affiliated with the World Federation of Trade Unions. Their support for this petition can be extremely valuable.

3. Build the WIDF and its constituent national organizations as strong anti-fascist, pro-democratic forces for peace in the world. The onslaught of reaction in America and in the world can be stopped if the peoples of the world organize effectively for peace and progress.

21

For New Approaches to Our Work Among Women

Claudia Jones

Political Affairs 27, no. 9 (August 1948), pp. 738–43

The draft resolution places as the central task before our Party the build-ing of the people's anti-monopoly and peace coalition against American imperialism. It likewise stresses the imperative need for the people's coalition, and particularly the working class, to fight aggressively on those issues which can win the support of every section of the popula-tion that can add solidity, numbers, and strength to the battle against American imperialism.

The resolution, however, does not sufficiently stress the need for the people's coalition to fight for the special social, economic and political needs of the masses of American women. Nor does it emphasize the Party's vanguard responsibility in organizing and winning working-class women to the anti-imperialist camp.

The resolution does not adequately emphasize the developing counter-offensive of the women themselves, as evidenced in their growing interest in the new people's party and in their fight against high prices, war, and for democratic liberties. While the resolution notes that a mood of resistance is growing among American women, it does not sufficiently expose the attempts being made by the monopolists to influence them.

The importance of winning American women, especially in working-class and Negro communities, to militant resistance to Wall Street's program of fascism and war, can be fully understood only if we correctly assess the decisive role American women can play in the political life of the nation.

To begin with, women represent over half of the nation. Moreover, there are nearly 16 million women wage-earners, one-fifth of whom are heads of families. Thirty-seven million women are housewives in cities or on farms. Eight per cent of these are working mothers. There are forty-seven million women eligible to vote in the United States—over a million and a half more than men!

As regards their degree of organization, nearly 30 million women are organized in various types of clubs and national women's organizations which are, in the main, bourgeois-led.

Wall Street imperialism has not been lax in recognizing the potentially powerful political force that women represent. It is paying increasing attention to reaching and influencing them. As part and parcel of its general reactionary offensive, it has, since the war's end, unfolded a tremendous ideological campaign, to influence the minds of the people along reactionary channels as regards American women.

Heart of its ideological campaign is the false Hitlerite slogan that "women's place is in the home." This slogan is primarily designed to obscure the source of the many existing inequalities in the social position of women in the United States. It further seeks to obscure the fact that the many social and economic advances made by women during the anti-fascist war are today being undermined.

No sooner was the war ended than a drive was made to send women back into the kitchen. In place of employer eulogies to "angels with dirty faces" women are discovering that because of their sex they have two strikes against them today in competing for jobs.

Furthermore, the majority of job openings are in clerical, sales, and service fields, which means that rates received by women workers are lower than those they received in wartime jobs. There are growing trends which show that these postwar employment difficulties are falling most heavily on Negro women, who were the first to be fired in the layoffs especially in the heavy industries. We are beginning to witness a growing trend in which Negro women wartime workers are being forced back into domestic work because no special fight has been put up to secure jobs for them in basic industry by the trade unions. Generally, a retraining job program must be outlined and fought for by the trade unions, if the wartime skills gained by women are not to be completely obliterated. While women are "still a major factor in industry, in the whole national economy, and in the labor movement" as the draft resolution notes, their widespread ouster from heavy industry during reconversion has resulted in a general falling off of their membership in the trade unions.

The drive of reaction, has on the whole, not succeeded in ousting women from industry. This is due mainly to their determination to remain in industry and trade union protection won in some industries during the war. As evidenced in numerous polls, moreover, work for these women is a necessity, to make ends meet, because of invalid husbands, sickness, inadequate wages of their menfolk, support of their families, etc.

The present reactionary attack on the position and condition of women in industry should be a challenge to progressive trade unions to organize women workers. The demands for a retraining program, for equal pay for equal work, for protective legislation for women, which monopoly capitalism seeks to remove by Constitutional amendment, loom today as some of the major issues with which to reach the women wage earner. Some reactionary successes in wiping out progressive legislation and in extending the working day for women occurred last year with very little protest by the trade unions. The emasculation of the appropriations by the G.O.P.-controlled Congress has also seriously crippled the valuable work of the Women's and Children's Bureaus of the Department of Labor.

Side by side with attempts to put women back into the kitchen has come a serious reduction of the all too inadequate social services. The wartime nursery program for working mothers has been cut down to a minimum. The threatened new rise in the price of milk menaces the health of millions of children. The refusal of Governor Dewey to appropriate funds for the all-too-few child care centers in New York State is an index of the callous attitudes which prevail in both of the major parties toward the needs of children.

It is around such issues that millions of women can be reached in the communities. Concern for the health of their children, for adequate medical and nursing services, for correcting the completely inadequate and obsolete conditions in the public schools, are burning issues in the minds of millions of women. Around such issues we can help women to more deeply understand the real significance of the Marshall Plan. We can show them that the Marshall Plan and the Truman Doctrine means sacrificing the living standards and the educational system of the people. We can show them that the drive to militarize and draft our youth means retrenchment in higher education and discouraging the enrollment of our young people in the colleges. We can above all expose the reactionary essence of monopoly capitalism, which on the one hand clouts the women with rocketing prices, housing shortages, hysterical threats of war; while, on the other, it woos them with free movies, speakers, etc., on the glories of American "free enterprise."

The drive of American reaction to force women into a reactionary path must not be permitted to succeed. The burning problems of the American women, if correctly understood and fought for by the people's coalition, can succeed in making the masses of American women, and especially the working-class women, a powerful force for progress. It is clear therefore that in such a situation our Party must correctly assess its own activities as regards work among women, if it is to play its vanguard role in this important sphere of the struggle for peace and progress.

Let us estimate the extent to which we have progressed in this vital sphere since the emergency convention.

In February, 1947, our Party established a National Women's Commission. Its establishment marked a significant reaffirmation of the importance of Communist work among women.

Our Commission has functioned rather regularly, and we were able in the course of the year to establish twelve similar commissions on a state scale. These exist in the following districts and cities: Ohio, Michigan, New York, Chicago, Eastern Pennsylvania, Western Pennsylvania, San Francisco, Los Angeles, Seattle, Washington, New Jersey, and Houston.

These commissions were established in most cases as a result of special women's conferences called by our Party districts and sections. This has proved a healthy means of assessing their needs, concrete problems and ties in the community and of raising Party sensitivity as a whole to the needs of women in general.

It has proved valuable likewise in convincing many women comrades (skeptical with justifiable reasons) that our Party was serious about this phase of work. This skepticism will not be eliminated solely by the formation of women's commissions; it will only be eliminated if our Party as a whole really begins to tackle these problems theoretically and practically.

A general weakness of our work has been failure to sufficiently integrate the work of these commissions with that of other Party departments. This is indicative of a general tendency to relegate this phase of work to the women themselves, and to consider questions of policy with regard to mass work of women the sole responsibility of the commissions and our women comrades in mass organizations.

If we ask ourselves why this situation exists, I believe we would have to conclude that it is primarily due to the fact that our Party has failed to place the question of theoretical understanding of the woman question as a "must" for every Party member. Absence of this theoretical understanding has resulted in failure to combat male-chauvinist tendencies which are rampant in our Party. It has resulted in failure consistently to assign women comrades to mass work, without which we can never root our work in this sphere among the working-class and Negro women particularly.

The recent establishment by our National Board, at the initiative of Comrade Foster, of a special sub-committee to deal with theoretical aspects of the woman question, marks the first serious step in the necessary process of equipping our Party to overcome this serious weakness.

As regards Party organization generally, we are only beginning to find the special methods and forms necessary for greater activization of our women comrades. Some of the forms which have brought results and which should be further developed are:

1. National cadre and regional schools for theoretical training of our women comrades.
2. Daytime classes for our women comrades. Such classes have been held in practically all major districts. The Kings County Party organization in New York City pioneered in this form and has since established a continuous daytime program for women comrades. This form is especially appropriate for rapidly equipping many of our women with an elementary knowledge of basic Marxist-Leninist principles.
3. Guidance of the work of our women comrades in mass organizations. There is much underestimation still of the importance of mass concentration work among women. When we consider the inadequate size and influence of the existing anti-fascist and progressive organizations among women, especially in the working-class, Negro, and nationality organizations, we can more fully appreciate the need of real attention to this phase of work in order to enable our women comrades to do effective mass work and Party building.
4. Concrete organization of services for Party women. The continued organization of services, "baby sitter" funds and services for Party women can prove very helpful in enabling many of our Party women to do mass and Party work.

The work of the National Women's Commission still suffers from many weaknesses. These can be listed as follows: 1) A failure to make the decisions and experiences and problems of the Commission the property of the entire Party; 2) failure to equip our Party more regularly with facts on trends among women and to organize an exchange of experiences between districts; 3) failure to integrate our trade-union women comrades in the work of the Women's Commissions. In connection with all our tasks, there is need for Party literature on the women question. Our press has to make a basic turn in its attention to, and coverage of, the problems of women.

Our Party nationally has a women's membership of close to forty per cent. While in most districts our women are demonstrating that they are capable of carrying out many-sided Party responsibilities equally well with men, there is not as yet sufficient recognition of their capabilities or their promotion into leadership posts on all levels. A notable exception is the California district, where, on a county, section, and club level, women Communists hold positions in administrative, educational, legislative and mass posts. This process must be speeded up in our entire Party.

Of special importance is the need to tap deeply the tremendous potential and organizational abilities of our Negro women comrades.

Generally in the Negro liberation movement, South and North, it is the Negro women who are leading and symbolizing many of the struggles for equality by the Negro people. Greater attention to the triple handicaps of Negro women can help to strengthen our Party life and the building of Negro and white unity.

Time is short. We are still in the process of catching up with our past weaknesses in this phase of work when, under Browder revisionism, work among women was liquidated as part of the whole liquidationist policy which then prevailed in our Party. But, since its national emergency convention, our Party has chalked up a proud record of militant struggle for the needs of the people, women and men, who must mutually join in a fight against the warmongers and pro-fascists as a necessary prerequisite for the attainment of our ultimate goal of socialism. The working-class women of America will respond to the message of our Party if we but organize our work in such a way as to speak out, and give leadership in struggle, on the needs and issues facing them.

SECTION IV
Winning Peace at Home and Abroad

The eleven pieces collected in the fourth section attest to Black Communist women's interconnected organizing work at home and abroad. More than half of these chapters initially appeared in Paul Robeson's and Louis Burnham's *Freedom* newspaper. The paper brought together a dynamic community of young Black radical women writers who shared the paper's commitment to anti-imperialism, anticolonialism, Black liberation, and the working class.[1] This cadre included Vicki Garvin, Dorothy Hunton, Lorraine Hansberry, Eslanda Goode Robeson, Dorothy Burnham, and Yvonne Gregory.

Immersed in the labor movement, Vicki Garvin joined the CPUSA in 1947. She was on *Freedom*'s editorial board and worked actively to organize and promote the National Negro Labor Council (NNLC).[2] Garvin's chapter, "Union Leader Challenges Progressive America," describes the improvement of the deplorable conditions of Black women workers as the "acid test of democracy."[3] Garvin emphasizes that marriage and a family are no path to security for Black women; they need secure union jobs. Dorothy Hunton was married to William Alphaeus Hunton Jr., a party leader who also served as the executive director of the Council on African Affairs (CAA) and a key member in the Civil Rights Congress (CRC). As Cold War–era reaction intensified in the early 1950s, the CAA was targeted as a subversive organization. Hunton himself was sentenced to six months in prison for refusing to comply with orders from the House Committee on Un-American Activities to turn over names of contributors to the CRC bail fund. Dorothy Hunton's chapter describes her emotional struggle dealing with the blow of her husband's arrest. The initial shock and despair transform into an understanding that the work of freedom fighters such as Sojourner Truth and Harriet Tubman remains unfinished. Hunton declares, "The time has come when we Negro women, especially, must unite and work together for the freedom and dignity of our people."[4]

Lorraine Hansberry, who became a celebrated playwright for *A Raisin in the Sun*, started as a clerical worker at *Freedom*.[5] The two chapters from Hansberry in this section reflect her attention to international political concerns. The first reports on Egyptian demands for freedom from British imperialism, noting that the Egyptian women's movement had trained some 250 young women for guerrilla combat. The second describes the Inter-American Peace Conference held in Montevideo, Uruguay. Hansberry attended the conference in place of Paul Robeson, whose passport had been canceled by the US State Department when he refused to sign an affidavit testifying that he was not a member of the Communist Party.[6] Her account of the conference connects the violence, poverty, and immiseration afflicting the people of Latin America with the war in Korea: both are instances of "Yanqui Imperialismo." The chapter from Eslanda Goode Robeson, Paul Robeson's wife, similarly opposes US militarism in Korea. Her scathing critique draws a parallel between the treatment of Chinese and Korean prisoners of war in US camps with the conditions facing incarcerated Black people in the US South. In each instance, the oppressors "speak for" the imprisoned—so whom should we believe?

The last two of the *Freedom* articles selected for this section are from Dorothy Burnham and Yvonne Gregory. Married to *Freedom*'s managing editor, Louis Burnham, Dorothy Burnham was a long-time CPUSA member and activist in the Southern Negro Youth Congress. Her piece describes the conditions facing sharecroppers in the US South. Gregory's article uses the incident of the physical attack on the singer Pearl Bailey by racist thugs in a New Jersey nightclub to reflect on the death of another great singer, Bessie Smith. Smith bled to death from injuries sustained in a car crash in Mississippi. No hospital in the town where the crash occurred would admit her because of her race. Gregory draws out the ways the music of the blues expresses the sorrow and anger of Black people.

Section IV also contains two statements issued by the Black women's political organization Sojourners for Truth and Justice (STJ). The organization cited inspiration from Sojourner Truth and Harriet Tubman as it located the ongoing struggle against lynching and white supremacist violence on the long road from bondage to freedom. Initiated by Louise Thompson Patterson and the poet and actor Beulah Richardson, the group's leadership included, among others, Thompson, Dorothy Hunton, Eslanda Goode Robeson, Alice Childress, Charlotta Bass, and Shirley Graham Du Bois. STJ fused Black nationalism, popular front organizing, communist theory, and gender analysis to advance people-centered human rights and radical politics.[7]

Finally, this section concludes with pieces from Claudia Jones and Charlotta Bass, respectively. Jones was the highest-ranking woman in the CPUSA. In 1951 she was arrested for violating the Smith Act. Passed in 1940 as the Alien Registration Act, this law made it a crime to advocate or to organize a group that advocated the overthrow of the United States government. As a party leader, Jones had long been under FBI surveillance. "International Women's Day and the Struggle for Peace," originally given as a speech and later published in *Political Affairs*, was cited in the indictment that led to her arrest and conviction.[8] Noting the rising global opposition to US production of the hydrogen bomb and the emerging nuclear arms race, Jones calls for the rallying of American women into the international movement to stop US monopoly capitalism's drive toward war and fascism. American women must be linked in solidarity to the ongoing peace struggle of anti-imperialist women around the world. Jones describes the reactionary "Hitlerite" anti-woman ideology being fostered to block women's social and economic participation. The lie that "women's place is in the home" attempts to conceal the fact that monopoly capitalism is the real source of workers' problems. But this lie is not confined to the ruling class. It also pervades the progressive movement more broadly, including the party. Uprooting the ideology of women's biological inferiority thus requires sustained struggle. Jones writes:

> Failure to recognize the special social disabilities of women under capitalism is one of the chief manifestations of male supremacy. These special forms of oppression particularly affect the working women, the farm women and the triply oppressed Negro women; but, in varying degrees, they help to determine the inferior status of women in all classes of society.[9]

The chapter from Charlotta Bass also originated as a speech, one that was given in acceptance of the Progressive Party's nomination for vice president in 1952. Bass was the first Black woman to be nominated for this position by a US political party. The owner and publisher of the *California Eagle*, an influential Black newspaper, Bass was monitored by the FBI and suspected of being a member of the Communist Party (which she denied) because of her involvement in progressive politics and leadership role in the Soujourners for Truth and Justice. In her acceptance speech, Bass observes that fascism has taken root and blossomed in the United States, referencing the terrorism and lynching of Black people not just in the US South but all over the country and linking that violence to US imperialist violence in Asia and Africa. She vows: "We support the movement for freedom of all peoples everywhere—in Africa, in Asia, in the Middle East, and above all, here in our own country. And we will not be silenced by the rope, the gun, the lynch mob, or the lynch judge."[10]

22

International Women's Day and the Struggle for Peace

Claudia Jones

Political Affairs 29, no. 3 (March 1950), pp. 32–45

On International Women's Day this year, millions of women in the world-wide camp of peace headed by the mighty land of Socialism will muster their united forces to make March 8, 1950, a day of demonstrative struggle for peace, freedom and women's rights.

In our own land, there will be over fifty celebrations. On New York's Lower East Side, original site of this historic American-born day of struggle for equal rights for women, and in major industrial states, such as Illinois, Ohio, Michigan, Pennsylvania, California, Massachusetts, and Connecticut, broad united-front meetings of women for peace will be head. "Save the Peace!" "Halt Production of the A-Bomb!" "Negotiate with the Soviet Union to Outlaw Atomic Weapons!"—these are the slogans of women in the U.S.A. on International Women's Day.

The Struggle for Peace

The special significance of this holiday this year, its particular meaning for labor, progressives, and Communists, and for American working women generally, is to be found in the widespread condemnation, among numerous sections of the American people, of Truman's cold-blooded order to produce the hydrogen bomb and to inaugurate a suicidal atomic and hydrogen weapon race.

Not to the liking of the imperialist ideologists of the "American Century" is the growing indication by millions of American women of their opposition to war, their ardent desire for peace, their rejection of the Truman-bipartisan war policy.

As in the Protestant women's groups, many women's organizations are opposed to the North Atlantic war pact, which spells misery for the masses of American women and their families. This development coincides with the policy stand of progressive women's organizations that have been outspoken in demands for peaceful negotiations of differences with the Soviet Union, for the outlawing of atomic weapons, for ending the cold war.

Typical of the shocked reaction to Truman's order for H-bomb production was the statement of the Women's International League for Peace and Freedom demanding that Secretary of State Dean Acheson "make clear by action as well as by words that the United States desires negotiations and agreement" with the Soviet Union. This is necessary, the statement added, to avoid "bringing down upon this nation the condemnation of the world." This organization also expressed its opposition to Acheson's suggestion for the resumption of diplomatic relations between U.N. members and Franco-Spain, as well as to the proposed extension of the peace-time draft law.

These and other expressions of opposition to the Administration's H-bomb policy by notable women's organizations and leaders merge with the significant grass-roots united-front peace activities developing in many communities. For example, in Boston, as result of a "Save the Peace—Outlaw the A-Bomb" peace ballot circulated last November, a permanent broad united-front women's organization, "Minute Women for Peace," has been established. In that city, within ten days, over 6,000 women from church, trade-union, fraternal, Negro, civic and middle-class-led women's organizations signed peace ballots urging outlawing of the A-Bomb. In Philadelphia, a Women's Committee For Peace has addressed to President Truman a ballot to "Outlaw the H-Bomb—Vote for Peace." Similar developments have taken place in Pasadena and Chicago. The wide response of women of all political opinions to these ballots is but an index of the readiness of American women to challenge the monstrous Truman-Acheson doctrine that war is inevitable. Emulation of these developments in other cities, particularly among working-class and Negro women, is certainly on the order of the day.

Indicative of the determination of women, not only to register their peace sentiments, but to fight for peace, is the coalescing on a community basis, following such ballotings, of women's peace committees. The orientation of these committees is to convene women's peace conferences, in alliance with the general peace movement now developing.

The widespread peace sentiments, particularly of the women and the youth in their millions, must be organized and given direction and effective, militant expression. This is necessary, since the monopolist rulers are doing everything possible to deceive the people to paralyze their will to fight for peace. Particularly insidious agents of the war-makers are the Social-Democratic and reformist labor leaders, the reactionary Roman Catholic hierarchy, and the American agents of the fascist Tito gang of imperialist spies, whose main task is to confuse, split and undermine the peace camp.

Hence, a fundamental condition for rallying the masses of American women into the peace camp is to free them from the influence of the agents of imperialism and to arouse their sense of internationalism with millions upon millions of their sisters the world over; to protest the repressive and death-dealing measures carried through against the countless women victims by Wall Street's puppets in Marshalized Italy, in fascist Greece and Spain; to link them in solidarity with the anti-imperialist women united 80 million strong in 59 lands in the Women's International Democratic Federation, who are in the front ranks of the struggle for peace and democracy.

In these lands, anti-fascist women collect millions of signatures for the outlawing of the A-bomb, against the Marshall Plan and Atlantic war pact, for world disarmament, etc. In the German Democratic Republic, five million signatures were collected by women for outlawing the A-bomb. In Italy, the Union of Italian Women collected more than 2 million such signatures for presentation to the De Gasperi government. In France, women conducted demonstrations when bodies of dead French soldiers were returned to their shores as a result of the Marshall-Plan-financed war of their own government against the heroic Viet-Namese. In Africa, women barricaded the roads with their bodies to prevent their men from being carted away as prisoners in a militant strike struggle charged with slogans of anti-colonialism and peace. And who can measure the capitalist fear of emulation by American Negro and white women of these peace struggles, particularly of the women of China (as reflected in the All-Asian Women's Conference held last December in Peking), whose feudal bonds were severed forever as a result of the major victory of the Chinese people's revolution?

These and other significant anti-imperialist advances, achieved in united-front struggle, should serve to inspire the growing struggles of American women and heighten their consciousness of the need for militant united-front campaigns around the burning demands of the day, against monopoly oppression, against war and fascism.

Reaction's Ideological and Political Attacks Against Women

American monopoly capital can offer the masses of American women, who compose more than one-half of our country's population, a program only of war and fascism. Typical of the ideology governing this war perspective was the article in the recent mid-century issue of *Life* magazine entitled "Fifty Years of American Women." That "contribution" did not hold out the promise to American women along the demagogic 2000 A.D. line of Truman's State of the Union annual message, but brazenly offered the fascist triple-K (Kinder-Küche-Kirche) pattern of war and a "war psychology" for American women!

The author, Winthrop Sargeant, drawing upon the decadent, Nazi-adopted "theorist," Oswald Spengler, propounded his cheap philosophy on the expensive Luce paper

> . . . that only in wartime do the sexes achieve a normal relationship to each other. The male assumes his dominant heroic role, and the female, playing up to the male, assumes her proper and normal function of being feminine, glamorous and inspiring. With the arrival of peace a decline sets in. The male becomes primarily a meal ticket and the female becomes a sexless frump, transferring her interest from the male to various unproductive intellectual pursuits or to neurotic occupations, such as bridge or politics. Feminine civilization thus goes to pot until a new challenge in the form of wartime psychology restores the balance.

The real intent of such ideology should be obvious from its barbarous, vulgar, fascist essence. The aim of this and other numerous anti-women "theories" is to hamper and curb women's progressive social participation, particularly in the struggle for peace. This has been the alpha and omega of bourgeois ideological attacks upon women since the post-war betrayal of our nation's commitments to its wartime allies.

Such ideology accompanies the developing economic crisis and penalizes especially the Negro women, the working women and the working class generally, but also women on the farms, in the offices and in the professions, who are increasingly entering the struggle to resist the worsening of their economic status.

Not always discerned by the labor-progressive forces, however, is the nature of this ideological attack, which increasingly is masked as attacks on woman's femininity, her womanliness, her pursuit of personal and family happiness. Big capital accelerates its reactionary ideological offensive against the people with forcible opposition to women's social participation for peace and for her pressing economic and social demands.

None of these attacks, however, has been as rabid as the recent "foreign agent" charge falsely leveled by the Department of Justice against the Congress of American Women on the basis of that organization's former affiliation with the Women's International Democratic Federation.

Only the most naive, of course, are startled at the attack against this progressive women's organization, whose policies, domestic and international, were always identified with the progressive camp. The C.A.W. leadership, in its press statement, answered the continuing attack of the Justice Department, which demands "retroactive compliance" with the undemocratic Kellar-McCormack Act, despite the organization's disaffiliation from the W.I.D.F. (under protest). The statement pointed out that this organization has been harassed from its very birth precisely because of its advanced policy stand and activities for peace, child welfare and education, Negro-white unity and equal rights for women. Incumbent on labor-progressives is the expression of full support for the struggles of women against these and other attacks and for the National Bread and Butter Conference of Child Care to be held in Chicago on April 15–16. The call for this conference indicates a broad, united-front sponsorship that includes C.A.W. leaders and demands use of government surpluses and the diversion of war funds to feed the nation's needy children.

Economic Conditions of Women Workers

Any true assessment of women's present status in the United States must begin with an evaluation of the effects of the growing economic crisis upon the working women, farm women, workers' wives, Negro women, women of various national origins, etc. The ruthless Taft-Hartley-employer drive to depress the workers' wage standards and abolish labor's right to strike and bargain collectively, as well as the wholesale ouster of Negro workers from many industries, was presaged by the post-war systemic displacement of women from basic industry. While women constituted 36.1 percent of all workers in 1945, this figure was reduced to 27.6 percent by 1947. Despite this, there still remains a sizable force of 17½ million women workers in industry, approximately three million of whom are organized in the trade unions, the vast majority still being unorganized.

The sparse economic data available show that the burdens of the crisis are increasingly being placed on the backs of women workers, who receive unequal wages, are victims of speed-up and face a sharp challenge to their very right to work. Older women workers are increasingly being penalized in the growing layoffs. Close to 30 percent of the estimated 6 million unemployed are women workers.

Side by side with this reactionary offensive against their living standards, women workers have increasing economic responsibilities. More than half of these women, as revealed in a survey by the Women's Bureau of the U.S. Department of Labor, are economic heads of families. The continued expulsion of women from industry, the growing unemployment of men and youth, as well as the high, monopoly-fixed prices of food and consumer goods generally, are impoverishing the American family and taking a heavy toll on the people's health.

Impoverishment has hit the farm women to an alarming degree. Almost 70 percent of all farm families earned less that $2000 in 1948, when the growing agricultural crisis was only in its first stage.

Women workers still find a large gap between their wages and those of men doing the same work, which the wages of Negro women are particularly depressed below the minimum wage necessary to sustain life.

There are increasing trends toward limited curricula for women students and limited opportunities for women in the professions. Employment trends also show increasing penalization of married women workers who constitute more than half of all working women.

The attempt by employers to foment divisions between men and women workers—to create a "sex antagonism"—is an increasing feature of the offensive to depress the wages of women and the working class in general. Male workers are being told that the dismissal of married women and the "return of women to the kitchen" will lead to an end of unemployment among the male workers. But this whole campaign against "double earning" and for a "return of women to the kitchen" is nothing but a cloak for the reactionary, Taft-Hartley offensive against wages, working conditions and social security benefits, with a view to a wide-scale dumping of workers, male as well as female.

It must be frankly stated that there has been lethargy on the part of progressives in the labor movement in answering and combatting this insolent demagogy. It should be pointed out that the German finance capitalists also used this demagogic line prior to the rise of Hitler. By perpetuating the lying slogan that "woman's place is in the home," monopoly capital seeks to conceal the real source of the problems of all workers.

Consequently this is a question of attacks, not only against the masses of women, but against the working class as a whole. When we deal with the situation of women workers, we do so, not only to protect the most exploited section of the working class, but in order to rally labor-progressives and our own Party for work among the masses of women workers, to lead them into the emerging anti-fascist, anti-war coalition.

Trade Unions and Women Workers

There is every evidence that working women's militancy is increasing, as evidenced last year in strikes in such industries as electrical, communications, packinghouse and in strikes of teachers and white-collar workers. Have labor-progressives grasped the significance of the vital need for a trade-union program based on concrete knowledge of the conditions of the woman worker, an understanding of reaction's attacks on her, economically, politically, socially?

Some Left-progressive unionists are beginning to tackle this problem as a decisive one. In New York District No 4 of U.E., splendid initiative was shown by the official establishment of a Women's Committee. Men and women unionists participate jointly to formulate a program and to combat the growing unemployment trends, especially the ouster of married women and their replacement, at lower wages, by young girls from high schools—a trend that affects the wages of all workers. In this union, also, conferences have been held on the problems of the women workers. Similarly, in Illinois, an Armour packinghouse local held a women's conference with the aim of enhancing the participation of Negro and white women workers; as the result of its educational work and struggle, it succeeded in extending the leave for pregnancy from the previous three-month limit to one year.

But these instances are exceptions and not the rule, and it would be incorrect if we failed to state that attitudes of male supremacy among Left-progressives in unions and elsewhere have contributed to the gross lack of awareness of the need to struggle for women's demands in the shops and departments. This bourgeois ideology is reflected in the acceptance of the bourgeois attitude of "normal toleration" of women in industry as a "temporary" phenomenon. This dangerous, tenacious ideology must be fought, on the basis of recognition that the dynamics of capitalist society itself means the tearing of women away from the home into industry as a permanent part of the exploited labor force. Marx and Engels, the founders of scientific socialism, more than one-hundred years ago exposed the pious hypocrisy of the troubadours of capitalism who composed hymns about the "glorious future" of the family relationship under capitalism; they noted the fact, which many progressives too readily forget, that "by the action of modern industry, all family ties among the proletarians are torn asunder . . . The bourgeoisie has torn away from the family its sentimental veil, and has reduced the family relation to a mere money relation" (*Manifesto of the Communist Party*).

The absence of a special vehicle to deal with the problems of women workers in the unions has undoubtedly contributed to dealing with these problems, not as a union question, but solely as a woman's question. It is of course, both. But it must be tackled as a special union responsibility, with the Communists and progressives boldly in the forefront. In many instances this approach would improve rank-and-file struggles for wage increases, against speed-up and around other concrete demands, and would also win militant unionists for active participation within the emerging rank-and-file movements. In this connection, it is also necessary to examine the just complaints of many women trade unionists, particularly on a shop level, who are concerned over the trend toward fewer elected women officers, and the relegation of women merely to appointive positions, as well as the unnecessary pattern of "all-male organization" union structure on many levels.

This entire question requires that we take into account also the position of the wives of trade unionists.

Indicative of the growing militancy of workers' wives is the role of miners' wives, hundreds of whom, Negro and white, recently picketed the empty tipples in the mining camps of West Virginia in support of the "no contract, no work" struggle of their fighting husbands, sons and brothers. Similarly, in the longshore trade, during the Local 968 strike in New York, wives of workers, particularly Negro and Italian women, played an outstanding role. Likewise, in Gary and South Chicago, wives of steel-workers issued open letters of support for the miners' struggle at the steel plant gates, collected food, etc.

Reactionary propaganda is not at all loath to exploit the wrong concepts of many workers' wives, who, because of political backwardness stemming from household drudgery, lack of political participation, etc., often adopt the view that it is the union, or the progressive movement, that robs them of their men in relation to their own home responsibilities.

Attention to the organization of wives and working men by labor progressives and Communists therefore becomes an urgent political necessity. And key to avoiding past errors is the enlisting of women themselves, with the support of the men, at the level of their readiness to struggle.

The Equal Rights Amendment

In the context of these developments and attacks upon women's economic and social status, one must also see the recent passage of the Equal Rights Amendment in the U.S. Senate by a 63–19 vote. The original amendment, sponsored by the National Women's Party, proceeding from an equalitarian concept of women's legal status in the U.S., would have wiped out all protective legislation won by women with the assistance of the trade unions over the past decades. Objection to the original amendment by labor-progressives and by our Party led to the formation of a coalition of some 43 organizations, including such groups as the Women's Trade Union League, the U.S. Women's Bureau, the American Association of University Women, C.I.O. and A.F. of L. unions, the National Association of Negro Women, etc.

A proper approach to such legislation today must primarily be based on recognizing that it is projected in the atmosphere of the cold war, carrying with it a mandate for drafting of women into the armed forces, for the war economy. Without such recognition, the present Amendment, which now urges no tampering with previously won protective legislative gains for women workers, might serve as an effective catch-all for many unwary supporters of equal rights for women.

Despite this danger, Left-progressives should not fail to utilize the broad debate already taking place to expose women's actual status in law; some 1,000 legal restrictions still operate at women's expense in numerous states, and minimum-wage legislation does not exist for over 1 million Negro women domestic workers. A demand for legislative hearings and the exposure of the reactionary attacks now prevalent in numerous state legislatures against the legislative gains of women workers are necessary to guarantee that no bill for equal rights for women becomes the law of the land without proper safeguards protecting the special measures meeting the needs of women workers. Perspective of a necessary referendum carrying a 37-state majority necessary to the bill's passage should not obscure the possibility that passage of the legislation in its present form, or minus the protective clause, could serve as a means of bipartisan electoral maneuvers for 1950 and the passage of the Amendment in its original reactionary form.

A Rich Heritage of Struggle

Before 1908 and since, American women have made lasting contributions in the struggle for social progress: against slavery and Negro oppression, for equal rights for women and women's suffrage, against capitalist exploitation, for peace and for Socialism. Special tribute must be paid those heroic women who gave their lives in the struggle for Socialism and freedom: Elsie Smith, Anna Damon, Rose Pastor Stokes, Fanny Sellins, Williana Burroughs and Grace Campbell. In this period of the U.S. monopoly drive to war and world domination, reaction pays unwilling tribute to the role of the Communist women leaders by its deportation delirium. The present-day struggles of progressive and Communist women merge with the traditions and contributions of such great anti-slavery fighters as Harriet Tubman and Sojourner Truth, of such militant women proletarians as the textile workers of 1848, of such women pioneers as Susan B. Anthony and Elizabeth Cady Stanton, of such builders of America's progressive and working-class heritages as Kate Richards O'Hare, Mother Jones, Ella Reeve Bloor, Anita Whitney and Elizabeth Gurley Flynn.

March 8 was designated International Women's Day by the International Socialist Conference in 1910, upon the initiative of Clara Zetkin, the heroic German Communist leader, who later electrified the world with her brave denunciation of the Nazis in Hitler's Reichstag in 1933. Already in 1907, Lenin demanded that the woman question be specifically mentioned in Socialist programs because of the special problems, needs and demands of toiling women. Present at the 1910 conference as a representative of the Russian Social-Democratic Labor Party, Lenin strongly supported and urged adoption of the resolution inaugurating International Women's Day. Thus did the American-initiated March 8 become International Women's Day.

The opportunist degeneration of the leadership of the Second International inevitably reduced the struggle for the emancipation of women to a paper resolution. Interested only in catching votes, the Socialist parties paid attention to the woman question only during elections.

Lenin and Stalin restored and further developed the revolutionary Marxist position on the woman question. Thus, Stalin declared:

There has not been a single great movement of the oppressed in history in which working women have not played a part. Working women, who are the most oppressed of all the oppressed, have never stood aloof, and could not stand aloof, from the great march of emancipation (*Joseph Stalin: A Political Biography*, p. 65)

Lenin and Stalin taught that the position of working women in capitalist society as "the most oppressed of all the oppressed" makes them more than a reserve, makes them a full-fledged part, of the "regular army" of the proletariat. Stalin wrote:

> . . . The female industrial workers and peasants constitute one of the biggest reserves of the working class . . . Whether this female reserve goes with the working class or against it will determine the fate of the proletarian movement . . . The first task of the proletariat and of its vanguard, the Communist Party, therefore, is to wage a resolute struggle to wrest women, the women workers and peasants, from the influence of the bourgeoisie, politically to educate and to organize the women workers and peasants under the banner of the proletariat . . . But working women . . . are something more than a reserve. They may and should become . . . a regular army of the working class . . . fighting shoulder to shoulder with the great army of the proletariat . . . (Stalin, *ibid.*)

Women Under Socialism

Complete emancipation of women is possible only under Socialism. It was only with the October Socialist Revolution that, for the first time in history, women were fully emancipated and guaranteed their full social equality in every phase of life.

Women in the U.S.S.R. are accorded equal rights with men in all spheres of economic, state, cultural, social and political life (New Soviet Constitution, Article 122).

But equal rights in the U.S.S.R. are not just formal legal rights, which, under bourgeois democracy, are curtailed, where not denied in reality by the very nature of capitalist exploitation. In the Soviet Union, full enjoyment of equal rights by women is *guaranteed* by the very nature of the Socialist society, in which class divisions and human exploitation are abolished. In bourgeois democracies, equal rights for women constitute at best a programmatic demand to be fought for, and constant struggle is necessary to defend even those rights that are enacted into law.

In the U.S.S.R. equal-rights articles in the law of the land are but codifications of already existing and guaranteed reality. No wonder Soviet women express such supreme confidence in Socialism and such love for the people. Their respect for other nations, their profound sympathy with the oppressed peoples fighting for national liberation, is based on the firm conviction that their Socialist country is the decisive factor and leader in the struggle for peace.

Marxism-Leninism rejects as fallacious all petty-bourgeois equalitarian notions. Equal rights under Socialism do not mean that women do not have special protection and social care necessitated by their special function (child bearing, etc.) and special needs which do not apply to men.

Comrade Foster's Contribution

The Communist Party of the U.S.A. has many positive achievements to record during the last 30 years in the field of struggle for women's rights and in promoting the participation of women in the struggle against war and fascism.

Outstanding was the recent participation of Party women and of the women comrades who are wives of the 12 indicted leaders of our Party in the mass struggle to win the first round in the Foley Square thought-control trial. And in the continuing struggle against the frame-up of our Party leaders we must involve ever larger masses of women.

Under Comrade Foster's initiative and contributions to the deepening of our theoretical understanding of the woman question, a new political appreciation of our tasks is developing in the Party. Party Commissions on Work Among Women are functioning in the larger districts and in smaller ones. International Women's Day will mark a high point in ideological and political mobilization and in organizational steps to intensify our united-front activities among women, particularly around the peace struggle. As a further contribution to that end, a well-rounded theoretical-ideological outline on the position of Marxism-Leninism on the woman question is being prepared.

Comrade Foster called for theoretical mastery of the woman question as vitally necessary to combat the numerous anti-woman prejudices prevalent in our capitalist society, and the "whole system of male superiority ideas which continue to play such an important part in woman's

subjugation." An important guide to the Party's work among women are
the following words of Comrade Foster:

> The basic purpose of all our theoretical studies is to clarify, deepen
> and strengthen our practical programs of struggle and work. This is
> true on the question of women's work, as well as in other branches of
> our Party's activities. Hence, a sharpening up of our theoretical analy-
> sis of, and ideological struggle against, male supremacy, will help our
> day-to-day work among women . . .

Comrade Foster particularly emphasized the ideological pre-
conditions for effective struggle on this front:

> But such demands and struggles, vital as they may be, are in them-
> selves not enough. They must be reinforced by an energetic struggle
> against all conceptions of male superiority. But this is just what is
> lacking . . . An ideological attack must be made against the whole
> system of male superiority ideas which continue to play such an
> important part in woman's subjugation. And such an ideological
> campaign must be based on sound theoretical work (William Z.
> Foster, "On Improving the Party's Work Among Women," *Political
> Affairs*, November 1948).

Party Tasks

Following Comrade Foster's article in *Political Affairs*, nine Party
Conferences on Work Among Women were held with the active participation of district Party leaders. Two major regional schools to train
women cadres were held. An all-day conference on Marxism-Leninism
and the Woman Question held at the Jefferson School of Social Science
last summer was attended by 600 women and men. These developments
evidence a thirst for knowledge of the Marxist-Leninist teachings on the
woman question.

But it must be frankly stated that it is necessary to combat all and
sundry male supremacist ideas still pervading the labor and progressive
movements and our Party. The uprooting of this ideology, which
emanates from the ruling class and is sustained by centuries of myths
pertaining to the "biological inferiority" of women, requires a sustained

struggle. Failure to recognize the special social disabilities of women under capitalism is one of the chief manifestations of male supremacy. These special forms of oppression particularly affect the working women, the farm women and the triply oppressed Negro women; but, in varying degrees, they help to determine the inferior status of women in all classes of society.

Progressive and Communist men must become vanguard fighters against male supremacist ideas and for equal rights for women. Too often we observe in the expression and practice of labor-progressive, and even some Communist, men glib talk about women "as allies" but no commensurate effort to combat male supremacy notions which hamper woman's ability to struggle for peace and security. Too many labor-progressive men, not excluding some Communists, resist the full participation of women, avow bourgeois "equalitarian" nations as regards women, tend to avoid full discussion of the woman question and shunt the problem aside with peremptory decisions. What the promotion of a sound theoretical understanding of this question would achieve for our Party is shown by the initial results of the cadre training schools and seminars on the woman question, many of whose students have begun seriously to tackle male supremacist notions in relation to the major tasks of the movement and in relation to their own attitudes.

The manifestation of bourgeois feminism in the progressive women's movement and also in our Party is a direct result of the prevalence of male superiority ideas and shows the need for our women comrades to study the Marxist-Leninist teachings on the woman question. According to bourgeois feminism, woman's oppression stems, not from the capitalist system, but from men. Marxism-Leninism, just as it rejects and combats the petty-bourgeois "equalitarianism" fostered by Social-Democracy, so it has nothing in common with the bourgeois idiocy of "the battle of the sexes" or the irrational Freudian "approach" to the woman question. These false ideologies must be combatted by women labor-progressives and in the first place by women Communists. Key participants in the fight against these ideologies, and in the fight to enlist the masses of women for the pro-peace struggle, must be the advanced trade-union women and women Communists on all levels of Party leadership. All Communist women must, as Lenin said, "themselves become part of the mass movement," taking responsibility for the liberation of women.

We must guarantee that women cadres end isolation from the masses of women, by assigning these cadres to tasks of work among women, on a mass and Party basis. The Women's Commissions of the Party must be strengthened. All Party departments and Commissions must deal more consistently with these questions, putting an end to the false concept that work among women represents "second-class citizenship" in our Party. A key responsibility of all Women's Commissions is increased attention and support to the growing movements of youth.

We must gauge our Party's work among women by our effectiveness in giving leadership and guidance to our cadres in mass work, with a view to concentrating among working-class women and building the Party. To this end, further, working-class and Negro women forces need to be promoted in all spheres of Party work and mass activity.

An examination of our work among women is necessary in all Party districts. There is need of Party conferences on the problems of working women and housewives. The good beginnings of examining the long neglected problems of Negro women must become an integral part of all our future work among women. This arises as an imperative task in the light of the militancy and tenacity of Negro women participating in struggles on all fronts.

Experience shows that a major area of our work should and must be in the field of education, where monopoly reaction and the Roman Catholic hierarchy concentrate in a policy in inculcating militarist, racist, pro-fascist ideology in the minds of our children; of victimizing progressive teachers, of conducting witch-hunts, etc. Where good work has been carried on in this sphere, victories have been won, as in the defeat of reactionary legislative measures directed at progressive teachers. In developing struggles to alleviate the frightful conditions of schooling, particularly in Negro, Puerto Rican, Mexican and other working-class communities, Communist and progressive women have an opportunity for developing an exceedingly broad union front for successful endeavor.

By connecting the struggle against the seemingly little issues of crowded schoolrooms, unsanitary conditions, lack of child care facilities, etc., with the issues of reactionary content of teaching—racism, jingoism, etc.—the political consciousness of the parent masses can be raised to the understanding of the interconnection between the demand for lunch for a hungry child and the demand of the people for economic security; between the campaign for the dismissal of a Negro-hating, anti-Semitic Mae Quinn from the school system and the fight of the people for democratic rights; between the protest against a jingoistic school text and the broad fight of the people for peace.

In keeping with the spirit of International Women's Day, tremendous tasks fall upon our Party. The mobilization of the masses of Americans, together with the enlisting and activation of women cadres, for heightened struggles for peace and for the special needs of oppressed womanhood, is indispensable to the building and strengthening of the anti-fascist, anti-imperialist, anti-war coalition. In working for a stronger peace movement among the women as such, we must draw the masses of women into the impending 1950 election campaign and thereby, on the basis of their experiences in the struggle, help raise their political consciousness to the understanding of the bipartisan demagogy and the hollowness of Truman's tall promises. Large masses of women can thus be brought to a full break with the two-party system of monopoly capital and to adherence to the third-party movement. In the course of this development, with our Party performing its vanguard task, advanced sections among the working-class women will attain the level of Socialist consciousness and will, as recruited Communists, carry on their struggle among the broad masses of women upon the scientific conviction that the final guarantee of peace, bread and freedom, and the full emancipation of subjected woman-kind, will be achieved only in a Socialist America.

23

Union Leader Challenges
Progressive America
Vicki Garvin (Vice President, Distributive, Processing and Office Workers)

Freedom 1, no. 11 (November 1950), p. 5

If it is true, as has often been stated, that a people can rise no higher than its women, then Negro people have a long way to go before reaching the ultimate goal of complete freedom and equality in the United States.

Latest figures on the job status of Negro women dramatically point up the inescapable fact that they are at the very bottom of the nation's economic ladder. A glance at the record shows that the average Negro woman in the U.S.:

- Earns only $13 per week.
- Is forced into the dirtiest, least desirable jobs.
- Puts in abnormally long hours.

By and large, Negro women today are living and working under conditions reminiscent of the plantation era, even though slavery was ostensibly abolished by constitutional amendment some 85 years ago. When it's considered that seven out of every 10 Negro women workers are chained to menial service jobs as farm hands, domestics, etc. Where in addition to low pay and deplorable working conditions, human dignity is least respected, it can readily be seen that raising the level of women generally and Negro women in particular is an acid test for democracy at this crucial point in history.

Low Pay in Boom

Even during the peak period of World War II when pay envelopes were considered to be fatter than ever before, domestic workers, both Negro and white, averaged a take-home pay of only $339 per year.

In New York City, where one half of all Negro women at work are domestics, labor officials admit that the present average work day is 13 and 14 hours long. In the South, the situation is complicated by the fact that while only 50 percent of white women workers have found employment as clerks, saleswomen and factory workers, Negro women for all practical purposes are barred from these "white collar" and semi-skilled jobs. In fact, the income of the average Negro family in southern rural areas is a sub standard $942 yearly.

The Negro woman worker, whether married or single, faces the additional burden of feeding one or more dependents besides herself. As a member of a family whose average income in urban centers is but $42 a week, Negro women have no choice but to find employment to help meet basic food, clothing and shelter needs.

Wife Must Work

In the case of white families, where the average income is $75 weekly, the pressure upon children to leave school and seek work is not nearly so severe as it is among Negroes. Yet, significantly, more than half of all Negro college students are women. The reverse is true of white students.

Getting a husband is not the answer for the Negro woman's search for security and release from back breaking toil, for the proportion of Negro women who enter the labor force after marriage is much higher than the one out of five rate for white women. When most Negro women think about marriage and children, it is almost a foregone conclusion that she will become a co-breadwinner.

The added income the Negro wife and mother provides is vital, for white men have a virtual monopoly on the best paying jobs available in the U.S. Ninety per cent of all skilled jobs and 80 per cent of semi-skilled jobs. Negro men are thus limited in their opportunities to provide a decent livelihood for their wives and families, being restricted to unskilled labor and menial tasks.

There is a big gap between the income of the Negro and the white man, with $3,000 and over the annual income of seven out of 10 white males, while only three out of 10 Negro men are similarly paid. Veterans who served together in World War II are also paid on the basis of color; the Negro GI's paycheck is $20 less than that of his white comrade in arms.

More Broken Homes

Broken homes are another part of the exorbitant price Negro women must pay for their oppressed status. In five southern cities recently surveyed, 85 per cent of all Negro working class women were supporting families where the man of the house was missing. Setting aside any reserves for unemployment, old age, illness and accidents is out of the question for this section of the population, burdened as they are with substandard wages, job insecurity, and indebtedness.

The familiar "last hired, first fired" policy for Negroes works a double hardship on women. Their jobs are immediately curtailed when slack seasons and similar "accidents" occur in the national economy. Today, twice as many Negro women are without work, relatively, as white women. The lack of training courses and a national FEPC makes job placement even more difficult.

It is an unfortunate fact that the areas where Negro women are concentrated are as yet unorganized. Employers, therefore, are free to ride roughshod over these un-protected workers. However, in a few cities, Negro women benefit from unions in industries such as food and tobacco, meat packing, electrical, hotel and restaurant, laundry, wholesale and warehouse, and white collar offices. Negro women have participated in militant struggles to win contracts and better working conditions. It is a matter of record that where given the opportunity to enter industry and become a part of the trade union movement, Negro women have demonstrated their loyalty and ability to fight for the best interests of all workers. Despite tremendous handicaps, Negro women have fought their way to the top in many unions.

Historically, it is the burning desire of every Negro woman to be free, to live and work in dignity, on equal terms with all other workers. Negro women are eager to undertake a greater role to give substance to freedom and democracy, to help build an America of peace and abundance.

It is the responsibility of progressive trade unions and women's organizations to spearhead a militant and far-reaching program that will:

1. Maintain Negro women in industry.
2. Provide opportunities for training, up-grading and employment in all categories of work.
3. Eliminate wage differences.
4. Extend coverage of social welfare legislation to industries and occupations now excluded.
5. Promote Negro women leadership at all levels of trade union activity.

Negro working women, with their long tradition of militancy, stand ready to be an integral part of the struggle for progress.

Let's join forces now!

24

Proclamation of the Sojourners for Truth and Justice

Sojourners for Truth and Justice, September 1951

We, a representative group of Negro women from different sections of the nation, assembled in Washington, D.C., on September 29, 1951, at the home of Frederick Douglass, to unite in dedicating ourselves to fight unceasingly for the freedom of our people and for the full dignity of Negro womanhood, DO HEREBY PROCLAIM:

For too long has the Government of this land turned a deaf ear to our plea for justice—Far too long have we tolerated the double anguish of being both victim of the mob and victim of the government—We refuse any longer to watch our children die a thousand deaths by mobs, hooded or unhooded, by starvation and disease.

We are sick and tired of being second-class citizens in this our country which denies us dignity and honor in any of its forty-eight states.

We are indignant at the policy of government which forces our sons, husbands, sweethearts and brothers into a Jim-Crow army to fight in the name of democracy in foreign lands where they must face frame-up court martials, while at home neither they nor their people are free.

We insist that only when our government abolishes the lynch justice of Mississippi, when it does away with the Ciceros and Peekskills, only when it moves to enforce the 13th, 14th and 15th Amendments to the Constitution of the United States—then and only then can it speak as a free nation for a free world.

WE CALL UPON OUR GOVERNMENT TO PROVE ITS LOYALTY TO ITS FIFTEEN MILLION NEGRO CITIZENS—BY—

The passage of an anti-lynch law that provides the death penalty for the lynchers and indemnity for widows and orphans of the lynch victims . . .

The passage of an anti-poll tax law and representation of the Negro people in every phase of the political life of our nation. Taxation without representation must end *now* . . .

The passage of a fair employment practice law to insure our right to earn our bread in dignity and with equal opportunity in all fields of endeavor . . .

The immediate freedom of Mrs. Rose Lee Ingram, sentenced to life imprisonment for defending the honor of all womanhood, as the first step in ending the indignities heaped upon Negro women everywhere in our land . . .

The dropping of all persecution and prosecution of our great leaders, that they may be free to carry on the fight for the full freedom of our people unhampered, and the mobilization instead of all agencies of government to track down and prosecute vigorously those who burn, murder and pillage the Negro people . . .

The coming together of our government with the other great nations to work out the guarantees for permanent world peace, so that we, along with all other women everywhere, may live and rear our children in a free, secure and peaceful world.

IN the spirit of Sojourner Truth and Harriet Tubman, we declare that:

"WE SHALL NOT BE TRAMPLED UPON ANY LONGER"

We shall resist all attempts to muffle our voices or shorten our strides toward freedom.

To this end we shall strive to unite all Negro women, and extend our united hands to every freedom and peace loving individual in our nation who wants to march together with us down freedom road.

We, the SOJOURNERS FOR TRUTH AND JUSTICE do declare that this proclamation is but the beginning of a new phase of our battle for full dignity.

OUR HANDS ARE TO THE PLOUGH
AND WE SHALL NEVER TURN BACK!

WE SHALL SECURE TRUTH AND JUSTICE!
OUR PEOPLE SHALL BE FREE!

25

Where Are YOU Hiding?

Dorothy Hunton

Freedom 2, no. 1 (January 1952), p. 4

A Present-Day Sojourner Truth Finds "An Abiding Sense of Personal Freedom"

"Six months for contempt of court!" These were bitter words for me to comprehend and accept when my husband was sentenced on July 9, along with the other trustees of the Civil Rights Congress bail fund, because of their refusal to betray their trust and turn over the records of the bail fund to the court.

The days that followed were also bitter. As I struggled with myself to find my way in those early weeks, I was suddenly shocked into the realization that I was not at all the person I had thought I was. In fact, I discovered that I had the same weaknesses that I had so often pointed out in others. The heavy blow almost smothered me for a while. It was not easy to see things objectively, impersonally. It was not easy to understand why everyone else did not react just as I did to this terrible thing.

But somehow I managed to recover my balance. I came to see my problem and what had happened in the proper focus of the people's forward march toward freedom and peace. I had been afraid. But now I was no longer afraid.

Believe me when I say that the struggle was not easy. At last, however, came the satisfaction of a deeper understanding of my place at the side of all those men and women—especially among my own people, the

Negro people—who are determined, whatever the personal cost, to make this a decent world in which to live.

This understanding brings with it not only an abiding sense of personal freedom but also a sense of great responsibility to one's fellow men. There is much work to be done, and few there are who are willing to serve. But serve we must, if we wish to be free.

We hear so much about loyalty today. Loyalty, as I understand it, is not something that is demanded of one. Loyalty is recognition of the truth and the determination to follow it. It is loyalty to principles, to ideals, and to the fulfillment of those ideals in our daily lives. This to me is the real loyalty, certainly something altogether different from the loyalty oath business that we see today being used to make this country of ours into a nation of panic-driven sheep.

But we need not be discouraged, those of us who have remained loyal to our ideals. Indeed, I am not. For this is a new day, a new era. And the places of those who have fallen by the wayside will be filled by new and stronger soldiers ready to join hand in hand with those who are determined to complete the unfinished work of the Harriet Tubmans, Sojourner Truths and Frederick Douglasses.

Where are the twentieth century Sojourners, Tubmans and Douglasses?

Where are YOU hiding? Do you know there's no hiding place down here, and that you cannot find a safe place for yourself and loved ones as long as your brothers and sisters are still strung up on trees or shot in the back? The time has come when we Negro women, especially, must unite and work together for the freedom and dignity of our people.

The record I have set down here my husband was able to glimpse piecemeal in the sequence of my letters to him in jail. He saw what was happening to me, how I found myself. As I was proud of what he had done in defense of his ideals, so I am thankful to be able to say, that he too was proud of the new wife that this experience gave him. And so now that the long months of waiting have passed and he is back home once more, we can count the hardship of our separation not as a punishment and loss but as an opportunity and gain.

26

Egyptian People Fight for Freedom
Lorraine Hansberry

Freedom 2, no. 3 (March 1952), p. 3

In November, 1951, some 250,000 Egyptian people marched in stark, sober quiet through the streets of Alexandria, one of Egypt's largest and most famous ancient cities. Their trek to the palace of the king passed 300,000 equally silent massed Egyptians. The next day in Cairo there was an almost identical demonstration. Then a voice broke the meaningful silence of the march: "We will spare no sacrifice until the Valley of the Nile is free from imperialism."

This was one of many warnings to the British imperialists of the Egyptian people's weariness of the 70 years of brutal foreign rule and exploitation. The building of the Suez Canal took some 20,000 Egyptian and Sudanese lives. It has since bulged the pockets of British, French and American interests, while a bitter Egyptian writer commented only three years ago:

"Ninety-nine per cent of the peasant population are sick not with one disease but two or three . . . and 80 per cent of the population are illiterate . . . The present income of a peasant family is now less than $40 a year."

The average Egyptian, then, lives to be somewhere around **27 years old.**

This was the Egypt which, a couple of months after the November demonstrations of silence, struck out in organized force against its oppressors. British occupation troops had murdered some 40 Egyptians at Ismailia, and all Egypt broke into anti-British demonstrations. In Cairo, everything that bore a British flag or label was burned or wrecked, and great throngs of angry patriots demonstrated before the government building for their **immediate independence.**

This is the same country where for months 75,000 Egyptian workers have refused to load food or water or anything else for the British. And this is the same Egypt, the traditional Islamic "cradle of civilization," where women had led one of the most important fights anywhere for the equality of their sex.

Last February, Madam Doria Shafik, president of the Daughters of the Nile (Bent el-Nil), the foremost women's movement in Egypt, led a thousand Egyptian women right into the halls of the parliament and demanded feminine representation. **And significantly, it was this same women's movement that in January offered some 250 trained young women for guerrilla combat service against the British in the canal zone.**

The "warnings" are over. The Egyptian people, like other African peoples, are tired of the exploitation and humiliation of the foreign rule of a white supremacist, imperialist nation. They will no longer tolerate domination by a nation which, after the last war, rolled heavy tanks right up to the palace gate of King Farouk, to guarantee by force the choice of a pro-British Egyptian premier.

One writer describes the guerrilla movement as being constantly reinforced by workers, students, peasants, the local police and Egyptian army officers.

American and British newsmen and frightened diplomats have tried again to label this new surge of a colored people for freedom. "Nationalistic fanaticism," they call it; "losing Egypt to the Reds," a "threat to world peace," etc. It is clear, though, that the only threat to world peace is the imperialist powers' insistence on keeping British tommies on Egyptian soil.

A French correspondent, Pierre Courage, writes from Cairo: "It is not a matter of a straw fire, a flame of passion exasperated by the crimes of colonialism, but of a profound movement which has already gone so far that it can be considered **irreversible.**"

In other words, the Egyptian people intend to be free.

27

Our Cup Runneth Over

Sojourners for Truth and Justice, March 23, 1952

Statement issued by the Sojourners For Truth and Justice, relative to the murder by bombing of Mr. and Mrs. Harry T. Moore of Mims, Florida

The racist bomb that on Christmas Day shattered at once the humble home and valiant lives of Mr. and Mrs. Harry T. Moore was the climactic drop to the bitter cup of grief and outrage poured for the Negro people of this nation in the year 1951.

In February, we shuddered and cried aloud at the legalized murder of seven of our sons in Martinsville, Virginia. In May, we walked, wired, phoned and wrote together with our sister Rosalie McGee to save the life of her husband in Laurel, Mississippi. In July, our brimming cup had to contain the outrage of Cicero, Illinois, and, in November, the lawless murder of Samuel Shepherd and brutal wounding of Walter Irvin, as they lay helpless and handcuffed on a Florida road, pierced the side of every Negro mother.

. . . But on December 25th, the birthday of the consciousness of the brotherhood of man, a day when even the lowly pine offers up its greenness to be adorned with lights of love and a star of promise, a bomb exploded in the little town of Mims, Florida, and our brimming bitter cup spilled over. That special hope that is Christmas fled the hearts of fifteen million black Americans; goodness was wounded, mercy dead. And the whole world looked with shocked and angry eye at Mims wherein that peace for which He came was slain and all mankind mocked.

Black women the world over know too well the tearless grief of Mrs. Rosa Moore, whose 71 years of sacrifice gave to the world a fighting son of the Negro people, Harry T. Moore ... too well the anguish of Mrs. Annie Warren Sims, who, at the bedside of her dying daughter, said goodbye to her son, M/Sgt. George Sims, returning to Korea, to fight for the kind of democracy and freedom that murdered her brave daughter, Harriett Moore. We know the empty loneliness with which Anne and Evangeline, daughters of Mr. and Mrs. Moore, must begin anew their shattered lives.

Truly, our cup runneth over!

Indignation, courage and determination to fight transcends our grief and mourning, and, drawing upon the spirit of that other brave Harriet, who, in the long hours of bondage, fought for the freedom of our people till the chains of slavery gave way to emancipation ...

THE SOJOURNERS FOR TRUTH AND JUSTICE, an all-Negro women's organization dedicated to fight for full freedom of the Negro people and full dignity of Negro womanhood, call upon every Negro woman in the United States to close ranks, join hands in an unbreakable bond of unity and carry on where Harry and Harriett Moore left off.

We, the Sojourners For Truth and Justice, have raised our voice in protest to the Governor of Florida. We will march again to Washington, but this time in thousands, and there cry in a loud voice to the President and all government officials till the walls of hate and injustice come tumbling down.

We will not be quieted until the death of our sister Harriett Moore and her husband Harry T. Moore is avenged, and until every man, woman and child can walk this land from Florida to Maine, from Virginia to California, in full dignity. Then, and only then, can we have a Christmas Day of peace on earth, good will to men.

28

"Illegal" Conference Shows
Peace Is Key to Freedom

Lorraine Hansberry

Freedom 2, no. 4 (April 1952), p. 3

Up and down the Americas, some people have already been murdered, scores have been tortured, thousands have been imprisoned and thousands more have fled their homelands in exile. Throughout Latin America, the interventionist policy of the United States Government has made the very word PEACE illegal.

In Brazil, a young woman was murdered in the streets; a young boy had instruments of torture placed under his gums, because he collected signatures for peace. In Argentina, no one may organize for peace without fear of imprisonment.

When all nations and all peoples need it so desperately, peace in the Americas is illegal.

One hour after my plane landed at Montevideo, the capital of the small South American republic of Uruguay, I was warmly embraced by one of the great women of the Americas, Maria Rosa Oliver, of Argentina, the secretary of the Inter-American Sponsoring Committee of the Inter-Continental Peace Congress.

Senora [*sic*] Oliver told me that the conference had been officially banned in Uruguay. The U.S. Government, leading the nations of the world in the most extensive armaments race in the history of mankind, did not want this conference to take place.

This particular conference had been called by the representatives of 179 million people who suffer some of the worst colonial exploitation of any area of the world, and who stand to lose the most from a third world war.

Representatives of delegations had been summoned to police headquarters and had their passports checked. Police were everywhere, watching, being obvious in their presence.

Senora [*sic*] Oliver explained: **"Of course, despite all intimidation, the Congress will be held."**

There were over 250 delegates from nine countries: Paraguay, Brazil, Venezuela, Argentina, Puerto Rico, Chile, Colombia, Uruguay and the United States of North America. Delegates from the West Indies, Mexico, Canada, Peru and Panama had been stopped in their own countries in some cases and held at foreign borders in others.

Every effort of the U.S. State Department was being made to stop this conference. So brazen was the U.S. Government's role that Mr. Cassidy of the U.S. Embassy at Montevideo personally sat in on some of the police questioning.

Dock workers in Montevideo were on strike for higher wages (for Uruguay is one more country in South America where the stranglehold of U.S. interest has sent the cost of living skyrocketing). **And they included in their demands the demand that the Congress of Peace be held.**

Delegates had been driven alone to the "plenary session," given plates of food and instructed to be prepared to get up and dance in the event the police should arrive. A pianist was posted at the piano to provide light music immediately if need be. Behind drawn blinds the reports were given quietly and fast and without applause.

One after the other the nations of the Americas reported. The United States delegation learned that Paraguay was a typical example of what the war drive of their nation was doing in South America. There is martial law in Paraguay, and a child of 11 needs a police permit to attend school. The wealth of the nation, cotton, is drained out to make gunpowder for a war the Paraguayan people have no sympathy for.

Of this nation, the U.S. Government demands troops for the murder in Korea.

The Paraguayan delegates told how in 1947, when the people of the country revolted, the U.S. air force was sent against them. Today, almost every family in the country has one member in political exile.

The representatives of each nation who rose to speak had similar situations to describe. The Chileans told of the robbery of their copper, which can be exported only to the United States, at the prices the United States sets. The Puerto Rican delegate described the transformation of his country into a big military base.

It became clear from their charges that the key to the freedom of these peoples is peace. They understood it and spoke out against all war.

A young lawyer of Argentina spoke, Leonor Aguier Vasquez of Buenos Aires. Twenty-six years old, she had been a member of the International Women's Commission which investigated atrocities in Korea.

"I can tell you about 10-year-old children who have been raped. I can tell you about whole forests and fields which have been burned so that people will starve to death. I can tell you about women and children who have been strafed from the air when they attempted to put out the fires . . .

"The people of Korea no longer raise the white flag of mercy, for they expect none. What I have seen in Korea is not war at all. It is the extermination of a people."

In the special women's session I heard the delegates tell of the struggles of the women in their countries for peace. Many have been jailed, like Eliza Brenco, of Brazil. One young woman 23 years old had been killed in a street demonstration.

In the name of the Negro people of the United States, I was given a beautiful bouquet of red carnations by the women of Brazil; a lovely hand-made handkerchief from the women of Paraguay; a traditionally costumed doll from the women of Uruguay.

At the meeting of the women I was voted the honor of sitting on the presidium. When I entered the meeting of the youth, the entire gathering stood and applauded. Everywhere I spent hours signing autographs and being interviewed by the press. **Everywhere I was warmly embraced and asked to bring greetings to my people, and to tell them how great was the admiration of the peoples of the Americas for their struggles.**

At 10 o'clock on a Saturday night, representatives from all the delegations mounted a huge platform that stretched across one end of the city's main plaza. Behind was an enormous blue and white sign that could be read for blocks: PAZ! (Peace!)

Powerful loudspeakers carried the voices of the speakers through the heart of the city. Jammed into the square were at least 5,000 citizens of Uruguay.

The authorities said there must be no mention of the name of a foreign power. And so there wasn't, from the platform. But again and again it was shouted from the crowd: **"Yanqui Imperialismo!"**

The chairman of the U.S. delegation, Mary Russak, rose to speak. **"We of the peace movement in our country feel great responsibility for what is happening in your country and in all the countries of Latin America. We pledge ourselves to return to our country and fight for peace."** She was cheered.

It was my turn to make the presentation of the U.S. delegation's gift to the Uruguayan host peace committee. I started: "In my hand I hold a message from a man whose name in our country is synonymous with the word peace . . ." And as the translator got out this much, the ovation broke. From everywhere went up the cheer: **"Viva Robeson!"**

There was no need to call his name; 8,000 miles from home, 5,000 people stood cheering the man who could not himself be with them, because the same State Department that wishes there were no peace congresses at all, anywhere, refused to grant him his passport.

This was the final victory. **The Inter-Continental Congress for Peace had been held.** The peoples of the Americas, North and South, had come together. Somehow, resolutions had been introduced, discussed, approved and printed by the end of the Congress, and a great open air meeting had been held for the ears of all Uruguay.

In fact, the banning was extremely unpopular with the people in this country where written in the streets was the slogan: "NO URUGUAYANS TO KOREA!"

The conservative press had editorialized about "the Congress that wasn't seen or heard—THAT WAS!"

The fact that 50 per cent of the people of all Latin America are undernourished, while only 3 per cent of the land is cultivated; that national governments are held in economic subservience to a United States bent on war, were facts too powerful to be stifled.

The representatives of the Americas came together and said in their great call to the peoples:

"If you do not wish to be the victims of military plans which will involve the sacrifice of our youth in the fields of battle of Korea, or in other wars which are not in the defense of our countries, then sign— SIGN FOR A PACT OF PEACE!"

29

Southern Officers Treat Korean POWs Like Negroes in the South

Eslanda Goode Robeson

Freedom 2, no. 7 (July 1952), p. 5

The prisoner-of-war issue seems to be the great stumbling block to truce in Korea, so let's have a look at it.

The United States says our military are holding 170,000 North Korean and Chinese soldiers and civilians in war prison camps. Our military, practically none of whom speak or understand the Korean and Chinese languages, insist that only 70,000 of these prisoners want to go home.

Now how did they find out which prisoners want to go home, and which want to stay "on our side"? They got some interpreters to ask them. And who were the interpreters? South Koreans and Chiang Kai-shek-Formosa-Chinese.

To fully understand this situation, let us suppose there are 170,000 Negro prisoners in a prison camp in the deep South. And let us suppose these Negroes speak a very difficult foreign language, which their captors neither speak nor understand.

So they get, as interpreters, members of the Ku Klux Klan and white lynchers like Sheriff Willis McCall to go into the camps and interview the Negro prisoners, to find out which ones want to go North and take their chances, and which want to remain in the deep South to work on the peonage farms, plantations, chain-gangs and in the lumber camps.

The Ku Klux Klansmen go into the camp, where nobody can see or hear, and they start asking—which means they start **telling!**

Now if you were a Negro prisoner in such a dangerous situation, what would you say? What would you do? What **could** you do? And who is to prove what you said and did?

This screening goes on for a long time, until reports begin to seep back into your prison camp stating that most of you want to stay with the Ku Kluxers. Then you know you must do something to let the outside world know this report just isn't true. But what to do?

Well, suppose you grabbed the Boss of the prison, and held him prisoner? That should tell something to the people outside who are interested. So you do, and it does. The outside world begins to ask questions.

Something like this must have happened at the prisoner-of-war camp on Koje Island: The South Korean and Formosa-Chinese interpreters are to the North Koreans and Chinese prisoners what the Ku Klux Klan interpreters would be to Negro prisoners: poison.

When the desperate prisoners on Koje **did** capture Brig. Gen. Francis Dodd, the Boss of the prison camp, and held him prisoner for four days, the outside world **did** start asking questions.

If, as reported, 100,000 of these 170,000 prisoners don't want to go home, but want to come to "our side," why then did they grab the big Boss of "our side"? It just doesn't fit.

The negotiations for the rescue of General Dodd tell the story: the prisoners demanded an end to forcible screening, re-arming of some prisoners, killing and ill-treatment of other prisoners.

When General Dodd was finally released and the terms of his release had to be made known, the military in Korea and the Defense Department in Washington rushed into the full-time job of explanations and denials. They said, over and over, offering no proof, that:

1. The prisoners had always been treated humanely, according to the Geneva Convention Rules of War. (It is important to note, by the way, that the United States never signed this international agreement.)
2. The screening of prisoners has never been forced.
3. None of the prisoners have been re-armed.

It should be remembered that the Geneva Convention provides that "prisoners of war shall be released and repatriated without delay after the cessation of hostilities." This is not only the rule, it is also the general custom. Until now, that is.

But the United States wants to keep 100,000 prisoners of war after the cessation of hostilities.

Secretary of State Dean Acheson said at the United Nations less than a year ago that the North Koreans were so low they had a long way to go before they could even be called barbarians.

That was less than a year ago, and now here we are, deeply concerned for these "lower-than-barbarians," welcoming them to "our side," protecting them from returning to their own fellow countrymen.

Well, maybe of the 170,000 "lower-than-barbarians," the 100,000 which our military want to keep are all special exceptions. But that does seem to be a lot of exceptions, doesn't it?

There seems to be a great deal about the Korean War which Truman says isn't a war, that is hidden from the people. As for instance, just how are we defending freedom and democracy in Korea by burning up the land and killing off the men, women and children?

It would be fine if Truman, or the candidates for election to his office, would explain all this in words of few syllables, so we, the voters, could understand.

30

Southern Tenants and 'Croppers Talk About Need for Organizing

Dorothy Burnham

Freedom 2, no. 10 (October 1952), p. 2

For the past few weeks millions of boys and girls have been trooping back to school and I can't help thinking of little Jeannie, a nine year old friend who won't be back until mid-October.

Jeannie lives in one of the southernmost parishes of Louisiana. Her father is a tenant farmer. The owner of the farm her father rents is Mr. J., the biggest landowner in the parish. He is also the head of the school board.

During September Mr. J. has hundreds of bales of cotton to be picked. Jeannie and her brothers and friends are needed to work for him, so he decreed that school won't open until October 11. Meanwhile, Jeannie's brother, who is 13, is wondering what **he** will do when school does open, **for there is no Negro high school in the entire parish.**

The state and parish officials claim they do not have enough money to provide decent schools for Negro children. But they refuse to tax the big landlords to raise the revenues out of the wealth they enjoy from the back-breaking toil of thousands of little children like Jeannie.

For instance, for the thousands of acres which Mr. J. owns he pays a tax of only 39 cents per acre. In other Southern states the rates are Alabama, 26 cents; Georgia, 30 cents; South Carolina, 31 cents and Mississippi, 32 cents. Contrast this with the $1.72 per acre tax which New York farmers pay or the $1.92 for California or the high of $4.54

which the farmers of Massachusetts pay, is there any wonder that the elementary school in Jeannie's parish is a hundred-year-old frame fire trap and that one teacher must teach eight grades in the same room?

Jeannie has a cousin, Paul, who was with the U.S. Army in Italy and France. After World War II Paul was anxious to get home to farm. As a GI he was entitled to a loan to buy a farm, but no one in the parish would sell him or any of the other Negro GI's land. The white land owners wanted Negroes to remain tenants and sharecroppers.

Paul's problem of being unable to buy land is a Southwide problem. The cold facts of the 1950 census show that land ownership among small Negro and white farmers is steadily declining. The ownership of the land is falling into fewer and fewer hands.

In Georgia, for example, the average-sized farm in 1945 was 83 to 218 acres. In 1950 the average size was 126–544 acres. In every county of the Black Belt in Georgia the average farm size has increased. And for the same period, 1945–1950, the number of Negro farm **operators** has **decreased** from 70,411 to 50,357. "Operators" in the census figures includes cash tenants as well as owners.

Everywhere one hears that tenants and croppers are being driven off the land in the Southeast. The greater part of them become part-time farm workers and part-time unskilled laborers in the unorganized saw mills, cotton seed plants and other small industries.

Throughout the cotton belt of the old South it is a common thing to hear farmers talk of the need to organize again. Former GI's like Paul, farmers who remember the days of the Tenant Farmers Union, others who have gotten together and won the right to vote, see the need for a Southwide farm laborers, sharecroppers, and tenants organization. The demands of these farmers is for a minimum hourly wage for farm laborers, the right to buy and own the land they till, an extension of the New Deal farm projects which have been discontinued during the Korean War. They also want federal health, education and farm-housing programs which will really meet their needs, the extension of crop and livestock loans to all farmers on an equal basis and the right of family-size farmers to sit on all local government farm bureaus.

Such an organization of farmers would make a big contribution to the fight for economic security in the United States.

Dorothy Burnham is secretary of the Committee for a Free South, with offices at 257 Seventh Avenue, New York. The Committee is organized to raise moral and financial support for movements working in the South for the economic, political and social advancement of the people of that region.

31

Pearl Bailey Incident Recalls Life and Death of Bessie Smith

Yvonne Gregory

Freedom 2, no. 11 (November 1952), p. 7

Last month, when the outrageous attack against Pearl Bailey by several white men was made public, many people remembered the terrible manner in which Bessie Smith, Empress of the Blues, had died just 15 years ago. In Mississippi on a theatrical tour, in 1937, Miss Smith had an automobile accident in which she was severely injured. No hospital in the town of Clarkesdale would take her in because of her color and the great singer bled to death.

One of our younger poets, Myron O'Higgins, wrote "Blues for Bessie"—in which he said:

> "Well Bessie, Bessie, she won't sing de blues no more
> Cause dey let her go down bloody, Lawd, travellin from door to door"

It is possible to hear Bessie Smith's voice today on records. The listener who never heard her in life, and whose ears are accustomed to the screeching or distorted moanings of the majority of today's vocalists, is hardly prepared for the great bell that tolls out its notes of deep sorrow and the anger of a people. As the powerful voice commands silence and attention in a room today, the listener is reminded of something which the cartoonist K. Simms Campbell had to say back in 1939: "When blues were sung by a woman, the voice, that is, the female voice, carried tragic implications—the rich overtones of the cello—the man always imparted background on a guitar or piano—she was the hub of the family—black America crying out to her, sons and daughters."

"Ma" Discovered Bessie

The earliest recorded blues singer, Gertrude "Ma" Rainey, is generally credited with having "discovered" Bessie Smith. Bessie, born in Tennessee about 1896, was a small girl of 11 or 12 when Ma Rainey visited that southern state with a road show. The older woman heard the little girl sing and was so impressed with her voice and personality that she took her as a pupil and started her on her great career. That was around the turn of the century and whenever a show or a preacher or a singer came to small southern towns, people came from miles around to hear them, much as they do today.

Bessie Smith soon stood before such audiences and in the people's language, sang the people's blues. She would sing, **"If the blues was money, I'd be a millioneer, 'cause I can't be satisfied, I can't be satisfied"** ... and the people with their aches and their laughter would understand and take her to their hearts. When she smiled at them, she and the people were one, and then her trumpet voice would ring out for all of them, singing ... **"I was born in Georgia and my ways are underground."** Or she would sing to the farmers and the turpentine workers ... **"Woke up this mornin' the blues all round my bed, went to eat my breakfast and the blues all in my bread . . ."** and they knew that she understood their life and suffered with them.

Today, in these same areas, and in the big cities north and south, some of the biggest audiences come to hear the gospel concerts of popular women singers like Sister Rosetta Tharpe, Mahalia Jackson, Marie Knight and others. As Alan Lomax, folklorist put it: "The blues have crept into the churches in the guise of 'gospel songs.'" An elderly gospel singer said it even more clearly while explaining just what kind of music it was she sang. First she played a few unmistakable blues chords on her guitar and sang, **"Blues get in you, you holler like a baby chile."** Then she said, "When I was young down home, I learned to play the box, learned all that sinful music, too. Now I don't sing **that** music no more." Whereupon she folded back the sleeve of her grey gown, twanged some very similar chords on the guitar and sang a line or two from "Move On Up a Little Higher," a popular gospel song that is an obvious first cousin to the blues.

Today it's Mahalia Jackson's gospel music; or it is Pearl Bailey singing "Tired of the life I lead, tired of counting things I need"; yesterday it was Bessie singing, "Down in the Dumps"; day before yesterday Ma Rainey sang "Backwater Blues." But yesterday, today and tomorrow, the blues are an unbreakable thread in the life of our people and in the life of all Americans. Alan Lomax says: "The blues have more than any other song-form, become **the American song,** much as **'cante hondo'** is the national song form of Spain or the **'corrido'** is the national ballad form of Mexico."

If this is true, and it is also true that Negro women are among the greatest interpreters of this art form, then we can look forward to the day when all the people will honor Bessie Smith, Empress of the Blues, and wipe away from our national memory the shame of her death.

"Don't talk about it
'Bout it, if you do I'll cry.
Don't crowd around me,
Round me, if you do, I'll die."

32

Acceptance Speech of Mrs. Bass
Charlotta Bass

Speech accepting the Progressive Party's nomination of Charlotta Bass for vice president, March 30, 1952, from *Forty Years: Memoirs from the Pages of a Newspaper* (Los Angeles: C. A. Bass, 1960), pp. 145–9

This is a historical moment in American political life. Historic for me, for my people, for all women.

For the first time in the history of this nation, a political party has chosen a Negro woman for the second highest office in the land.

It is a great honor to be chosen as a pioneer—and a great responsibility. But I am strengthened by thousands on thousands of pioneers who stand by my side and look over my shoulder—those who have led the fight for freedom—those who led the fight for women's rights—those who have been in the front line fighting for peace and justice and equality everywhere. How they must rejoice in this great undertaking which here joins the cause of peace and freedom.

These pioneers, the living and the dead, men and women, black and white, give me strength and a new sense of dedication.

I shall tell you how I come to stand here. I am a Negro woman. My people came to America before the Mayflower. I am more concerned with what is happening to my people in my country than in pouring out money to rebuild a decadent Europe for a new war. We have lived through two wars and seen their promises turn to bitter ashes.

Two Negroes were the first Americans to be decorated for bravery in France in World War I. That war was fought to make the world safe for democracy. But when it ended we discovered we were making Africa safe for exploitation by the very European powers whose freedom and soil we had defended. That war was barely over when a Negro soldier, returning to his home in Georgia, was lynched almost before he could take off his uniform. That war was scarcely over before my people were stoned and shot and beaten in a dozen Northern cities. The guns were hardly silenced before a reign of terror was unleashed against every minority that fought for a better life.

Then we fought another war. You know Dorie Miller, the spudpeeler who came out of his galley to fight while white officers slept at Pearl Harbor. And I think of Robert Brooks, another "first" Negro, and of my own nephew. We fought a war to end Fascism whose germ is race superiority and the oppression of other peoples.

Yes, we fought to end Hitlerism. But less than seven years after the end of that war, I find men who lead my government paying out my money and your money to support the rebirth of Hitlerism in Germany to make it a willing partner in another war. We fought to destroy Hitlerism—but its germs took root right here. I look about me, at my own people, at all colored peoples all over the world. I can see the men who lead my government supporting oppression of the colored peoples of the earth who today reach out for the independence this nation achieved in 1776.

Yes, it is my government that supports the segregation by violence practiced by Malan in South Africa, sends guns to maintain a bloody French rule in Indo-China, gives money to help the Dutch repress Indonesia, props up Churchill's rule in the Middle East and over the colored peoples of Africa and Malaya. A few days ago Churchill's general in Malaya terrorized a whole village for refusing to act as spies for the British, charging these Malayan and Chinese villagers who enjoyed no rights and no privileges—and I quote him literally—for "failing to shoulder responsibility of citizenship." But neither the Malayan people, nor the African people who demonstrated on April 6, took this terror lying down. They fought back.

Shall my people support a new war to create new oppressions? We want peace; we shall have freedom. We support the movement for freedom of all peoples everywhere—in Africa, in Asia, in the Middle East, and above all, here in our own country. And we will not be silenced by the rope, the gun, the lynch mob, or the lynch judge. We will not be stopped by the reign of terror let loose against us and against all who speak for peace and freedom, and a share of the world's goods—a reign of terror the like of which this nation has never seen.

For forty years I have been working as editor and publisher of the oldest Negro newspaper in the West. During those forty years I watched the tide of racial hatred and bigotry against my people and against all people who believe the Constitution is something more than a piece of yellowed paper to be shut off in a glass case in the archives, but is a living document, a working instrument for freedom.

Yes, during those forty years, THE EAGLE stirred in her nest, led the struggles of my people, taught them to work with labor as the one group that could break down racial differences and open the door for the Negro people. I have stood watch over a hope to protect a Negro family against the outrages of the Ku Klux Klan. I have fought the brazen attempts to drive Negroes from their homes under restrictive covenants. I have challenged the great corporations which extort huge profits from my people, and forced them to employ Negroes in their plants. I have stormed city councils and state legislatures and the halls of Congress demanding real representation for my people.

I have fought not only for my people. I have fought and will continue to fight unceasingly for the rights and privileges of all people who are oppressed and who are denied their just share of the world's goods that their labor produces. I have walked and will continue to walk in picket lines with union members for the right of all men and women, of all races, to organize for their own protection and advancement. I will continue to cry out against police brutality against my people, as I did in the famous Zoot Suit riots in Los Angeles in 1944, when I went into dark alleys and rescued scared and badly beaten Negro and Mexican American boys, some of them children, from the clubs of city police. Nor have I hesitated in the face of that most un-American "Un-American Activities Committee"—and I am willing to face it again. And so help me God, I shall continue to tell the truth as I know it and believe it as a loyal citizen and a good American.

As I stand here on this platform presenting the cause of the Progressive Party, I cannot help but hark back to the thirty years I spent in the Republican Party as an active member. Often as a member of the Republican Party I was as bewildered and as hopeless for the future as the children of Israel when they marched through the Red Sea and failed to envision the other side. I remember 1940, when I was chosen Western Regional Director for Wendell Willkie's campaign for the presidency.

Willkie stood for One World. But when I reported to Republican Headquarters in Chicago, I found two worlds—upstairs was a world for white Republicans and down below was the world for Negro Republicans.

No, I could not see the future clear in the Republican Party, as the children of Israel could not see their future. But if you remember, when the liberation came to these victims of Pharaoh's hate, after they had crossed their final Jordan, they dragged from the bed of that river twelve stones and built a monument to commemorate the rolling away of the burdens of their bondage. As a member of the great elephant party, I could not see the light of hope shining in the distance, until one day the news flashed across the nation that a new party was born. In 1948, in the Progressive Party, I found that one political world that could provide a home big enough for Negro and white, for native and foreign-born, to live and work together for the same ends—as equals.

Here in this party was the political home for me and for my people. Here no one handed me a ready-made program out of the back door. Here I could sit at the head table as a founding member, write my own program, a program for myself and my people, that came from us. In that great founding convention in Philadelphia, in 1948, we had crossed the Jordan. There we shared in the labor of building a platform stone by stone, choosing candidates, creating a new political party—as equals.

Now perhaps I could retire. I had helped to found a home for my people. I looked forward to a rest after forty years of continuous struggle.

But how could I retire, and where could I retire as long as I saw what Frederick Douglass saw and felt what he did—the need "to stand up for the downtrodden, to remember those in bonds with me."

Could I retire when I saw that slavery had been abolished, but not destroyed; that "democracy" had been "saved" in World War I, but not for my people; that Fascism had been wiped out in World War II, only to take root in my own country where it blossomed and bloomed, and sent forth its fruits to poison the land my people had fought to preserve? Could I retire without thinking of Dorie Miller, of Robert Brooks, of my own nephew, John Kinloch who gave up a brilliant career, helped set up the first mixed regiment of white and Negro troops, and then went ahead of them to die in the Battle of the Bulge? I think often of John who was to take over my beloved paper, of John who died that those for whom he fought might enjoy the freedom and the liberty for which he laid down his life.

I could not retire and step aside when Rosa Lee Ingram and her two boys had been railroaded to jail for defending themselves. Could I turn a deaf ear to Rosalie McGee? Where was the Shangri-la in these United States where I could live and breathe in dignity? Where my people enjoyed the rights for which their sons and nephews died? In the North there were the Trenton Six demanding justice; in the Middle West was Cicero. In the South there stood Amy Mallard, and the Martinsville Seven, and unnamed hundreds of unavenged deaths that cried out. There was no rest in Florida—there a cross was burning and a bomb that killed Harriet Moore and her husband; and white "justice" snuffed out the life of Samuel Shepherd, threatened Lee Irvin. Across the land in California, the Bailey home was dynamited and other Negro families threatened with the same fate.

No, this new uprising of terror was not confined to the South. It spread throughout the country, goaded and inflamed by persons in high places who created hysteria every time they opened their mouths. In New York, just a few miles from where I live, they stoned my people at Peekskill—and a governor of a great state defended them. Only last week a Yonkers policeman shot and killed Wyatt and James Blacknall—and he was held on only a minor charge!

Where were the leaders of my nation—yes, *my* nation, for God knows my whole ambition is to see and make my nation the best in the world—where were these great leaders when these things happened? Why was my President silent when Harriet Moore died? And why did he not call on the governor of Florida, a fellow Democrat, on his visits to Key West? What did General Eisenhower say or do about mob lynchers and legal lynchers of my people? General MacArthur rode through Georgia in triumph, like another general 85 years ago, but MacArthur drew the applause of the Klan, the Moore dynamiters, the lynchers.

What were these great leaders who talked so grandly about freedom and spent even more grandly to crush it—what were they doing about my people losing jobs in Detroit while profits were piling up?

To retire now meant to leave the world to these people who carried oppression to Africa, to Asia, who made profits from oppression in my own land. To retire meant to leave the field to evil. For there is an evil that stalks in our land, an evil that strikes at my people, that would enslave all people, that would send up the world in flames, rob us of our earnings to waste on arms, destroy our living standards, corrupt our youth, silence and enslave us with Smith Acts, McCarran Acts, passed by concentration camp Congressmen.

I believe in a world of good and not a world of evil. A month ago doctors in New York City announced the discovery of a new drug that promised a real cure for tuberculosis, that dread killer. Only last week, I looked at the pictures of the patients who had offered themselves to try out this new drug. I looked closely at these pictures. I counted the faces. There were ten patients shown. Eight of these ten were Negroes. And seven of these eight were Negro women.

Those pictures symbolize the plight of our people today. Yes, and the promise of tomorrow. Tuberculosis is not a disease of race. It is a disease of poverty. It strikes my people hardest because, North and South, Negro workers earn less than half what white workers earn. It strikes my people who live in Chicago who live 90,000 to the square mile. It strikes my people who live in Harlem, 4000 to the square block, so crowded that on the same basis all of America could be put into half of New York.

This is what we fight against. We fight to live. We fight that my people and all people may live. We want the $65 billion that goes for death to go to build a new life. Those billions could lift the wages of my people, give them jobs, give education and training and new hope to our youth, free our sharecroppers, build new hospitals and medical centers. The $8 billion being spent to re-arm Europe and crush Asia could rehouse all my people living in the ghettoes of Chicago and New York, and every large city in the nation.

We fight that all peoples shall live. We fight to send our money to end colonialism for the colored peoples of the world, not to perpetuate it in Malan's South Africa, Churchill's Malaya, French Indo-China, and the Middle East.

You have called me to lead the fight against evil, the fight for human life and human dignity. I am indeed proud to answer the call from this party of progress. Can you conceive of the party of Taft and Eisenhower and MacArthur and McCarthy and the big corporations calling a Negro woman to lead the fight in 1952? Can you see the party of Truman, of Russell of Georgia, of Rankin of Mississippi, of Byrnes of South Carolina, of Acheson, naming a Negro to lead the fight against enslavement?

I am stirred by the responsibility you have placed upon me. I am proud that I am the choice of leaders of my own people, and leaders of all those who understand how deeply the fight for peace is one and indivisible with the fight for Negro equality.

I am impelled to accept this call, for it is the call of all my people and a call to my people. Sojourner Truth and Harriet Tubman would approve.

Frederick Douglass would rejoice, for he fought not only slavery but the oppression of women. Above all, Douglass would counsel us not to falter, but to "continue the struggle while a bondsman in his chains remains to weep." For Douglass had that calm resolution which held fast while others wavered, that steadfastness which helped to shape the party of Abraham Lincoln and hold it fast to the fight for abolition.

I make this pledge—to my people, the dead and the living—to all Americans, black and white. I will not retire nor will I retreat, not one inch, so long as God gives me vision to see what is happening and strength to fight for the things I know are right. For I know that my kingdom, my people's kingdom, and the kingdom of all the peoples of the world, is not beyond the skies, the moon and the stars, but right here at our feet—acres of diamonds—freedom—peace—and justice—for all the peoples of the world—if we will but stoop down and get them.

I accept this great honor. I give you as my slogan in this campaign— "Let my people go!"

I accept the nomination for the candidacy of Vice President of the United States of America on the Progressive Party ticket.

SECTION V

The Struggle Continues: White Supremacy and Anticommunism

The last section comprises writings spanning 1953 to 1956 that track the continuation of political and economic struggle in the context of an intensifying white supremacist and anticommunist backlash. Some of the chapters refer directly to experiences with McCarthy-era political persecution and its toll on Black activists and their families. As Black political leaders were increasingly targeted as subversives, Black Communist women persisted in their efforts to build unity across struggles against oppression domestically and internationally. A minority in the United States, Black people were part of the global majority fighting for liberation—and winning key victories.

The excerpt from Esther Cooper Jackson's biography of her husband that begins this section recounts the life of James E. Jackson, a Communist Party leader hounded by the FBI and charged with "harboring dangerous thoughts and spreading radical ideas" under the Smith Act. More than a biography, Cooper's earnest advocacy describes how her husband's study of communism led him to the view that "the Negro people have a powerful ally in the white workers and that it is to the self-interest of both to unite in common struggle."[1] The doctrine of white supremacy was a tool of landlords and big business to oppress all the poor people in the South. Cooper Jackson also emphasizes that "the most burning problems of every Negro and every worker" extend far beyond the borders of the United States. If we presume that they are merely domestic, "our nation will soon become a benighted wasteland of 'super patriotic' bigots."[2] The two articles by Vicki Garvin included in this section continue the theme of labor unity as they emphasize the imperative of organizing unions committed to full equality for Black workers and mobilizing white workers in defense of Black rights.

Eslanda Goode Robeson's "Unrest in Africa due to Oppression" envisions a universal freedom struggle. Linking together struggles for independence in Africa, Indonesia, and India with those of workers, women, and Black people in the United States, she announces, "Their victories are our victories."[3] Dorothy Burnham's "American Women Join World Peace Crusade" likewise emphasizes the commonality of the struggles of the oppressed against white supremacy, colonial oppression, and war. Her article reports on the World Congress of Women held in Denmark in June 1953. The Congress was organized by the Women's International Defense Federation (WIDF), an international women's peace association organized against fascism, militarism, colonialism, and war.[4]

This section includes two short exemplars of Alice Childress's regular *Freedom* column, "A Conversation from Life." The fictional column was written from the perspective of Mildred, a Black domestic worker. Though they differ in tone from the other writing collected in this volume, we include these pieces because of the way they reach out to Black working-class women. Indeed, Mildred was one of the most important "voices on the Left theorizing and representing black women workers into the 1950s."[5] Through Mildred, Childress provided Black women "with a theory of labor rights, authorization for dissent, and a language to speak against injustice."[6]

The remaining chapters open windows into the second Red Scare, not least FBI surveillance, investigations by the House Committee on Un-American Activities, arrests, indictments, convictions, jail sentences, and the generalized mobilization of the Cold War state apparatus against Black communist leaders. In these writings, Black Communist and Communist-adjacent women defend their husbands and comrades. Two chapters are excerpted from the pamphlet defending party leader Benjamin J. Davis Jr. after he was convicted under the Smith Act. The pamphlet was written by Claudia Jones and introduced by Eslanda Goode Robeson. Jones locates the persecution of Davis in the longer history of the Black struggle for freedom. "The very core of *all* Negro history," she writes, "is *radicalism* against conformity to chattel slavery, *radicalism* against the betrayal of the demands of Reconstruction, *radicalism* in relation to non-acceptance of the status quo!"[7] The chapter from Dorothy Hunton describes rallies organized in defense of Paul Robeson after the US State Department revoked his passport and support mobilized on behalf of W. E. B. Du Bois, who was indicted as an agent of a foreign power for his peace activism. Hunton brings out the imperialist and colonialist dimensions of US persecution of Black communist leaders such as her husband, William Alphaeus Hunton Jr., the executive director of the Council on African Affairs. He worked tirelessly in support of anticolonial struggles, raising funds for relief and trying to direct more attention to the movement for African freedom. Hunton writes, "For three years after his release from prison, Alphaeus fought a losing battle with the government in defense of the right to advocate and support the cause of African freedom."[8]

The final chapter comes from the memoir of Charlotta Bass, who was described as being pro-Communist by a California un-American activities committee. Because of this, her sorority revoked her membership. Bass observes that she had never been a member of any organization advocating the overthrow of the US government. In fact, she had spent her life defending democracy.

33

Excerpt from *This Is My Husband: Fighter for His People, Political Refugee*

Esther Cooper Jackson

March 1953, published by the National Committee to Defend Negro Leadership, pp. 5–36

It is a great effort to write these words. Memories pour through my brain and fill my heart. It is hard to capture in words that which ought rightfully be told in song: words are flat and dead things but a song has life and soul, and nourishes dreams, and joy, and hope, and glorious deeds, like the story of my husband. It is a hard thing to confine oneself merely to making words about one's beloved upon whose face one has not looked for what seems an eternity of time. I want so much to have now his warm comradeship; to hear again from his lips those winged words of exciting promise as he would give voice to his confident dreams of a free and bountiful new life for the world's humble peoples.

Background

For nearly two years now, my husband has been a hunted and harried "fugitive" in his own land. The agents of the FBI—who in the whole history of their organization have never found a single one of the lynchers of more than five thousand of my people—have subjected his family and his friends to the unrelieved terrors of constant "surveillance" and "interrogation" in their relentless search for the whereabouts of my husband and his colleagues.

Our children especially have been the target of their vindictiveness. For a year and a half now FBI agents have been watching and shadowing our daughters and their young friends everywhere. Last year they made attempts to have our younger daughter, Kathy, expelled from a city-supported nursery school. But this attack was doomed to failure. The people of the community and throughout the city were enraged by this obvious persecution of a child because of the political beliefs of her father. The Department of Welfare was forced to withdraw its ridiculous order expelling little Kathy from nursery school after protests began pouring in from citizens of all political beliefs and from all walks of life.

The Baltimore *Afro-American*, commenting on the harassment of our family, had this to say in its February 23, 1952, issue: "More than a month ago, Harry T. Moore and his wife were murdered by foul bomb assassins in Mims, Florida. The FBI went through the motions of 'investigating' but no arrests have been made. It looks like some of those FBI boys frittering away their time trailing innocent four-year-old children down the streets of Brooklyn could be more profitably employed tracking down bomb-throwing killers in the everglades of Florida."

Yet today the surveillance continues. Even as I write this my hand shakes with hatred for these cruel and vicious manhunters of the true leaders and heroes of the people. Through the window of my apartment I have seen them sitting in their cars, glaring searchingly at every passer-by and waiting impassively to trail me to work, to the park, to school with our daughters. When they sit there no one speaks to them. Even the children of the neighborhood cut off their laughter and shroud their small faces in grim expressions of scorn when they pass by them. Oh yes! The celebrated FBI "laws" know they are in enemy territory here. They are sealed off from all the "tongues" in the community by an unbreachable wall of hatred which is the historic fate of the persecutors of the just.

In his hometown, too, where my husband's family is under constant surveillance, these FBI hunters are scorned. Especially is this true in the community around his father's drug store. These people were his friends and neighbors in that ghetto with its awful poverty, its hardworking men and women—happy hunting ground for police gunmen, rent-gougers, loan sharks.

There, upstairs above the store, my husband was born. From the age of 6 to his 23rd birthday, he often worked there with his father. The people and the life of that community were his first teachers, and I believe that some day men will write that he in turn was one of their greatest teachers. My husband dearly loved the working people of that neighborhood. It was the soul-killing drudgery of their toil and sufferings, yet ever-hopeful spirit and striving for better things, that inspired him to write, to speak, to join in and to lead struggles in their behalf.

Jackson Ward

The community where my husband was born and lived in early childhood was named Jackson Ward for the swashbuckling general of the slavemasters' rebellion—Stonewall Jackson. Today, although it is still referred to as Jackson Ward, only the oldest residents will tell you that it was named after the Confederate General, Stonewall Jackson. The tobacco workers will tell you that its name derives from the fact that this neighborhood was the scene of a great strike of tobacco workers which was led by my husband in the late Thirties!

My husband is among those men and women indicted under the Smith Act, a thought-control law sponsored by that poll-tax Congressman from Virginia, Howard W. Smith. This Act makes it a "criminal conspiracy" to teach or advocate or circulate any ideas which paid informers may testify implies "intent" to overthrow the government by force and violence. Supreme Court Justice Hugo Black declared in a minority opinion in reference to the eleven leaders of the Communist Party convicted under the Act, "These petitioners were not charged with an attempt to overthrow the government . . . The charge was that they agreed to assemble, talk and publish certain ideas at a later date." And two outstanding Negro attorneys, Richard E. Westbrooks and Earl B. Dickerson, argued that "The inevitable effect of the Supreme Court decision on the Smith Act is to undermine, if not destroy, effective protest with regard to government practices and policies inimical to the welfare of Negroes."

My husband is charged with harboring dangerous thoughts and spreading radical ideas which, at some future time, may help the common people to organize and make America a truly democratic nation: a nation in which the workers will toil to enrich *themselves* and not a small set of exploiting industrialists, a nation in which poor farming folk will own the land they till.

Let me now put down some of the highlights of my husband's life, gathered from relatives, friends, and from my ten years of full and happy life with him.

Early Home Life

Although he grew up in a miserably poor neighborhood, the same in which his father was born, my husband enjoyed certain privileges and advantages which had been denied to his playmates. His parents had the advantage of a college education and reared their children in a reasonably comfortable house with adequate clothing, plentiful amounts of food and good medical attention.

As a druggist in this community of poor laboring people, his father quite naturally became in their eyes a person of high accomplishment. His mother enjoyed great prestige, respect and authority among the people. She was one of the earliest Negro women college graduates—a woman of striking beauty with warm sympathies for the problems of others.

As his parents were to the community, so they were to their children, examples and symbols of the possibility of accomplishing some measure of culture in spite of all obstacles of discrimination prejudice and poverty. This was no small factor in helping the children of the family retain their natural self-confidence when they began—at such an early age—to come up against the soul-crushing proscriptions which confront all Negro children growing up in Jim Crow America.

The Du Bois Influence

An additional family influence on the course of my husband's development was that his father was of that band of self-made intellectuals, the sons of slaves, who fought their way out of the mire of poverty, inspired by the forever glowing star of hope that was born in the glorious decade of the Reconstruction years. The outstanding figure of that generation was Dr. W. E. B. Du Bois, and my father-in-law counted himself among his followers.

They were inspired by the *Credo* of the Niagara Movement delivered by Dr. Du Bois at Harpers Ferry in 1906. He said, "*We will not be satisfied to take one jot or tittle less than our full manhood rights. We claim for ourselves every single right that belongs to a freeborn American, political, civil and social; and until we get these rights we will never cease to protest and assail the ears of America . . . First we would vote; with the right goes everything . . . Second. We want discrimination in public accommodation*

to cease . . . Third. We claim the right of free men to walk, talk, and be with
them that wish to be with us . . . Fourth. We want the laws enforced against
rich as well as poor; against Capitalist as well as Laborer; against white as
well as black . . . Fifth. We want our children educated . . . Either the
United States will destroy ignorance or ignorance will destroy the United
States . . ."

In the realm of economics my father-in-law and his friends were
enamored of the Horatio Alger mythology. They envisioned the emer-
gence of a large monied Negro business class as both a possibility in the
America free enterprise market of the turn-of-the-century, and as a
necessity to ensure a minimum of economic independence and self-
sufficiency to the Negro masses. On the political front the letter of the
United States constitution was their doctrine and banner. They
demanded with Du Bois every right enjoyed by white citizens. They
were uncompromising foes of segregation and the foremost advocates
and believers in the power of widespread popular as well as intensive—
that is, liberal, classical—education. They were for the education of the
whole man to enable him to exercise all the functions as citizen in a
democracy, as against the policy of conciliation of Booker T. Washington.

I am told that my father-in-law participated in the struggle against
the institution of the one-man Jim Crow trolley cars; in this battle he
was beaten bloodily and jailed, but not before he had defended himself.
This struggle resulted in tying up the whole trolley car transit system for
hours!

His drugstore-home was a kind of headquarters for other battles of
Richmond Negroes against the assaults of the white supremacists. He
was among that pioneer band that won one of the earliest victories
against the restrictive residential covenants in regard to housing during
the 1920's. Only recently a struggle led by the National Association for
the Advancement of Colored People and other Negro organizations has
resulted in the historic Supreme Court decision making such covenants
unenforceable by law.

At the outset of the anticipated participation of our country in World
War I, before the then-renowned "Young Men's Forum" at the Ebenezer
Baptist Church, my father-in-law spoke against our entry into the war.
He characterized it as an imperialist war of thieving nations whose
hands would be forever stained with the innocent blood of the outraged
African and Asian peoples.

An Answer to the Klan

Following World War I, though my husband was scarcely out of his crib, he, like most Negro children born in the South, was early aware of the fact that returned veterans were met everywhere in the country by the unbridled terrorism of the KKK. The local authorities, the planters and the industrialists were determined to erase from the minds of returned veterans, through the instrument of the Ku-Klux-Klan, any notions of equality that they might have brought home with them from France.

The Klan rode in Atlanta, St. Louis, Tulsa, Chicago, Washington, and many other places on its mission of putting "uppity" Negro servicemen "in their place." The Klan committed wholesale acts of murder, raping, lynchings and burnings in dozens of Negro neighborhoods across the country. The present master of the FBI bloodhounds, J. Edgar Hoover, whose men are with such energy sniffing around the peaceful homes of thousands of law abiding citizens, vindictively seeking the whereabouts of my husband and his colleagues today, gave the orders to the government's manhunters then! But not a single one of those murdering Ku Kluxers did he choose to arrest and bring to justice, although they committed in broad daylight hundreds of overt acts of force and violence in contemptuous disdain for the highest laws of the land!

When the Klan advertised its intention of invading the Negro neighborhood in Richmond where my husband's family lived, the community formed a self-defense association, and then waited to receive the would-be invaders. When an informer passed the word to them that the people had prepared to defend themselves, the Klan discreetly did not choose to ride through that part of town!

Furthermore, my husband's family, like those of hundreds of thousands of other Negroes throughout the South, was always a part of the every day struggle for human dignity against the tides of white supremacy, arrogance, and ignorance, which everywhere seek to drown the spirit of the Negro people of the Southland. In his store, my father-in-law has always insisted that every salesman address him as "Mr." or "Dr.", and refer to his wife as "Mrs." He demanded that they exhibit this evidence of simple decency as a condition for doing business with them.

College Days

In February of 1931, at 16, my husband entered Virginia Union University and was elected President of the Freshman class.

The "youth of the slums" generally affected a scornful and hostile attitude toward the "college boys." They looked upon the students' cultured speech as a showy "putting on of airs" and a mockery of their own. They resented their better-dressed appearance, their singing and horseplay and derisively characterized them as thinking themselves "somewhat better than us." My husband shared this viewpoint for a while, rather ridiculously strained to keep himself "pure" of any real identification with the manners of the collegian.

However, he soon saw the injustice of this one-sided view of the college student. He saw that the bulk of them weren't the "arrogant conceited asses" that he and his friends might call them, but hard-working young men and women, toiling at odd jobs after school hours and throughout the summer months; denying themselves the small pleasures, and along with their parents pinching and saving that they might buy the tools of a higher learning and "make something really worthwhile" out of their lives. It was the same old aspiration and struggle for freedom he had heard as a child from the lips of his father's friends at the back of the store.

On Freshman Day, my husband made a speech in the college Chapel. In the speech, entitled, "The World Beyond the Campus," he painted a graphic picture of the stark realities of Negro life in the city and he asked his fellow students to dedicate their lives to the people as the sole motive and justification for their more favored circumstances.

The Discovery of the Communist Movement

On the strength of this speech, my husband was elected among the delegates to attend an interracial Seminar in North Carolina. Here for the first time he came in contact with white people who did not consider themselves the natural superiors of Negroes, or at least did not go out of their way to impress this feeling upon him. Here he met for the first time a Communist, a brilliant student of the labor movement, and others determined to fight for full democratic rights for the southern people, black and white.

From that summer of 1931 onward my husband read everything that he could find on the world's socialist movements. He discovered that Marx, a German, and Lenin, a Russian, had given hope to oppressed people everywhere by their scientific research and writings on the origins of poverty and tyranny and had pointed out the solution for these evils which had been plaguing mankind for generations.

Through the study of communism, my husband discovered that the Negro people have a powerful ally in the white workers and that it is to the self-interest of both to unite in common struggle. He discovered that the goal of the landlord, big-business combination is to strip the poor people of the South of all means of expressing their will for a better life through the use of the odious doctrine of "white supremacy" and "legal" and extra-legal terror. He could foresee the awakening of a tremendous vote movement in the South which would challenge the rule of those so long in the saddle. He found that the task of correct leadership was to fight for this unity of the Southern people—Negro and white workers— to weld it, and to win allies for them in the nation and throughout the world.

Others, with full conviction, have chosen different paths leading to Negro freedom. Some still say education alone will do the job. Others propose to reach equality through success in business. Some would place complete reliance upon court decisions. Some few still see no hope in the U.S.A. and turn their eyes wistfully to Africa as a "homeland."

Marxism taught my husband to seek the answer *here* in an alliance of the Negro people with white workers for immediate social gains and the eventual establishment of a social system in which economic exploitation and Jim Crow oppression would be profitable to no one and would cease to exist.

Youth Activities

From the days of the Youth Seminar onward, Jack was more occupied with fighting for the rights of his people than with his classroom textbooks. Nevertheless, he graduated from college in less than the prescribed four years with an average assortment of grades. Though some of his professors ranked him as a superior student, he is better remembered by his classmates for his extracurricular activities; his organization of a Marxist Club and the Proletarian Students Party which won leadership of the student government and several of the other various campus organizations. They remember his leadership of the Cooperative Independents Club with its ambitious program "to train leaders for the deliverance of our people, through militant action, from every semblance of racial and class oppression." This group established contact with white students in nearby colleges and held a conference for the abolition of Jim Crow in education.

College Editor, Debater, Organizer

They recall his editorship of the student paper, "The Panther," with its militant editorials against war, for the freedom of the Scottsboro Boys, for academic freedom, and on other issues. They remember him as an ardent speaker. They recall the time when he and a colleague debated a team from Lincoln University on the subject, "Resolved: that Negroes Should Join the Communist Party" and how the galleries were packed with his colleagues from the unemployed council wildly cheering every reference that Jack made to the writings of William Z. Foster and James W. Ford to the evident dismay and discomfort of administration officials. They recall their participation with my husband in the picket lines before the A. and P. chain stores, and the "Free-the-Scottsboro-Boys" parades and "Hunger-Marches."

Receiving the degree of Bachelor of Science in Chemistry in 1934, my husband went to Washington, D.C. and entered Howard University—the Alma Mater of his mother and father. He graduated from the College of Pharmacy in 1937, completing the four year course in three years.

During his years at Howard, there was much militant activity among the students. The Young Communist League, the Marxist Study Circle and the Liberal Club were large and authoritative leadership organizations in the student body. They led anti-war strikes, and strikes against the high cost of living, and demonstrations for the passage of an anti-lynching bill. The students participated in many activities off the campus as well.

The Birth of the S.N.Y.C.

It was during his last year at Howard that Jack joined with the outstanding young leaders of the progressive Negro youth of that time in founding the Southern Negro Youth Congress. This organization, whose founding convention and first headquarters, was in Richmond, Virginia, wrote an heroic page in the organized struggles of the Negro people, and the joint struggles of Negro and white youth, in the South.

The motto of the Southern Negro Youth Congress, "We Shall Dream, Organize, Build—For Freedom, Equality, Opportunity," was heard far and wide throughout the Southland.

The first conference of the SNYC took place at a trying moment in the life of our country. The national economy was in partial bankruptcy; thousands of factories were idle and millions of adults were jobless; a whole generation of youth had come of age since 1930 who had never worked. Some serious-minded adults gravely pronounced in innumerable articles, books and speeches, that ours was a "lost generation." Such was the dismal future for the mass of the youth; but the outlook for Negro youth, what with all the multiple patterns of discrimination and oppression, was more hopeless yet. However, Negro youth, as the whole American people, refused to accept such a fate for themselves.

From 1933 to 1937 a wave of strikes occurred on the Negro college campuses. The issues included poor food, lack of social life, and free speech. These strikes were indicative of a new spirit among Negro youth which was in tune with the disaffection of youth elsewhere with the status quo which held for them only the prospect of a dole or job of menial capacity on WPA. Such were the ingredients and the background, the mood of the age, out of which my husband and his co-workers gave leadership to thousands of youth of the South for more than a decade.

The Southern Negro Youth Congress became the foremost instrument of the southern Negroes' struggle for justice, suffrage rights and job opportunities. The glorious history of the brave struggles of that organization is indelibly related to the activities of my husband and myself along with a devoted band of other young people who led the S.N.Y.C.

The Tobacco Workers Strike of 1938

Immediately upon graduating from the University in 1937, my husband returned home and plunged into the drive of the Southern Negro Youth Congress to organize the tobacco workers into the new house of organized labor, the CIO. Like his colleagues in the SNYC, he was a volunteer organizer, working full time as a pharmacist in his father's drug store for his livelihood.

The betterment of the lot of the tobacco workers had long been his determination. When a child, every day when the quitting whistle blew, he would take his post in front of the store and bid "good evening" to the hurrying line of workers till the last straggler had passed.

The tobacco workers were the most exploited of all the local working people. The Giant Export Leaf Plant employed great numbers of cripples, old folk and mere children. They worked ten and twelve hours a day for as little as a dime an hour in steam filled, dust-beclouded, dark cavernous sheds. The foreman was invariably some sadistic white-supremacist who delighted in driving and screaming at the workers as though he was some overseer on a slave plantation. Following the long blast on the evening whistle, the workers would pour out of the factory with loud cries and laughter—glorying in the end of another day endured in spite of "Mr. Charley." They were joyful to taste the fresh air and empty their lungs of the foul tobacco dust of the factory, if only for a little while.

The Whole Community Joins In

Inside the factory there were rules against laughing, and rules against talking, and rules against getting up from one's stool, and rules—and rules—and rules. So once out on the streets the workers would laugh and shout to one another at the top of their lungs. The younger ones would indulge in horseplay in the streets, sometimes stopping traffic. Often the women workers would link their arms and march six abreast down the sidewalk.

Yes, after the closing whistle blew, for ever so little a while, the street belonged to the workers. The swinging strength of their numbers gave them the power before which all else had to give way. So, down the street they would come, the strong helping the lame and the sick, bearing great loads of barrel staves and boxwood chips on their heads—firewood for their cold flats. Their shoulders would be draped about with burlap sacks against the chill wind which tore at their thin garments.

My husband helped organize these workers at the Export Leaf Factory of the British-American Tobacco Company, and led them in a strike struggle which resulted in a union victory and a substantial improvement in all of their wage and working conditions.

Following on the heels of this victory in 1938, contracts were won and strikes were conducted at several other plants. In one of these strike struggles—at the I.N. Vaughn Plant—my husband was brutally assaulted by the police and arrested. Over a score of workers were also arrested and many were beaten during this long and hard-fought strike. Nevertheless, in the end the workers won recognition for their union.

All of these union organizing activities were financed by the local efforts of the workers. They had formed a network of committees which made collections on street corners and canvassed house to house; they impressed the ministers into taking special collections at their churches for the strikers; local merchants were waited upon by committees of workers to make contributions of foodstuffs, to extend credit and other services. The whole community was involved in making that fight of the tobacco workers for a decent wage from the giant Wall Street-London Corporation a success. The initiative taken, the success achieved by the tobacco workers gave a new confidence to all sections of the Negro people and inspired a wave of struggles among the white workers as well. (There hadn't been a big strike in Richmond since the Street Car Strike of 1903.)

The Negro teachers rapidly built up their organizations in a determined struggle for equal pay.

Big movements unfolded in support of the demands for cheap public housing.

The movement for the right to vote developed with a new burst of energy.

Experience Strengthens Conviction

One day my husband received an invitation to make a field study for a year of various aspects of the status of the Negro in several southern states as a part of the Gunnar Myrdal Study of the "Negro in America." This offer proved to be the bridge my husband needed for the solution of his dilemma. The Myrdal Study job gave him the opportunity for a year of intensive study and testing of his own abilities over the broader canvas of the whole South. He traveled throughout the South, talking with the people and studying the program and leadership technique of all the leaders there of any importance.

As a result of this trip he became thoroughly convinced of the superiority of the program advanced by the Communists and of his own ability to provide the kind of leadership which could unite that program with the yearnings and urgent needs of the masses of the South. He saw that only through the end of white supremacy in the southern states could exploitation and oppression end for all the southern people.

Furthermore, the enormity of the Jim Crow crimes and the huge scale upon which he saw them being committed against the people in the deep South steeled him in his resolve to devote his entire energies toward realizing needed, long overdue social changes.

Jack bid his parents an affectionate good-bye in the spring of 1940 and went to Birmingham, Alabama, where he joined the staff of the Southern Negro Youth Congress. He had made his decision.

The Southern Negro Youth Congress

It was during his brief stay at Fisk University while working on the Gunnar Myrdal Study of the "Negro in America" that I met my husband. What impressed me most about him at that time was his sincere and passionate desire to change the Jim Crow South and to unite Negro and white in bringing about that change. I was then at work on a detailed study of domestic workers in relation to trade unionism which was to be my thesis for a Master's Degree in Social Science. His suggestion and criticisms on the development of my thesis were most helpful. He advised me to take the completed study to the CIO and try to interest them in the unionization of this important group of exploited workers. However, I did not get very far on this proposal with leaders of the CIO in Washington, D.C.

At that time I lived in a settlement house, organizing group activities for the children of the neighborhood, in exchange for room and board. Jack often stopped to play with the children, to toss them a ball, to examine a drawing or painting, to lift a young child on his shoulders. He was never too busy to return a child's warm smile.

I remember our first "date" and how he fell asleep in the movies before we had hardly settled in our seats. He often told our daughters of this meeting and that it seemed we had known each other a lifetime.

A Cherished Letter

After our brief meeting in Nashville, we began to write each other frequently. A letter which I read many times these days, one of my most cherished possessions, is one on the stationery of the Tobacco Stemmers and Laborers Industrial Union. Jack wrote, "*Already I have missed the glorious Fisk hospitality and most especially your contribution to the joyous stay I had there. Of all the happy memories of my trip my acquaintance with you will stand out in bold outline—a native unselfishness, a will to serve and to sacrifice, an ardent devotion to our cause, symbolized in the youthful beauty of a charming lady—and that's Esther to me.*"

Our courtship continued through the mails. We exchanged gifts, somehow always remembering the holidays that we had been too busy to observe before.

Already a part of many student activities, I moved to Birmingham and joined the staff of the Southern Negro Youth Congress and at the following convention was elected one of the officers.

In 1941 Jack and I were married and made our home in Birmingham for the next six years. It was in that steel city of the deep South in 1943 that our first daughter, Harriet Dolores, was born. We named her for the heroic woman fighter, Harriet Tubman.

Our friends and associates shared the many grueling experiences and triumphs of years of struggle on a multitude of issues in the Southern Negro Youth Congress. There in the very depths of the Klan-ridden, Jim Crow Southland we fought upon the very front lines of the southern people's fight for the vote, peace, jobs and democracy. The fact that salaries were small and irregular never once dampened our spirits or blunted the ardor of our enthusiasm. The energy that was poured into the cause of building the fighting unity and leading in the people's struggle came from the people themselves.

A Communist Leader

My husband, who had previously been a volunteer teacher of Marxism-Leninism in several states of the South, was elected State Chairman of the Communist Party of Louisiana in the fall of 1946. His tenure was short lived, however. One of his first functions was to address a public meeting celebrating the Twenty-ninth Anniversary of the socialist revolution in which the oppressed Russian people wrested their freedom from the corrupt and reactionary Tsarist regime and took the government in their own hands. The leaflet advertising the New Orleans meeting stated, "The American Revolution of 1776, the French Revolution of 1789 and the Russian Revolution of November 7, 1917, are the great landmarks in the advancement of mankind toward a universal condition of economic security, brotherhood, peace, democracy and freedom."

While he was speaking, a mob escorted by the police, attacked the meeting and Jack and a number of his colleagues were arrested and imprisoned.

When his case came to trial, the main contention of the prosecution was that, by making a favorable reference to the Soviet Union, my husband had thereby provoked the patriotic "true-Americans" in his audience to acts of force and violence against himself and his comrades; hence he was guilty of inciting to riot and criminal mischief which threatened the security of the state!

During the same period a mob surrounded the house where he lived in New Orleans and tried to break in a window and seize him. The attempt was thwarted. But when the police arrived they promptly arrested him—the victim! In spite of a lynch-charged courtroom and hysteria-inciting newspaper headlines and radio bulletins, my husband conducted himself in prison and in the courtroom in a most heroic fashion, reflecting credit to the cause of his work. The charges were later dropped.

The Ford Workers

From Louisiana in 1947, we moved to Detroit. In the same year our second daughter, Kathryn Alice, was born. My husband became a leader of the Communist auto workers at the great Ford plant. The Communists were an important factor in the leadership of the big struggles of the Ford workers against the man-killing speedup, Jim Crow employment and job classification policies; and, in behalf of unity and democracy within the labor unions.

The militant Ford workers have become an outstanding element in the ever growing resistance movement of the American people against the efforts of a Big Business–dominated government to scrap the Constitution, junk all democratic processes, and impose an openly fascist rule upon the country.

In 1949 my husband became Southern Regional Director of the Communist Party and in the following year, an alternate member of its National Committee. Once again he returned to the area of his birth— the region and the people of this country whom he loves above all others—as a leader of workers and farmers—as a Communist leader.

It was not for long that my husband and his comrades were to be able to go about their work in relative peace. The power-hungry monopolists in our country became frustrated and enraged by the world-wide resistance of the organized will of hundreds of millions of people to their program for world domination. They struck a cowardly and vengeful blow at the Communist Party and their leaders. Eleven leaders were indicted under the provisions of the Smith Act. They were railroaded through a trial based on the evidence of paid informers, and imprisoned. In its garroting of the Constitutional rights of those Communist leaders, the government impaled the democratic rights of all Americans of whatever political persuasion.

Attacks on Negro Leaders

The war drive of the rulers of America and their assault against civil liberties, led to increased attacks upon Negro leaders and the Negro people as a whole. It matters not whether they are Communists, non-Communists or anti-Communists, Negro leaders are being persecuted as "dangerous subversives," threatened, jailed, deported, lynched. In the forefront of these leaders are the Smith Act victims such as Benjamin J. Davis, now serving a five-year prison term in the Jim Crow Terre Haute Federal Penitentiary and Henry Winston, now a political refugee.

The conviction of the eleven leaders was quickly followed by the indictment and arrest of dozens of others; among them were the Negro leaders, Claudia Jones, Pettis Perry, and my husband. Jack and several others chose to find a way to continue their struggles for peace and democracy in spite of the fascist-like law under which they were indicted.

By their example they have warned all Americans who cherish their liberties that they cannot long remain free people and still live with these Smith and McCarran laws, laws which have instituted in our land such a system of thought police that men and women are arrested and imprisoned—not for any crime that they have committed, but merely for the ideas they hold or the books they have read.

The "Foreign Agent Slander"

They accuse my husband of taking his "dangerous ideas" out of books of "foreigners"—men like Stalin and Lenin. Whatever the power, the effect, or influence of my husband's ideas upon the future conduct of the masses of the people of this country in general and in the South in particular, no sensible person can believe that it requires the dictates of some foreign Communist leaders, living or dead, to have caused him to advocate a program of social reforms.

Our government's traditional two-facedness is notorious and obvious to all: it indulges in loud proclamations about democracy, equality and freedom and at the same time reveals in life a picture of great privilege and riches for the few owners of the national wealth and a miserable existence of poverty, ignorance and want for the millions.

Especially in the South, the Negro people face disfranchisement, segregation and Jim Crow. The facts of life in the southern town where my husband was born and grew up motivated his search for truth and a way out for himself and his people.

Should that search for answers to the most burning problems of every Negro and every worker stop at the continental borders of the United States? Concede this and our nation will soon become a benighted wasteland of "super patriotic" bigots.

The Heritage of Jefferson and Douglass

Jefferson knew this and never ceased to draw inspiration from the great French Revolution in the early development of the United States, just as our revolution served as a catalytic agent among the French people and throughout 18th century Europe. Jefferson noted that the "flames kindled on the Fourth of July, 1776" had spread to France. Similarly the first blows at the institution of slavery in the Western Hemisphere were made when the people of Haiti and the West Indies won their emancipation from French and British slave-holders. The movement for emancipation in the West Indies gave great stimulus to the American anti-slavery movement. In the words of Frederick Douglass, *"British example became a great lever in the hands of the American abolitionists. The downfall of slavery under British power meant the downfall of slavery ultimately under American power and the downfall of Negro slavery everywhere. The cause of human liberty is one the whole world over."*

What was true in the days of Jefferson and Douglass is all the more true today. But how far have we come from their ideals!

Today Congress would deny us the rich heritage of peoples of other lands. Under the McCarran-Walter Law they would keep from our shores great leaders of world science and culture who may not agree that the so-called "American way of life" is the best and only way for mankind. They would also bar migration of peoples who do not fit into a Hitler-like classification of Anglo-Saxon superiority. Under this law the West Indian people are practically denied admission to the United States, and other darker peoples are limited to insignificant quotas.

This nation was built by "foreigners"—by men and women who brought to the New World the then "foreign" idea of democracy. The best democratic heritage of this land includes the millions who have come here, the ideas and the labor they have contributed to the building of the United States, and ideas which we have borrowed from other people. The people of France presented this nation with a great statue which stands in New York Bay in honor of those who came here from other lands.

But today the Statue of Liberty must hang her head in shame.

For Peace and Brotherhood

No, it is not *dictation* from any foreign source which caused my husband to dedicate his life and talents to the struggle for a new social order. Rather, in the course of the struggle for a better life he discovered the answer to the problems of our times in ideas which have grown as an integral part of the history of our country. That these ideas have been adopted in other lands simply indicates that mankind, facing common problems, eventually arrives at common answers.

My husband and his colleagues exploited no man, lynched no man, sent no mother's son off to die in an unjust futile struggle against peace-loving nations on the other side of the world! The men who did these things are the real criminals-at-large, not my husband! All of his life he was worked for peace among the nations and an end to war; for brother-hood among the peoples and an end to Jim Crow; for the prosperity of the masses and an end to poverty.

My husband and his colleagues have acted in the great tradition of Frederick Douglass and the abolitionists who defied the Fugitive Slave Law of 1850 (that infamous law also had the endorsement of the Supreme

Court!) and chose to carry on their fight as "fugitives" rather than obediently surrender their cause to the jailers of liberty.

They know, like Douglass, that, "He is the best friend of his country, who at this tremendous crisis dares to tell his countrymen the truth, however disagreeable it may be."

The people of America must aid the Smith Act victims, those men and women who stand in the forefront of the struggle to preserve America's democratic heritage, just as in the past they have come to the aid of freedom's fighters.

Amnesty must be granted and all political prisoners freed.

The frame-up trials of the communists must be stopped and an end brought to the witch hunts of the FBI thought-police.

The courts must rule against and Congress must repeal the fascist-like Smith and McCarran Laws.

The People Can Win

If millions of citizens, Negro and white, workingmen, professionals and business people—all who cherish democracy and fear its final destruction in our land—speak up, we can halt persecution for political beliefs in our country.

Some people, old friends and complete strangers, sometimes stop me to commiserate with me over the fate of my husband. They express deep human sympathy and pity. I thank my friends but I tell them that I am not one to be pitied but to be congratulated.

I AM PROUD OF MY HUSBAND AND HIS COLLEAGUES! I have the wonderful satisfaction of knowing that my husband has labored to find a path that will lead my people and all those who are heavily burdened into an age of peace and security—an era wherein all the people will live as brothers, wherein the happiness of many will be the highest concern of all, where there will be neither poverty, nor ignorance, nor prejudice.

My husband and his colleagues not only believe they have found a way that will lead to such a happy future for the people but they have the will, the courage and the great strength of the working people to make that dream come true.

I am sure that the people of this country and especially my own, the Negro people, will join in the defense of my husband and his brave comrades!

34

Unrest in Africa due to Oppression

Eslanda Goode Robeson

Freedom 3, no. 6 (June 1953), p. 11

When, at the United Nations, I had the good fortune to be granted special interviews with the delegates from Liberia and Ethiopia, I learned many things. Not the least of these was that it is not simply the color that is tending to unite Africans among themselves and with other peoples as never before. Most important, it is a common resistance to **oppression.**

The struggle of the African people in Kenya for the return of their land; the struggle of the African, Indian and colored people in South Africa against segregation and discrimination; the struggle of the North African people in Tunisia and Morocco for control of their land, resources and internal affairs; the struggle of the people of Indo-China and Malaya for control of their natural wealth—all these are closely related to the struggle of the Negro people here in these United States for truly representative government and full equality.

And these struggles are essentially another part of the successful struggle of the peoples of India and of Indonesia for self-government and independence. Their victories are our victories.

And, to go a little further back in history, the successful struggle of the Chinese people under the War Lords, and of the Russian people under the Czars, for control of their land, resources and government, were and are part of the whole picture, and their victories are also our victories.

The struggle of women, and labor, and minorities here in the United States and everywhere for equality, human rights, and truly representative government are all part of this same picture.

Same Pattern

In this universal struggle by people everywhere for freedom, there is always the same general pattern:

There is always the beating of drums and the calling to arms, the name-calling, the flood of pious declarations of peaceful intentions, the "benefits" of civilization by the oppressors, who scream about the evil intentions, the savagery and backwardness, the troublemaking, disloyalty, subversiveness and sedition of the people who insist upon equal rights, self-government, human rights, an end to oppression, and payment for services rendered.

In this general pattern there is always the jailing and exile and persecution of the freedom leaders, the confiscation of their lands and resources, the use of **real** force and violence—the army, navy, air force. There is always the attack upon the freedom organizations, the banning of the publications, the forbidding of public meetings, the threats and the terror.

From Jail to Power

North, East, South African leaders against oppression; Malayan, Indochinese, American freedom leaders are now in prison or in exile. Not so long ago freedom leaders in India, Indonesia, and the Gold Coast in West Africa came out of prison to lead new governments. **Just so freedom leaders now in prison and in exile will soon also lead new governments.**

In this world struggle of people against colonialism and oppression the local circumstances and methods of resistance may vary, but the objectives are always basically the same—in Asia, Africa, the Americas—the objectives are self-government, independence, freedom, equality, human rights.

In South Africa and in India the method is and was organized passive resistance. In Kenya it is active resistance. In West Africa it was strike, boycott, demonstration. In North Africa it is now active resistance. In Indonesia it was war. In Malaya and Indochina it is war. In the United Nations it is the ever-growing consolidation of the Arab-Asian-African bloc.

Part of Majority

I believe all this double-talk of the Western nations about Free Nations, Free World, Democracy, the Four Freedoms, Human Rights and Peace is reverberating and will echo back to blast the colonialism and oppression right on out of existence. Too many people in too many places have set their sights on Freedom and will not settle for anything else. When more than two-thirds of the population of the world decide—as they have decided now—that human rights must be fought for, then that's it, brother, that's **it**. And we American citizens, Negro and white, who are insisting upon equality and our civil rights no longer find ourselves a minority, but part of a fighting—and winning—world majority. I feel comfortable and confident with so many people on our side, fighting oppression.

35

American Women Join World Peace Crusade

Dorothy Burnham

Freedom 3, no. 3 (September 1953), p. 3

When 1,865 visitors and delegates convened in the World Congress of Women in Copenhagen, Denmark this past June they expressed the will for peace of hundreds of millions of women in all parts of the world. Among the delegates were seven women peace partisans from the United States, among them the author of this article.

It is a fine and heart-warming experience to greet and be greeted by women whose love of humanity has moved them to work together in the building of a great women's movement embracing millions of our sisters all over the world. And it is more than a pleasure to bring to the women peace fighters of the United States, fighters for the security of our homes and children, the deep affection and respect of the women of India, France, the Soviet Union, Africa—from all our sisters in the far corners of the globe.

Our delegation, though small in numbers, represented at the World Congress of Women the working women of the United States, the Negro women, women in professional and cultural fields, the foreign-born women, the peace fighters of our country. We represented the women who have been the victims of the Smith Act, McCarthyism, Taft-Hartley.

U.S. No Exception

Everywhere we went we were asked about the foremost peace fighters in America. The name of Robeson on the lips of any of us was an occasion for cheers. **Do you know him? Please give him our love!**

As the women made their reports on the economic conditions within their own countries, as they told of the starvation of children, of the long working hours for mothers and small children, they spoke bitterly of a U.S. foreign policy which prevented Marshall plan countries from importing the goods necessary for existence or exporting and selling on a free market the goods of their countries.

But had not the report from our own country carried an indictment of these very same industrialists, who have exploited the women workers of the United States for generations, whose Jim Crow hiring policies confine Negro women to the five lowest-paid job categories, where their earnings average less than half the salary of the white women workers?

Challenge to America

The mill-worker in Massachusetts, struggling to feed and rear a family on $35 a week has much in common with the women carpet workers in Iran; the Georgia mother pushed off the farm which she has share-cropped all her life to make room for cattle and machinery, has a common struggle with the women of Chile who move down from the hills, driven from their allotments, to seek water and food for their little ones.

The degree of starvation, misery and oppression may be a little different; the name of the oppressors is one and the same. Our salvation lies in unity with these women.

Many times in the course of the meeting American women were challenged directly and reminded of their responsibilities. It was as though these women of the world were saying, "Sister, you've got to move a little faster, you've got to talk a little louder, you've got to bring the majority of the U.S. actively to our side."

A Story of Shame

I remember the afternoon the Japanese women paused in their recital of the barbarities visited on their women by the American occupation troops to ask: "Do American mothers and wives know of the way their boys are behaving?" And I had to answer, yes, I know that American working men and the sons of workers, deprived for generations of the right to decent human relations with their own black brothers, are assured by "white supremacy" of the right to behave like animals where darker women are involved.

I thought of Mrs. Ingram, whose name had brought applause when mentioned, in the Georgia jail together with her two sons, for having defended herself from an attack by a white man. Mrs. Ingram and her neighbors, the black women of the United States know the fruits of white supremacy. It is our duty, the duty of all women of the United States who understand, to make American women know in what low esteem "white supremacy" ideas are held in the eyes of the civilized world. For are not our children, our sons, due a richer heritage than that bequeathed by James Byrnes and Herman Talmadge?

Why Russia Seeks Peace

And ever, as we discussed the rights of women, our thoughts and our talk would turn to the task of peace in the world. For we could not but realize that our struggle for medical care, for nursery schools, for decent wage scales, for food, for shelter, could only come to full fruition in a world at peace. For who could tell this story better than the women of the Soviet Union? They had made great strides, before 1941, in the building of nurseries, hospitals, schools and factories, in the winning of women's rights, only to see in five long years of war 17 million men, women and children killed and wounded, 1,710 towns razed to the ground, 70,000 small villages wiped out, 84,000 school buildings and 40,000 hospitals and medical buildings destroyed. It is no wonder that today as they bend their efforts to the rebuilding of their country, their first thoughts are—as are ours—of peace.

Large numbers of the women of the colonial countries, courageous and strong, having borne the brunt of the war-mad killers' savagery, could not even be present at the meetings. The women of Kenya who have seen their baby sons and daughters burnt and castrated before their eyes, whose villages have been destroyed wholesale, sent out their voices demanding of their British sisters a fiercer struggle against war and colonial oppression. And from the women of Korea there was a special message to American women: **"On behalf of the mothers of Korea, I call upon all of you, including the American delegation, to ask for an immediate end to this war. Only by fighting harder can you prevent your sons from being condemned, only by fighting harder can you prevent the senseless deaths of your sons. Only peace can insure the freedom of nations and the security of our homes."**

What We Pledged

It was this certainty that here were women who represented tens of millions more whose sacrifices on behalf of peace are unlimitable—this gave us the greatest feeling of strength. And this strength was reflected in the words of our final report to the conference:

"We will leave this Congress with deeper and clearer understanding of the historic task that lies ahead and with inspiration of the heroic women to whom we have listened—knowing that what is at stake is the rescuing of all that is best and most truly American in our country and the peace and security of the world.

"Through their own experiences in struggle our women will overcome their isolation and fear, learn their own strength and how that strength is invincible when joined with the surging movement of women all over the world. We pledge ourselves, sisters, to this task."

36

A Conversation from Life: Two Columns from *Freedom* Magazine

Alice Childress

Freedom 3, no. 8 (September 1953), p. 8

That's a pretty shade of nail polish, Marge . . . Oh, don't belittle your hands, child—I think they are lovely. Yes, I know you get tired of being a house servant . . . yes, you should have every right to be as much as you can be. But, when you come to think of it, everyone who works is a servant. Why, we couldn't live without the hands and minds of millions of working people.

Now you just look at anything in this room or in this apartment and try to point out something that working people didn't have their hands in . . . well you can stutter and stammer all you please, 'cause you can't name a solitary thing, be it cheap or expensive.

Take that chair you're sittin' in . . . can't you see the story behind it? The men in the forests sawin' down the trees . . . the log rollers . . . the lumber mill hands cuttin' up the planks . . . people mixin' up varnishes and paints . . . the artists drawin' the designs . . . all the folks drivin' trains and trucks to carry 'em . . . the loaders liftin' them off and on . . . all the clerks writin' down how many there are and where they're goin'— and I bet that's not half of the story.

Now Marge, you can take any article and trace it back like that and you'll see the power and beauty of laboring hands.

What the Hands Do

This tablecloth began in some cotton field, tended in the burning sun, cleaned and baled, spun and bleached, dyed and woven. Find the story, Marge, behind the lettuce and tomato sandwich, your pots and pans, the linoleum on the floor, your dishes, the bottle of nail polish, your stove, the electric light, books, cigarettes, boxes, the floor we're standin' on, this brick building, the concrete sidewalks, the aeroplanes overhead, automobiles, the miles of pipe running under the ground, that mirror on the wall, your clock, the canned goods on your shelf, and the shelf itself. Why, you could just go on through all the rest of eternity singin' the praises of labor.

So you can see we are all servants and got a lot in common . . . and that's why folks need unions. Well, for example Marge, suppose all you had was money and you wanted to make some more money . . . Oh hush, girl! I know you wouldn't, but let's suppose . . . Well, you'd hire ten people without any money who knew how to make tablecloths . . . and you'd sell them for four hundred dollars and pay the folks who made them one hundred of that . . . Marge, I didn't say you would do that . . . I'm only pretendin' . . . Well, never fear honey, we would form a union and tell you we wouldn't sew any more for you until you paid us fair . . . and then you'd either do that or make nothin'!

Who's Ordinary?

Why, not too long ago the workin' people in France folded their hands and everything stopped—the buses didn't run, the garbage wasn't collected, the stores shut up, and folks was in a fix.

Now, contrary to some opinion, I contend that healthy folks love to work, but "a servant is worthy of his hire . . . and they want decent pay and clean places to work where they won't be burnt up in no fire trap building, they want a little time to rest and enough pay to buy and enjoy some of the wonderful things they have made.

Yes, indeed, girl—I do get so tired of hearin' folks say, "I'm just an **ordinary** workin' man." Why workin' people are the grandest folks in the whole wide world . . . They set the steamships on the ocean and the lighthouse on the land . . . they give us our breakfast coffee and a roof over our heads at night . . . That's right, Marge, when workin' folks get together it should be with the highest respect for one another, because it is the work of their hands that keeps the world alive and kickin'.

Oh, Marge, what do you mean "you guess they're right nice." . . . I told you before . . . YOU HAVE BEAUTIFUL HANDS!

Freedom 4, no. 1 (January 1954), p. 4

Marge, there's an awful lot of upsets going on today. You can't pick up the newspaper without getting the tremors. Everybody is going around with a worried hang-dog expression. Too many people are frightened and tearful and worried and just plain heartsick.

Every word you read is Communist this and Communist that and McCarthy, McCarthy, McCarthyism. Everybody is being investigated to see if they think anything Communist. Air raid sirens are blowing all over the land and the whole populace is stirring and tossing with troubled dreams every night and the little children are crawling under their desks in school and holdin' their little hands over their heads—to protect them from **atomic blasts.**

The church is being investigated, the school is bein' investigated, the library shelves is bein' investigated, the Army is bein' investigated, the unions is bein' investigated, social clubs, political clubs, scientists, actors, writers, business people, housewives, the post office, the fire department, social workers, factory workers, store keepers, aunts, cousins, sisters, grandmothers, daughters, sons, brothers and husbands—all bein' investigated!

And for what? . . . Yes, that's what they say—to see if they are Communists or sympathize with Communists, or have ever belonged to any organization that had Communists in it, or if they have ever entertained a Communist or spoken to a Communist, or read a Communist paper or thought any thoughts that a Communist might also think.

Why, Marge, WHY? . . . Yes, they say that too—that Communism is wicked or keeps people from being free and is just outright awful . . . But the particulars are so skimpy . . . Why is it awful? "Because you'll lose your freedom," they say! The freedoms we prize so much, like—reading what you want, saying what you want, choosing your friends like you want, publishing any book or paper you want to publish, reading what you like, going to whatever church you want . . . every citizen in the land having equal rights to vote, serve on juries and all the rest of the equal rights that citizens are supposed to have . . .

Now, Marge, you just turn on your television set at almost any time and you will be sure to find some discussion ragin' about, "How we can stop Communism"—and it will be called some kind of "forum," and you will see that they have picked three or four more folks who **hate** Communism—to tell you what it is; and if by chance there is one person who is not too sure whether it's all that bad, he will sure wish he hadn't been there by the time the others finish ruining his reputation or his business or both.

But one thing you never see is a Communist sittin' in on it and explaining what he thinks Communism is—and defending it. That's not allowed!! No, mam!

Now if the object of McCarthy is to stop Communism and convince all the American people that it's bad, it seems to me it would be a short-cut for him to get a well-known Communist on television and rip into him in a open debate and show the people what a Communist thinks about . . . and if McCarthy is right he could pick his arguments to shreds. Why doesn't he do that? I ask you, **why?**

No . . . Instead there's a whole lot of hullabaloo about not allowin' Communist books on the library shelves, not allowin' Communists to write on newspapers or teach in schools, or act in plays; or speak their piece anywhere. In other words, they are tellin' the American public, "You just might believe every word you hear."

. . . That's very true Marge. There are folks that are speakin' out against terrorizin' the public, but most of 'em use the strangest reasonin'. They will say, "We must not be questioning and terrorizing **innocent** people." Now who in the devil can decide who is innocent beforehand? What they are sayin' really is: "Let's terrorize the Communists by fair means or foul and at the same time try not to bedevil folks who are not Communists."

Now I contend that terrifying and bedeviling are not fit methods to use on any citizen and we are all going to suffer much more until we wake up and defend the rights of Communists—defend their right to speak and be heard, to write and be read, to vote and to run for public office, to have the full benefits of trial by jury.

It is laughable, Marge, but I hear people everywhere beginning their sentences . . . "I am not a Communist, **but . . .**" Why does someone have to announce that they are not a Communist before they can tell me what they are thinking?

Well, the upshot of it all is just this . . . There is one thing in which I am agreein' with McCarthy . . . **If we are going to persecute people for what they read or think** there is nothing else for the persecutors to do but to keep the readin' and thinkin' matter out of sight and sound. Then we must raid the libraries and remove all books that the ruling body in this land deems unfit for our minds . . . we must suppress all movies that they think unfit . . . we must close all schools that they think unfit . . . we must close off every avenue that they think unfit and put away or do away with all people who have such ideas, close all churches and social groups that hold such ideas and purge every home in the land to root out such ideas—that is if we are ready to trade **Justice** in exchange for **Persecution.**

That's right, Marge. The question today is **not** McCarthyism or Communism. It is—American Justice.

. . . **What is its definition? You see, Marge, to me peace means a lot more than not bein' in a war. It means peace in your heart and mind; it means my neighbors and friends and all mankind growing in wisdom and love and understanding; it means finding a cure for cancer; it means feeding the hungry, making garden apartments out of the slums, stopping polio, opening up every school in the land to all races; it means friendship and laughter and freedom from fear; it means grownup folks not bein' ashamed to go to school and learn to read and write and enjoy this big, beautiful world; it means making it the social rage to belong to the millions rather than the "four hundred."**

That's right, Marge, there are two doors in front of us: Persecution or Justice, and it's up to the American people to decide which one it will be . . . I've made up my mind, Marge. How about you?

37

Introduction to *Ben Davis: Fighter for Freedom*
Eslanda Goode Robeson

National Committee to Defend Negro Leadership, Brooklyn, November 1954, pp. 1–3

We list many Negro women along with our heroes among the fighters for freedom—from slavery through abolition down to the present—from Harriet Tubman, Sojourner Truth, to Mary Church Terrell. And there are nameless unsung Negro women who have worked in the fields, kitchens, nurseries, factories to supplement the family income when our Negro men have been denied job opportunities and equal pay for equal work. Negro women move into new and dangerous areas with their men when breaking new ground in restrictive housing; they march beside their men on picket lines; they, together with their men, carry the fight against segregation in schools, transportation, etc.

Therefore it is not at all unusual to find a Negro woman, Claudia Jones, writing this pamphlet in defense of our beloved leader, Ben Davis, who is now immobilized in prison. Nor is it at all unusual to find me, another Negro woman, writing this introduction.

Claudia Jones, tall, attractive, warm brown woman, in her late thirties, is a brilliant and dynamic leader. Born in Trinidad, British West Indies, she came to the United States at the age of eight. She was quick and clever at school, but along with five million other young people had to leave school during the depression and go to work. Seeking jobs, and on the job, she came smack up against discrimination at every turn. Instead of futile complaining, she determined, as she said in a birthday speech, "... *to develop an understanding of the sufferings of my people and my class and to look for a way to end them* ..." She now holds a position of leadership in the Communist Party and plays a major role in the work for equality for women and for peace. For her beliefs, Claudia Jones was victimized by reaction and prosecuted under the Smith Act. She also faces deportation to her native West Indies under the Walter-McCarran Act.

Ben Davis is in prison because he has the courage of his convictions. I can't imagine a better reason for going to prison. When I was a little girl I used to think that only criminals, bad, wicked, evil people, dangerous to the community, were put in jail. Now I am a woman grown, living in a rapidly changing world, I know that very often, very good, very wonderful people are put in jail because they are dangerous—not to the community—but to the few, sometimes very wicked and corrupt people who are in power in the community.

Ben Davis, who was a chosen and freely elected leader and representative of the people of Harlem, and who served his constituents and the people of the great city of New York as Councilman honestly, consistently, constructively—reaped the strange reward of a prison sentence for his services. Widespread publicity of so unjust a reward to so just a man will help reveal and destroy the corruption and desperation behind such injustice and persecution. Hence this pamphlet. The term in prison will not destroy so strong and fine a man as Ben Davis, but will temper and refine the steel and humanity of which he is made.

If anybody should want to know why I, Eslanda Goode Robeson, am writing the introduction to this pamphlet about Ben Davis, an American Communist, now in prison, I will give some of my reasons here and now.

1. *First, Ben Davis is an old valued friend of mine, and of my family. We are proud to be numbered among his friends. It is an honor that we deeply cherish. We love the man.*
2. *Second, Ben Davis is an incorruptible leader and representative of the people who has the courage of his convictions. We admire and respect the man.*
3. *Third, Ben Davis is a militant advocate for the rights of the Negro people, and for all American citizens, at a dangerous time when such militant leadership is under continuous and violent attack. We must support and defend the man.*

38

Excerpt from *Ben Davis: Fighter for Freedom*
Claudia Jones

National Committee to Defend Negro Leadership, Brooklyn, November 1954, pp. 37–9

When things get thick
Some gents [thin] out
—AN OLD SAYING OF THE NEGRO PEOPLE

There have not been a few such gents and ladies who have so thinned out when the going got rough. They are among those who figuratively prefer the safety of their scalps and can down their troubled consciences, if they have any, by avoiding the rising glances of concern by our people who increasingly judge our leadership by their incorruptible and unpurchaseable characters.

Well, let us ask ourselves:

Then, there are those who tell us that to be radical and black means three strikes against us, or to be black and red is even worse.

Essentially this argument is one which counterposes patriotism to the nation's welfare; loyalty to radicalism, *real loyalty* to jingoism.

Well, let us ask ourselves:

Do not our people have a *right to have* radicals?

Yes—a *right!*

Do not our people have the *right to seek some radical solution* to their highly oppressed status?

And have a *right to be radicals?*

It would surely *seem* they have.

The very core of *all* Negro history is *radicalism* against conformity to chattel slavery, *radicalism* against the betrayal of the demands of Reconstruction, *radicalism* in relation to non-acceptance of the status quo!

Is there a conflict between being *radical* and *being loyal* to one's country?

History can best answer this question. For the history of our people is rich in example that because the oppression of our people comes from the ruling class, the very *survival* of our people required non-conformity to preserve the dignity of manhood and womanhood.

For example, when in 1850, Frederick Douglass said: *"that the whole framework of the American government is radically at fault"*[1] was he not expressing a radical thought? Was he being disloyal to the Negro people, to democracy, to the interests of the vast majority of the American people?

Or when Charles Langston, Negro secretary of the Ohio Anti-Slavery Society told a U.S. Court in 1858 about to jail him for violating the Fugitive Slave Act: *"I know that the courts of this country, that the governmental machinery of this country are constituted as to oppress and outrage colored men,"*[2] was he not expressing a radical idea fundamentally in the interests of the country?

When Sojourner Truth, demanding equality for Negro women told the First National Women's Rights Convention in Seneca Falls: *"I have borne five children and seen most all sold off into slavery and when I cried out with a mother's grief . . . none heard . . . And aren't I a women?"*[3] was she disloyal to the laws of the land, which not only denied legal, political and social rights to white women, but triply discriminated against Negro women?

When President Buchanan sent U.S. marshals to Frederick Douglass' home to arrest him after John Brown's heroic effort, in order to question him as to his knowledge of the event, was Douglass not radical in writing from Canada that: *"I have no apology for keeping out of the way of these gentlemanly U.S. marshals . . . I have quite insuperable objections to being caught by the hands of Mr. Buchanan."* Douglass also wrote from

---

1   From *A Documentary History of the Negro People*, by Herebert Aptheker.
2   Ibid.
3   *Sojourner Truth*, by Dr. Arthur Huff Fauset.

Canada he would never *"assume the base and detestable character of an informer."*

Now, Douglass may have disconcerted the slaveowners, but *"only base and detestable characters"* owe loyalty to exploiters and oppressors!

We can conclude as a result of these examples that the entire history of the Negro people has been one of *radical* solution to a sorely-oppressed status. We can also conclude that the finest patriots of the Negro people—Harriet Tubman and Frederick Douglass, Sojourner Truth and David Walker, Nat Turner and Denmark Vesey, Ben Davis and Henry Winston—those who have been assailed as radicals—are the staunchest fighters against slavery and Jim Crow, for freedom and equality. We can also conclude that the oppressors of the Negro people are the betrayers of the American nation. When, finally, we remember that history teaches that the only organized effort to overthrow the U.S. government through force and violence came from that class holding the Negro people in slavery, we can better judge who is truly loyal to America!

Who is loyal to America and its democratic traditions?

James Byrnes: governor of South Carolina, who equates the role of the NAACP and KKK, correctly assailed by Thurgood Marshall as *"fascist McCarthyism rampant with racism"*?

Or Ben Davis—whose eloquent voice against Jim Crow scathes Byrnes and all the racists even from behind prison bars?

YES, TO BELIEVE IN NEGRO FREEDOM MEANS TO BE RADICAL!

I believe with Ben Davis and his colleagues that this thought—Marxist-Leninist thought—contributes mightily to correcting the many evils in our society through peaceful effort.

You may not.

BUT you will agree that to disagree with a man's thoughts is no reason to jail him.

Instead of using his great talents and enthusiasm of deeply-held beliefs, Ben Davis is thrust into jail.

It is a disgrace to this country that Ben Davis ever went to jail or that he is kept there now.

39

White Advocates of Negro Freedom Continue Tradition of John Brown

Vicki Garvin

Freedom 5, no. 2 (February 1955), p. 8

Today a fighting and closely-knit Negro people are pressing forward to complete all the unfinished equal rights business tabled with the defeat of the Reconstruction governments

A striking feature of this crusade is that the "John Henrys" of the fight for equality do not struggle alone; increasingly they are joined by "John Browns" adding their blows against the walls of Jim Crow.

As this unity of Negro and white fighters for a democratic America develops, it strikes fear into the hearts of men in high places in government and industry.

Costly Adventure

What to do about it, then? Put a price on the heads of the "John Browns!" Make advocacy of Negro freedom—if not a crime—at least a costly adventure!

And so the history of the past years is marked by some outstanding examples of white Americans who have been willing to pay the price for advocacy of the constitutional rights of Negroes.

- Maurice Travis, secretary treasurer of the International Mine, Mill & Smelter Workers Union, brutally attacked in Bessemer, Alabama, in 1948 during a trade union struggle with a lily-white Steelworkers local to preserve a genuinely democratic union of Negro and white workers, almost paid with his life, and lost an eye.

- Professor Lee Lorch, who fought against Jim Crow housing by turning over his apartment in New York's Stuyvesant Town to the first Negro family to live there, was subsequently penalized with the loss of his teaching post at the City College. In 1950, Lorch was welcomed to the staff of Fisk University, but recently the 99 per cent lily-white trustee board decided to drop him. As Negro parents were escorting their children to formerly lily-white schools, Lorch sued the Tennessee Board of Education to admit his daughter to an all-Negro school. This action "angered many of the members of the board of trustees."

- The dragnet of persecution of decent whites has extended even to the courts. Judge Waites Waring of the Federal District Court in South Caroline committed the unpardonable "crime" of joining the forces of progress when he ruled against all-white primaries. Today, in retirement, he has been ostracized by former colleagues.

- Carl and Anne Braden, the courageous white couple in Louisville, Kentucky, broke the unwritten law by selling their home in a white community to a Mr. and Mrs. Andrew Wade, a Negro family. The Wades were bombed and forced to move. On December 13, 1954, Carl Braden was found "guilty" of sedition, and has been sentenced to 15 years in prison.

Violence—A "Last Resort"

The most dangerous extension of these repressive attempts to enforce the separation of Negro and white people, the better to exploit them, is the McCarthyite movement now underway, spearheaded by the misnamed National Association for the Advancement of White People, the American States Rights Association and the Citizens' Councils, substitutes for the infamous Ku Klux Klan.

These hate groups are well-financed and in many instances led by prominent men. Jeff Williams, member of the Mississippi House of Representatives, and vice-president of the State Veterans of Foreign Wars, spread the Citizens Councils from his state to Alabama. Aiming to maintain segregation at all costs, the Councils claim not to believe in violence—"except possibly as a last resort."

Democracy's Counterattack

But the real patriots of the United States will not be stampeded into violence, nor will they surrender their heritage of struggle so easily.

- Attorney Vincent F. Kilborn, former State Senator in Alabama, has said: "One reason I oppose this thing is that I happen to be a Catholic. If this group can do this to a Negro, they can do it to a Jew . . . a Catholic . . . a Baptist . . . and soon . . . to anybody."
- The American Civil Liberties Union is joining the defense in the Braden case. Several denominational alliances are beginning to face up to the issue of discrimination against Negroes.
- Undaunted, the United Packinghouse Workers Union, CIO, is stepping up its program for Negro rights in the South by proceeding with plans for an anti-discrimination conference in Atlanta, Ga., this month.
- Despite the failure of President Eisenhower for the second consecutive year to include a single recommendation for civil rights legislation in his annual message to Congress, the Negro people joined by labor are pursuing the fight for FEPC in many localities.

Guarantee of Progress

Today's challenge, as we approach the threshold of far-reaching changes, is addressed in the main to American white workers, to defeat the white supremacists in their domestic and foreign policies, to rise more boldly in support of Negro rights, and in so doing to help guarantee their own survival and opportunity to progress.

40

New Hope for Negro Labor
Vicki Garvin

Freedom 5, no. 3 (March 1955), p. 1

With the announcement that on February 9 the AFL and CIO agreed to merge the strength of their fifteen million members, the potential for decisive struggles to end job discrimination, the key problem affecting Negro working men and women, has been greatly increased.

In concentrating on the declared objectives of organizing the unorganized, winning additional economic gains, and increasing political activity, particularly in the legislative field, the new labor federation can certainly advance the pressing needs of Negro workers also. For with all their weaknesses and uncertainties, the trade unions have been the major instrument through which improved working conditions have been won, by and for white and Negro workers alike.

Only 7% Are Skilled

Especially following the formation of the CIO, many important gains have been made by Negro labor. Today 11 per cent of all industrial workers are Negro. Almost two million of the U.S.'s organized workers are Negroes: approximately one million in AFL unions and the rest in CIO and independent bodies.

But obviously much more needs to be done to change the conditions under which employers pay Negro families annual wages as yet but 56 per cent of white family income. After 60-odd years of trade union organization 57 per cent of all non-farm Negro workers are still in unskilled and service occupations, as against 15 per cent of whites. Today only seven per cent of all Negro laborers are in skilled crafts, as compared with 17 per cent of all white workers.

On the railroads, an old and highly unionized industry, nine out of every 10 Negro workers are in service, unskilled and common labor jobs. Even in many powerful CIO unions the problem of upgrading has yet to be seriously tackled. For example, in the auto industry at least 40 per cent of the foundry workers are Negro; yet in the tool and die division less than 3 percent are Negro. In the giant steel industry, practically all Negro workers are found in the eight lowest paid of some 32 worker classifications.

Women Doubly Handicapped

In textile, only a handful of Negroes are employed and in tobacco they are bunched mainly in the low-paid stemming and drying plants.

As for Negro women workers, six out of every ten are in domestic and service jobs. Only 20 per cent of Negro women hold industrial, sales and office jobs as compared with 59 per cent of white women workers in these categories.

It is natural then that considerable discussion is taking place around the question, "What is to be done to help solve the special problem of Negro workers" as a result of the AFL-CIO merger.

In order to fight most effectively for job equality for Negroes it is necessary to mobilize the combined strength of white and Negro workers against the power of discriminating industries. This calls for the organization of Negro workers on a full and equal basis with white workers and first-class membership in every union.

Jim Crow Not Dead

Although some progress has been made in that direction, there are still many powerful unions such as the AFL building trades and the Railroad Brotherhoods which have resisted setting their houses in order. With token exceptions, such unions have persisted in barring Negro workers from union membership or in maintaining Jim Crow locals.

Even the CIO which is credited with the most effective pioneering for job equality, has its own linen exposed by its failure to include Negro leadership among top national officers and/or policy-making general executive boards and in the top federation and in practically all its international affiliated unions. The record of the AFL and its affiliates on this score is far worse.

As now planned, the new federation will have three top officers, 27 vice-presidents and an executive council of 29 members. So far there has been no official statement as to Negro representation in any of these posts.

Statement of Principle

However, it is encouraging that many lessons learned from past defeats as well as victories in meeting employer attempts to "divide and rule" Negro and white workers, have helped to focus more attention on the question of Negro-white labor unity at this time.

It is significant that among the major principles incorporated in the merger is the following provision:

"The merged federation shall constitutionally recognize the rights of all workers, without regard to race, creed, color or national origin to share in the full benefits of trade union organization in the merged federation. The merged federation shall establish appropriate internal machinery to bring about at the earliest possible date, the effective implementation of this principle of non-discrimination."

This statement is undoubtedly a positive step, though its language has been criticized as "weak and vague." Michael Quill, president of the CIO Transport Workers, recently claimed that this provision is a watered-down version of the position that the CIO originally agreed to in the merger discussion.

Timing Important

If democracy is to "begin at home" it is necessary for the new labor federation to give leadership by example and incorporate in its new international constitution now being drafted a clear-cut clause binding on all affiliates, to the effect that there shall be no discrimination because of race, color, creed or national origin, in any aspect of union membership.

Equally important is the question of definite guarantees on the timing of the "establishment of appropriate internal machinery" to effect the principle of non-discrimination.

The Negro press and Negro trade union leaders, while greeting the merger as "of great value and importance to the Negro worker," have not neglected to caution vigilance.

In an editorial (3-5-55) the Oklahoma *Black Dispatch* declared: "A unified labor movement will still need to be prodded to the recognition of the necessity of cleaning its house entirely of the virus of racial discrimination . . . (We hope) . . . that the CIO pattern regarding equal rights will be retained."

Charles Hayes of Chicago, director of District 1, United Packinghouse Workers, CIO, commented: "The Negro cannot sit back and feel secure that in the merger all his problems will be solved . . . the Negro worker must become a union member and an active one."

And Willard Townsend, president of the United Transport Service Workers, CIO, pointed out that, "The challenge for stronger and more alert Negro leadership must be fully realized."

Organizing the South

When merger is completed, the AFL-CIO combined membership will comprise only 25 per cent of the entire American working force. In the midst of a multitude of problems and attacks, the labor movement is confronted with the growing problems of run-away shops, and the large reservoir of unemployed and unorganized, Negro and white workers in the South.

Here, surely, is a major challenge to the very existence and growth of democratic trade unions which, when diligently tackled, will immeasurably change the status of Negro workers and improve the living conditions of Negro and white families, North and South.

Louis Hollander, president of the N.Y. State CIO council declared at the recent convention of the Transport Workers Union: ". . . there are **hundreds of thousands of workers in the South who are being kept in slavery . . . Where there is no strong labor organization, where there is no industrial democracy, political democracy is nothing but a fraud."**

And AFL president George Meany declared at a meeting in Atlantic City a few weeks ago that, ". . . **the person who is unorganized because of a racial bar or discrimination of any kind is a threat to the conditions of those who are organized. Anyone who is underpaid, who has substandard conditions, threatens the situation of those in unions . . . The merger would mean more effective efforts to attain a fair employment practices bill on a national scale, and in attempts to assure civil rights in other fields."**

To the millions of Negro workers, South and North, who have long been eager to share the full benefits and responsibilities of democratic trade unionism, these forthright expressions are heartening. But these workers are also aware that continuous struggles must be waged within and with the labor movement for full economic citizenship and greater protection for all workers.

41

Prison: The Bail Fund Affair
Dorothy Hunton

Alphaeus Hunton: *The Unsung Valiant* (Richmond Hill, NY: D. K. Hunton, 1986), pp. 81–92

Along with the intensified practice of establishing guilt by unsupported accusations, and character assassination by alleged association, there grew steadily a pattern of linking the advocacy of full equality for Blacks and minorities with Un-Americanism. Frequently, in examinations designed to test the loyalty of applicants for government positions, the question was asked whether they believed in equality of the white and black races or entertained Blacks in their homes. It was not unusual in many areas for those defending non-segregated housing to be branded as Communists. Long ago those who pleaded for low cost housing had been called Socialist.

Bitter experience has taught us that the emotional attitude of a people can be nurtured and shaped by a cruel and clever government to any end the rulers may wish. McCarthyism spewed the menacing influence in the fifties. Drunk with power, the junior senator from Wisconsin, Joseph R. McCarthy, commanded national attention in his reckless crusade to eliminate so-called Communism from every aspect of American life. He constantly fed the public the big lie of our time, with his rabid, obsessive idea of security risks in the Federal Government.

In the early forties, the horrors of the Dies Committee investigations had set the precedent for the new McCarthy inquisitions. McCarthy's authority reached even into the U.S. overseas libraries, where hundreds of books by forty authors were yanked from the shelves by the State Department. Oddly, outstanding among the works singled out for elimination were the distinguished contributions on the subject of race discrimination, especially anti-Black oppression in the U.S. The purpose was, of course, to sow the seeds of suspicion of those writers who had the nerve to reveal or reject American racial inequalities. Weren't they adhering to the Red line? Consequently, their writings must be subversive.

In such an inhibitive atmosphere of red-baiting and war hysteria, Alphaeus organized a picket line of more than a hundred in front of Madison Square Garden to protest the refusal of the Garden to permit the Council to hold a concert-rally, featuring Paul Robeson. The event held in September of 1950 had two purposes; to protest the revocation of Robeson's passport, and to demonstrate public support for Dr. W. E. B. Du Bois, who faced a five-year jail term if convicted for his refusal to register under the Foreign Agents Registration Act, as chairman of the Peace Information Center.

After the demonstration, Alphaeus said:

> It is no accident that a progressive Negro organization, the Council on African Affairs, and a great Negro leader like Paul Robeson, have been made the first target of the proposed police state legislation. The fight to compel the Garden Corporation to reverse its stand is joined with the struggle to defeat the Wood-Mundt-McCarran-Kilgore repressive bills.

Among the untold number of organizations on the H.U.A.C.'s subversive list was the Council on African Affairs and the Civil Rights Congress. The **C.R.C.**, of which William L. Patterson was National Executive Secretary, derived from a merger of the International Labor Defense and the National Federation of Constitutional Liberties. It was formed in 1946 to conduct struggles for the legal defense of victims of American reaction. When private bonding companies refused to provide bail for progressives, but had no hesitation in granting it to gangsters, thieves and the like, it became necessary to provide some kind of fund, and a group of public minded citizens set up the **Civil Rights Bail Fund.**

Contributions came in from thousands of people from every political persuasion and every sphere of life. Four trustees were secured to administer the fund: Dashiell Hammett, the noted mystery novelist, who had been a part of the struggle for more than a decade; Frederick

Vanderbilt Field, editor and writer on the *Far East*, and a member of the prestigious Vanderbilt family; Abner Green, Executive Secretary of the **Committee for the Protection of the Foreign Born,** a man whom thousands of foreign born remembered with affection and gratitude, and Alphaeus.

Those four men held their sacrifices as unimportant in a just cause. For refusing to hand over the records to the committee, they were sentenced to six months in prison for contempt of court. Frederick Field, in violation of the Fifth Amendment, was subjected to double peril and sentenced twice; once for six months and once for three months for the same crime.

That fateful morning, July 9, 1951, when the gathering clouds of obstruction threw a shadow of gloom over our lives, is etched indelibly in my memory. Just two weeks previous we had moved into our own home, on a quiet block in Queens, New York. It was the only house owned by Blacks for years in that area. Its last owner was a close family friend who had recently died. Having visited her for many summers, I knew the neighbors in the adjoining houses—one German, the other Irish, and these acquaintances proved very valuable in the trying months ahead.

As Alphaeus and I sat at the breakfast table discussing the coming events of the day (he was to appear in court at 11:30 to answer charges against the Civil Rights Bail Fund), he casually commented on the fact that Field had been sentenced the day before and he expected the same fate. The impact of what he said did not really penetrate at the moment. The situation had never been seriously discussed prior to that morning. Alphaeus viewed the predicament in such a nonchalant manner that one would have thought he was merely going to the office as usual.

What if they locked him up immediately? We had made no plans to cover any problems that would arise. There had been no time to sit down and discuss seriously the numerous things that had to be done. The roof leaked; the furnace had to be replaced, and alterations made. How could I cope with all the new problems in that old house?

A million questions ran through my mind as we hurried to reach court on time. Like most wives, who more often than not are taken for granted and inadequately consulted on important issues that concern them as well as their husbands, I was left with the assumption that, somehow I would manage. Whatever the reason, I was totally unprepared to see Alphaeus put behind bars that morning.

A sense of numbness crept over me as I watched the courtroom procedure. Alphaeus had continued to answer the judge in his soft, quiet voice, refusing to disclose the names of the contributors. Now it was finished! The guard came forward, took him away, locked him up. Court was dismissed until afternoon when he would be sentenced. Dazed and bewildered, I walked out into the street, wondering what to do next. The need to talk to someone became more and more urgent as I racked my brain, searching for the right person. One had to be careful in that out-of-focused period when innocent people were often exposed to public scorn by mere association. Nevertheless, my friend Nellie Stanly, whose secretarial job in the school system could have been in danger by her friendship with us, put aside her family tasks and accompanied me to court.

"Six months for contempt of court," continued to ring in my ears as I prepared for bed that night, alone in our house amid unpacked barrels, boxes, and disarranged furniture. Never had I felt so devastated, crushed and utterly deserted. For the first time in my life I had to stand alone.

Yet from the agony and bitter experience of that day, a new insight into myself and the nature of emotional pressure emerged. That new and enlightening awareness dispelled any doubts I may have had about my ability to meet boldly any future calamities.

Those were frightening years, years that tried men's souls and spread distrust through the silence of fear that gripped the hearts and minds of progressive America. My German neighbor, an elderly, aggressive woman, who spent much of her time sitting on the bench in her front yard, was a plucky match for the inquisitive, the curious, and the F.B.I. who parked across the street in front of our house every day for weeks. Though I never saw them (they came after I left for work and pulled out before I returned), she kept me well informed; not only of them, but of the interviews by the press with certain neighbors.

The whole rotten affair distressed and depressed me, but it did not compare to the harassment and terrifying experiences heaped upon courageous Esther Jackson and her two small children during that period. Esther, now the managing editor of *Freedomways*, is the wife of Dr. James Jackson, who was then a leader in the Communist Party in the southern states. Jackson had been indicted under the Smith Act, but had become a political refugee. The F.B.I. was so vexed because he had slipped through their fingers that their agents inflicted systematic revenge on his family, down to their four-year-old daughter, who had a constant F.B.I. escort each day on her way to nursery school.

The Smith Act, a thought control law, placed new and unconstitutional restrictions on the right to freedom of speech and political association. It aimed to punish people for their ideas, and the right to advocate ideas distasteful to the rulers of our government; for acting together to achieve common objectives—such as uniting in the struggle against the threat of war, unbridled oppression, and economic hardships. The first victims to be tried and convicted were the top Communist leaders, among whom were two Blacks. Benjamin Davis, whose father served as a G.O.P. national committeeman in Georgia, was raised in luxury, Amherst-educated, and had a law degree from Harvard. Yet he turned his back on what could have been a life of leisure, to fight for a dangerous, and to him a just cause. The Harlem community elected him twice to serve on the New York City Council. He fought on many fronts with Henry Winston. Winston, who is still a stalwart Communist leader with a long courageous record of struggle for American youth, the rights of Blacks and the working class, was sentenced to eight years under a Smith Act frameup, and became totally blind as a result of deliberate neglect of his health in prison. Only after world-wide protest was he released after serving five years.

Recalling the Black man's direct experience through generations of historical struggles against "informers," and one that continues to have special significance for our efforts to achieve equality as citizens in all areas of American life, one is reminded of similar instances. Time and again, leaders of color have been confronted by official and unofficial despots with the demand: "Tell us the name of your associates!" Time and again those leaders refused to act as informers for the oppressors of their people, even at the risk of their personal liberty or lives. They refused to degrade themselves on the high moral ground that the cause for which they and their colleagues labored was just and to name their associates would be to betray them to the wrath of immoral, illegal, and prejudice-ridden forces of persecution.

"Who can remember the name of the craven slave who betrayed Denmark Vesey?" read the editorial of *Freedom*, Paul Robeson's paper, on which Alphaeus served as an Editorial Board member. "Or the miserable fellow who told his master the details of the plan when Nat Turner struck for freedom at Southhampton? Their names are buried with their bones in ignominious graves.

"Harriet Tubman and Sojourner Truth are the shining exemplars of our struggling womanhood; Douglass remains the paragon of unyielding leadership; John Brown is sainted in our midst; Vesey, Turner and Prosser clothed with life the words of a song which guided a whole people: 'Before I'd be a slave I'll be buried in my grave and go home to my lord and be free.'

"These men and women were trustees of our bloody struggles for freedom. They were worthy of their trust and history shows they merited the responsibility they cherished for their lives and liberation of millions of oppressed bondsmen. They would and did, protect their trust with their lives.

"Add to theirs the name of Hunton."

"I am sure you share my deep concern over the imprisonment of Dr. William A. Hunton for the refusal to betray his trust as an officer of the Civil Rights Bail Fund," wrote Dr. W. E. B. Du Bois, to a number of prominent Black citizens, August 8, 1951, for the **Special Committee on Dr. W. A. Hunton.** "I have come to know this fine man very well during my years of association with the Council on African Affairs. Quiet, studious, conscientious and absolutely uncorruptible, he is the worthy son of a fine and distinguished family from which he comes.

"A vindictive prosecutor and court have sent Dr. Hunton to jail for six months for so-called contempt of court. He does not belong there, and I hope you will join me in trying to get him out."

Dr. Du Bois' proposal was to ask several hundred Black leaders to endorse a petition to the President and Attorney General, urging an immediate pardon for Alphaeus. In that distressing episode in our history, it took courage and grit to sign a petition for one in Alphaeus's position. The Administration frequently ignored the petition and at times victimized the petitioners. Nevertheless, fifty-four Black leaders from twenty-two states affixed their names. Yet, the petition brought no response from the government. Alphaeus was denied bail, pending an appeal and he eked out his time at the Jim-Crow Federal Prison in Petersburg, Virginia, working in the small, poorly stocked library.

In September **An Open Letter to J. Howard McGrath,** U.S. Attorney General, concerning the four trustees appeared in magazines and newspapers across the country under the sponsorship of Elmer Benson, former Governor of Minnesota; Fred Stover, President of the Iowa Farmers Union; Robert W. Kenny, former Attorney General of California; William Hood, Secretary of Local 600, United Automobile

Workers; I.F. Stone, journalist, and Professor Robert Morss Lovett. Thousands of Americans from every state in the Union and from all levels of life gave their signatures and their dollars to bring the message to their fellow citizens. But it was of no avail.

McCarthy, the most infamous of the self-righteous chauvinists to undertake the ruination of innocent people's careers, aroused public anxieties about Communism to fanatical proportions. The reactions he provoked, the crudeness of his political style, and his debating tactics kept him in the news. Yet McCarthy did not work in isolation. The House Un-American Activities Committee, of which Richard Nixon was an energetic and inflexible member, existed long before and after. Public pressure, however, finally cut the senator down to size in 1955, after five years of blind untruths that deluded great numbers of people, and left behind untold damage to countless others, victims of a shattered society.

In the months following Alphaeus's imprisonment, I floundered through a rising tide of conflicting emotions. To be objective did not come easily. The indifference and unfeeling attitude of some people with whom I had been associated for twenty-five years, perplexed me. I suppose economics becomes closely connected to moral courage when one has passed the fanciful idealism of youth. Yet it seemed to make one's feelings known. The lack of concern for one's fellow member going through a shattering experience, when a kind, understanding word meant more than anything else, cut sharply and brought to light the true value of friendship. All this ushered in a deeper awareness of my place beside Alphaeus, and of our bond with all progressives working to make this a better world.

On my first trip to Petersburg, it was not a pretty sight to behold Alphaeus's tall, gaunt figure in his misfitting prison garb. His six feet four and a half inches posed a problem for the clothing manager, but they were not about to make any new uniforms for him. He had lost several pounds, which he could ill-afford, and his face looked haggard and drawn. Yet he complained only about the food. Surely the bed was too short, and his feet extended far beyond the end; they always did in a normal size, like many human devices that were a fraction too small or skimpy for his need.

Meetings and more meetings consumed my evenings while Alphaeus was away, especially those of Black women who came together to discuss and do something about the many grievances they carried in their hearts. The time had come to personally address the government for immediate and unconditional redress of injustices suffered at the hands of organized bigotry. To that end a committee sent *A Call to Negro Women* throughout the land to come to Washington, D.C., September 29 through October 1st, 1951, to demand an audience with the President, the Justice Department, and the State Department.

The Sojourners for Truth and Justice, as we were called, one hundred and thirty-two Black women from various sections of the country, and all walks of life, assembled in Washington at the home of Frederick Douglass; heard their proclamation read . . . "In the spirit of Sojourner Truth and Harriet Tubman," it declared, "we shall not be trampled upon any longer."

They were there to unite and dedicate themselves to fight unceasingly for the rights of our people, and for full dignity of Black womanhood. For three days the Sojourners held forth. A special appointment was made with Maceo Hubbard in the Civil Rights Section of the Justice Department. Mr. Hubbard, a Black, appeared painfully disturbed as sixty Black women entered his office while a single white government official stood with folded arms, surveying the group. A number of women had their say, and when they had finished, we felt a bit sorry for Mr. Hubbard, sitting behind the big desk, making it easier for some white official who was guilty of the crimes we related.

"Be sure to get Alphaeus on that plane," was the last remark I heard as I left New York to bring him home. A large delegation would be at the airport to greet him the following day, and to miss the scheduled flight would have been unthinkable. With one month off for good behavior, Alphaeus was released on December 9th.

The excitement of preparing for the trip, two sleepless nights, and the mixup and confusion among the friends who were to take us to the airport had left me in a frightful dither. I wanted to look my best and feel even better, but I felt and looked my worst. When the plane took off, I too took off, right in the paper bag before me for some relief. Little did my friend realize how sick I was, when she said, "For God's sake, Dorothy, smile," and presented me with a beautiful bouquet of red roses. I did try. It was Alphaeus's day, and I rejoiced in his return, but I thought any minute I would buckle under.

More than a hundred black and white friends greeted Alphaeus as he stepped off the plane at LaGuardia Airport in a misty rain. "Welcome home, Dr. Hunton," they cried. Some carried placards acclaiming him a

"Defender of the Bill of Rights." The present thrust in his hand by his friend and co-worker Dr. Herbert Aptheker delighted him. It was a copy of the *Documentary History of the Negro People* he had compiled, and which the Federal Prison Authorities in Petersburg refused to let him receive when it came in the mail.

"I wanted this book—with its priceless speeches and writings by Frederick Douglass and other great spokesmen of freedom, very, very, badly," Alphaeus said. "But the wardens thought it was too inflammatory, and feared it would cause a race riot if many of the prisoners read it. Many of the prisoners were sharecroppers and workers. They were very friendly and sympathetic and promised to help in the struggle for their people when they got out."

In late December, the Sojourners organized a reception for Alphaeus and me at Small's Paradise in Harlem. It was an evening of rejoicing; a moving event that I recall to mind with warmth and pleasure.

Disregarding my entreaties to stay home a few days to get himself together, Alphaeus wasted no time in returning to the office. A stickler for duty and the sanctity of obligations, he knew that may critical issues had developed in Africa during his absence, and he was eager to resume his work, always the pivot of his life.

"I'm glad to be back with you," he wrote in the first issue of *Spotlight on Africa* after his return. "It has been indeed heart-warming to receive the greetings and good wishes of many Council members and friends since my return to New York from my enforced 'vacation' . . . I want to take this means of saying, Hello to all you near and far, including especially my friends and colleagues in many sections of Africa.

"I come back to what prison inmates call the 'free world'—a world in which things are getting more and more difficult for the imperialist overlords. As we in the Council have long forseen, the explosive national resistance to foreign domination has spread from Asia to Africa. What does this mean to us in the United States? Plenty!"

The brutal armed suppression of the National Liberation Movements in Tunisia and Morocco was in full swing when Alphaeus returned. After two hours of picketing in support of the demand for Tunisian freedom and Security Council action to prevent an outbreak of war in North Africa, Alphaeus led a large delegation to the French Consul. In the meantime, South Africa's ten million non-whites continued their struggle through the heroic **Campaign of Defiance of Unjust Laws** during 1952.

In response to an urgent appeal from South Africa for aid of the children and families of more than 8,000 men and women who were sent to jail, during the campaign the Council collected and forwarded $2,500. Alphaeus also organized a picket line in front of the South African Consulate and the South African Delegation to the U.N. It was in connection with the campaign that he wrote the pamphlet, *Resistance with a Postscript for Americans.*

Scarcely a day passed where he did not grapple with some problem somewhere in Africa. South Africa had always been in the forefront, with the situation growing more acute daily. Now, Kenya. The basic cause of the conflict there was precisely the same. In February, 1944, Alphaeus wrote an article in the bulletin *What about Kenya?* in which he described the East African colony, twice the size of Great Britain and Ireland, as "one of the most extreme of Africa's sore spots." A vital part of Britain's extensive African empire, they constantly cracked down on any African organization united for self-rule. **The Kenya African Union** was the latest target; founded in 1944, it became the greatest movement for the Africans. Now, on October 21, 1952, its President, Jomo Kenyatta, and other leaders, had been arrested and a state of emergency was declared.

Britain's "dirty war" in Kenya was a long and brutal one. They used the suppression of the violent insurrection "Mau Mau," as an excuse of the most horrendous, genocidal crimes against the Kikuyu people. Alphaeus planned an all-day working conference (April 24, 1954) in Harlem, which resulted in a program of assistance, and setting up the **National Aid Committee.** Street corner meetings were held in order to give the busy Harlemite a vivid picture of events happening to his brothers and sisters in Kenya. He must be made to see the connection between colonialism and Jim Crow, and the common objectives for which Kenya Africans and Blacks in Mississippi and Harlem struggled.

For more than two hours speaker after speaker took the microphone and spoke their minds. The response was good. Passersby stayed to listen, bought "Africa Must Be Free" buttons, copies of the bulletin, and anything else concerning Africa. The meetings demonstrated the people's ready support for the Council's program to **Aid to Kenya Africans** if only they could get the truth, and know **how** to help.

With all the monumental problems confronting Alphaeus in running the organization, an additional one was added in June 1955. After months of harassment and investigations, the Council began its legal fight to continue functioning. The Federal Grand Jury in Washington subpoenaed Alphaeus to appear October 7, 1955. He had to present all correspondence with the African National Congress, and the South African Indian Congress, which jointly led the struggle in South Africa. As if that were not enough, they demanded all other correspondence from 1946 to 1955, all records of funds sent abroad, and all materials published or disseminated by the Council during the same nine year period.

The jury quizzed Alphaeus at length regarding funds and food sent to relieve the South African famine in 1946-7, and funds sent to aid the dependents of those jailed during the **Campaign of Defense of Unjust Laws.** The Grand Jury said it was concerned with whether the activities represented violation of the Foreign Registration Act.

Alphaeus replied that the Council of African Affairs had never been the agent of any foreign principal, and consequently had never considered the question of registration as such. The real issue in the case, he said, was the moral question of whether it was right or wrong for Americans to give assistance to Africans suffering and in dire need. The Justice Department counsel gave a clue to the underlying purpose of the proceedings, when he asked why Negroes in America should feel that they have any common cause with the people of Africa, and why the Council maintained that the U.S. Government should give no further loans or other aid to the South African Government. Those questions Alphaeus answered in no uncertain terms.

For three years after his release from prison, Alphaeus fought a losing battle with the government in defense of the right to advocate and support the cause of African freedom. Never endowed with a working fund, the non-partisan, non-profit Council on African Affairs (C.A.A.) ran solely on contributions, and was staffed mostly with volunteer help. Few volunteers were available for the many pressing office tasks, and Alphaeus found himself practically a one-man organization, persevering under the most trying conditions and working late into the night without pay. Though he never confided his anguish to me, I knew his heart was overcast with despair, while he tried unsuccessfully to disguise his inner feelings. It was infinitely more painful for me to watch him literally drag himself to the office day after day, being stripped of vitality and enthusiasm for life, than to experience it myself.

Yet, as I watched his shoulders droop more and more, and his steps began to falter, my anxiety for him mounted. Finally I could stand it no longer. "African freedom or no African freedom," I screamed, "it's sense-less to kill yourself from overwork, no matter how important the cause." As we sat on the divan trying to sort out our thoughts and emotions, after my sudden outburst, the silence deepened. Alphaeus lifted his tired, drained face, and his dark brown eyes, filled with sorrow, sought mine for a fleeting moment, as if in search for an answer to my unex-pected flareup. Slowly he drew me close and gently kissed my tears away, and in his quiet soft voice, calmly but firmly promised to stop.

At the Executive Board meeting June 14, 1955, to decide whether the Council should continue, Alphaeus reviewed the organization's work during his twelve years of activity. He stressed the importance of the pioneering character of the work. It had been the only organization of its type in the United States giving full attention to the African people's problems and struggles.

He then traced the reason for the rapid growth of American interest in Africa since 1952, which was reflected in popular and scholarly jour-nals and books, in academic and governmental circles, and in the emer-gence of new organizations with aims and programs of work similar to those of the Council. He spoke of the heightened concern with African and colonial problems on the part of Black organizations with other main interests.

"In view of the changed situation and the possibility of American support for the African people's freedom being expressed through a wide range of other existing groups," Alphaeus noted, "the Council is no longer needed to stimulate American interest in Africa as in the earlier period of its work and it should accordingly be dissolved."

He stated also that "continuing government harassment of the organ-ization had made it difficult if not impossible for it to function." He cited the various investigations to which the Council's finances and affairs had been subjected, and the intolerable strain which would be placed upon it by the hearing before the Subversive Activities Control Board, scheduled to start July 11.

Even so, Alphaeus said he would "recommend continuing to fight for the right to function, were it not for the considerations previously cited." Looking at the problem as a whole, he was convinced that dissolution of the Council was the only sensible course.

Thus Alphaeus ended twelve years of service to the organization and to the cause of African liberation in the face of great difficulties and personal sacrifice. He had tenaciously kept the faith, and had become a victim, along with countless others, of five years of demagogic hysteria, which found its outlet in hate, mistrust, and intolerance that in turn poisoned every facet of American life.

The closing down of the Council did not mean, however, that Alphaeus was giving up the fight, despite the pressures and blows from those who feared his voice as well as his existence. As Paul Robeson said, "Having done all, stand!" That Alphaeus did. It was a sad commentary on our times that one of the few organizations devoted to fighting the evils of colonialism had been red-baited into silence by a gestapo committee, which claimed a monopoly on what they termed "Americanism."

Letters poured in from wellwishers at home and abroad, expressing sadness regarding the dissolution of the Council. Alphaeus was gratified by the warm response. He had done all that was humanly possible to give the movement for African freedom momentum, and his unselfish and effective devotion to a momentous cause would not be forgotten.

In this desolate period of Alphaeus's life, dramatic developments were taking place in Asia and particularly Africa, which was no longer the "Dark Continent" but instead aglow, and in some places afire. He had been unable to attend the historic Asian-African Conference at Bandung, Indonesia, in April 1955, because of the critical situation surrounding the Council and its imminent closing. However, the powerful impact of the representatives of more than two-thirds of the world's population struggling against colonialism and racialism and in the interest of peace, prompted him to dedicate the last two issues of the bulletin April–May, 1955 to the conference.

A survey of the African press gave the impression that the subject was less publicized and discussed there than in the United States. It was not because of the African's apathy. The curtain of censorship and repression with which the rulers of Africa sought to keep its people isolated from the mainstream of world affairs—except when needed to fight European wars—was responsible.

To the African and Asian, the opposition to color discrimination is so deeply felt that nations, otherwise at odds, unite regardless of divisive ideologies, particularly when they have shared misery and humiliation. They met to impress on the world that it is possible to live together, meet together, speak to each other, without losing one's identity, and yet contribute to the understanding of matters of common concern. It was possible to develop a true consciousness of the interdependence of men and nations for their well-being and survival of the earth.

Bandung was a shining light and a landmark in the annals of civilization. It reflected the determination of the Asian and African people to be done with Western dictation, and their determination to think for themselves and decide their own destiny. That Third World alignment struck fear in the minds of the white imperialist nations, and it continues to have repercussions today.

42

In Retrospect: An Attack—An Answer
Charlotta Bass

Forty Years: Memoirs from the Pages of a Newspaper (Los Angeles: C. A. Bass, 1960), pp. 185–6

While working on this book I received the following letter, dated August 14, 1956.

"Dear Mrs. Bass:

"At the National Executive Board meeting of Iota Phi Lambda Sorority, held in Toledo, Ohio, on August 10, 1956, it was brought to the attention of the National Executive Board of said organization that your name has been listed in many connections in the Sixth Report on Un-American Activities in California, 1951.

"On August 16, 1956, the National Executive Board investigated said report and then acted upon this accusation and thereupon rescinded the honorary membership given you by Iota Phi Lambda Sorority in 1948 because of the foregoing.

"It is therefore, with deep regret, that I inform you that the honorary membership awarded you by the Iota Phi Lambda Sorority in 1948 has been and is hereby rescinded as such activities do not exemplify the ideals and aims of Iota Lambda Sorority since the listing of your name in many connections and activities are deemed to be unfavorable to good American Citizenship.

"Iota Phi Lambda Sorority therefore requests that you return to me the sorority pin given you at the time the honorary membership was conferred upon you, and that hereafter you desist and refrain from representing yourself as a member, honorary or otherwise, of Iota Phi Lambda Sorority or participating in any way in its activities."

The reception of such a letter brought neither shock nor surprise. As a matter of fact, it did not even emotionally disturb my ulcers. As I observed its contents, I primed my memory, which brought me to the point of looking up old records. My answer to my one-time "sisters" follows:

"No, I have never been investigated by that real un-American Activities Committee that stems from the National Capitol and swoops down on Los Angeles or Hollywood every so often, plunging its fangs into some activity, in either of those two cities, which it does not approve.

"But now I remember, back in 1948, I, along with many other citizens, some prominent, others not, was called to testify before the Senator Jack Tenney Committee.

"I wondered and am still wondering why my sisters—pardon me, Sorors! For that 'Sister' usage was a slip—allowed all this lapse of time before they began investigating!

"I realized that in your estimation, Sorors, I am a social and political outcast, and I accept my status in all humility.

"But what I started to say, is this: I did not seek admission to your organization. Back in 1948, when I published a newspaper and could be of service to your organization, you sought my co-operation and, of such as I had, I gave freely.

"It was in this same year, 1948, that Senator Jack Tenney called me to testify before his Committee. I answered his call and freely answered his questions, among which was 'Are you a Communist?' To this question, at that time, and should the same question be asked of me now, my answer was and would be: 'If you will explain the meaning of "Communist," I shall, according to my understanding, answer your question.'

"I would now ask you a question, Sorors. Why did Iota Phi Lambda wait nearly ten years to find out that my record of Un-American activities makes me unfit to be a member of your Sorority?

"This discovery should have been made, and applied, before you decorated me with an honorary membership. And, if my memory serves me correctly, in 1956 you invited me to be present and hailed me as your first selected honorary member at the Annual Meeting of the Sorority held the early part of the year in the Watkins Hotel. At that time, you mentioned some certain services I had done for the organization. You pinned a corsage on me. All of these favors, with others, I am proud to remember.

"But I am forced to remind you that a Greek Letter organization with your educational potential, should investigate the characters and reputations of persons before taking them into your sacred fold.

"I am sorry, but the pin you gave me was lost somewhere in Europe in 1950. Hence, in this case, I can only offer to pay for it.

"Back to the Senator Tenney investigation: If you will read the Fourth Report on Un-American Activities in California, you will discover that I was not the only victim of Jack Tenney's attack. Many law-abiding loyal Americans, both Negro and white, fell under the political lash of this man who, under the guise of public service, used his high office to punish these citizens who believed in and spoke out for freedom and justice for all Americans.

"During what may be described as Senator Tenney's reign of terror in and around Los Angeles, many important citizens and organizations were called to answer charges sprouted and grown out of Jack Tenney's morbid imagination.

"On Sunday, October 8, 1944, The American Youth for Democracy staged a Teenage Mock Congress at the Virgil Junior High School. The sponsors and consultants of the Congress were: Judge John Beardsley, Mrs. Harry Braverman, Reuben Borough, Dr. Ernest Caldecott, Philip M. Connelly, Dr. Franklin Fearing, Kenneth Howard, Mrs. Lucie McCollie, Carey McWilliams, Oscar Pattiz. William Pomerance, Earl Robinson, Everett Will and myself.

"Again, December 31, 1944, the American Youth for Democracy birthday fete was celebrated at the Roosevelt Hotel, Hollywood. Rex Ingram, Rev. J Raymond Henderson and Willis J. Hill were mentioned as supporters of the affair. The sponsors were: Mrs. Fay E. Allen, Floyd C. Covington, Rev. Clayton D. Russell, Dr. Ruth Temple, Mrs. Jessie L. Terry and myself.

"At a conference on 'Thought Control' held in the Beverly Hills Hotel, July 9, 1947, sponsored by the Arts, Sciences and Professions, I with fifty other individuals, was invited to read a short paper on various phases of thought control, together with suggestions on the strategy and tactics to be used in fighting the persecution by government committees.

"Among others who presented papers, were: Henry Wallace, Harlow Shapley, Norman Corwin, John Cromwell, Frank Kingdon, Morris E. Cohn, Sam Moore, Darr Smith, Milton S. Tyre, Harold Orr, Paul Draper, Ann Revere, Donald Ogden Stewart and Hugh de Lacy.

"In his report on Un-American Activities on this and subsequent meetings of like nature, Senator Jack Tenney accused the organization, its affiliates, and the speakers, of being Communists or Communist-front sympathizers.

"Among the prominent Negroes mentioned in the Tenney report were: Dr. Charlotte Hawkins Brown, Rev. J. C. Coleman, Earl P. Dickerson, Dr. W. E. B. Du Bois, and Langston Hughes. The writers the report accused of being pro-Communist were: Pearl S. Buck, Leland Stowe, Anna Louise Strong, Dr. Will H. Alexander, Adam Clayton Powell and Vito Marcantonio.

"In the Civil Rights Congress, it mentioned: Dr. H. Claude Hudson, Hugh MacBeth, Jr., Judge Stanley Moffatt, Artie Shaw, Louise Beavers, Dr. P. Price Cobbs, Rev. J. Raymond Henderson and myself.

"The Citizen's Committee for Better Education was supported by extreme leftists, so the report said, and fronted in 1947 for the election of Dr. H. Claude Hudson to the Board of Education. Dr. Hudson had been active in a number of Communist-front organizations, the report said. Dr. Hudson was also mentioned as the sponsor of a dinner that netted $15,110.00 to defend the 'Hollywood Ten.'

"I was accused of signing a letter to 'The People's World' in March, 1948, in defense of Ferdinand C. Smith. In reply to this accusation I said, 'I have signed many letters. I was especially interested in Claudia Jones because I believed her to be a victim of color prejudice, emphasized by the fact that she dared to be a liberal.'

"Daniel G. Marshall, Chairman of the Catholic Interracial Council and Vice Chairman of the Southern California Committee for a State FEPC and a member of the National Lawyer's Guild, was accused of being pro-Communist in February, 1948. In this same report, it was stated that Loren Miller, Los Angels Negro attorney, wrote for 'New Masses', and was a member of the John Reed Club and the Los Angeles Chapter of the National Lawyer's Guild.

"The American Jewish Congress held its conference in the Biltmore Hotel, February 7 and 8, 1948. Those who participated in the conference were: Daniel G. Marshall, Loren Miller, Mrs. Fred C. Pollock, William Strong, Marguerite Weiss, Nita Blackwell, Leon Clifford, Eleanor Grennard, Charles J. Katz, Milton Tyre, Philip Connolly, Mrs. Emanuel Kotkin, Dr. Franklin Fearing, Jaime Gonzales, Mrs. Milton Harris, Wellesley Aron, Rabbi Jehudah M. Cohen and Mrs. Phyllis Ziffren.

"All these were listed as pro-Communist. Rabbi Max Nussbaum was also given the 'red' smear because he sponsored a meeting of the American Youth for Democracy.

"Katherine Hepburn was smeared by the Tenney Committee when she dared to denounce certain major political parties and officials such as J. Parnell Thomas, Attorney General Tom Clark and others of the political hierarchy, when addressing a meeting in the Gilmore Stadium on 'Thought Control.'

"Senator Tenney said her speech was probably written by one of the 'red' writers in the Screen Writers Guild.

"Listed as Communist-front organizations in the 1948 report of Senator Jack Tenney were: The A.F. of L., C.I.O., and other trade union organizations, the American Legion, Disabled American Veterans, Veterans of Foreign Wars, the Amvets, the American Veterans Committee (the California section of the American Veterans Committee, it said, falls into the Communist dominated class and is a vociferous, dissident minority in National AVC affairs), many groups of the Democratic Party and also some of the Republican Party, the National Association for the Advancement of Colored People, the Bar Association and Medical Association.

"Miss Nita Blackwell, former secretary of the NAACP, was quoted in this report as saying that 150,000 Negroes who had recently come to Los Angeles were being crowded into filthy ghettoes and suffered from police brutality, which was true.

"I, with others, was reported as supporting the candidacy of Mrs. LaRue McCormick for the State Senate in 1948. In reply to this report I said, 'My support in this case was on the premise that women had the same right to aspire to high office as men.'

"In the face of these facts, it seems to me now that Iota Phi Lambda Sorority, its officers and members, have succumbed to a certain political propaganda employed by such organizations as the Ku Klux Klan, the White Citizens' Council, the Anti-Segregationists, race supremacists, bigots, who are determined to keep Negroes second-class citizens and submissive to their will."

In this book I have sketched the part played by THE CALIFORNIA EAGLE during my forty years administration. Many of the things I fought so hard for are not yet fully realized by some American citizens. I have never been, and am not now concerned about what the Jack Tenney Committee or his successors think of my loyalty to my country and government. But I am concerned about what this Negro sorority thinks. I am concerned because I know their problem is also my problem. It springs from the same source. My letter continues:

"I am sure that, if weighed in the same balance with yours, Sorors, my love of and loyalty to my country would not be less sincere than yours; as a matter of fact, when you use the Tenney Committee as a measuring rod to determine my loyalty and love of country, you are playing into the hands of the Eastlands, the Russells, the Walters, the McCarrans, the Gerald L. K. Smiths, and all the enemies of democracy; of those who refuse to obey the highest court's decision and order to desegregate the schools of the country; those who *promise* in glowing rhetoric in political campaigns to pass a Civil Rights measure making it possible for Negro citizens to vote in all the states of our United States of America, by throwing around them the legal protection obstructed by the unwritten 'lynch law' and mob rule to defend those who are trying to make the prescribed laws a reality.

"No, I am not mad. But I am sad, when I look around and see what it happening to us—to you and me.

"The policy of segregation and discrimination is a unique pattern, cut and applied especially for and to Negro citizens in continental U.S.A.

"I invite Iota Phi Lambda Sorority to look at the present handwriting on the wall in the year of our Lord, 1957.

"Take a look at your 85th Congress. For weeks, even months, a grand tussle has been in progress in the two law-making bodies of the nation. Men, some grave, some grinning, and others frowning, try to decide how to get around the long promised passage of a Civil Rights Law. Every day, week and month that these 'loyal' representatives of the people sit and wrangle costs the taxpayers money. Are these too big and strong for you to tackle? Individuals like myself are the object of your scorn and your determination to destroy—words are often sharper than swords.

"I am not ashamed to say that I gave forty years of devoted service in an effort to impress upon my government that as long as sixteen million sable-hued Americans are half-free, ours cannot be considered a free nation. It has been said that as long as there remains one slave in a country, that country is not free.

"In answer to your would-be attack on my loyalty, I shall endeavor to give you some of the facts that invited the investigation in my case.

"The Tenney Committee questioned me closely about my name being printed on the stationery of the American Youth for Democracy and the

298   The Struggle Continues: White Supremacy and Anticommunism

Junior NAACP. During the formation of both of these youth organizations, small groups came and solicited my encouragement and support. I gave this freely. Both groups held meetings in THE EAGLE office, particularly the Junior NAACP, which was organized under the leadership of my nephew, John Kinloch.

"At the first meeting, how well I remember that among the more than fifty young people who gathered around the punch bowl of pink lemonade and cookies I provided for them, were the upturned, smiling faces of Gertrude and Lillian Lomax! The only adults at the first meeting were Mrs. Ida Brandon and myself. It was a gathering of young people, planning a future course of action in the community in which they lived, that would guarantee them all the rights and privileges enjoyed by other Americans in the local universities, colleges, schools, and public places of recreation and resort.

"As an American, I have never been, nor would I ever be, a part of or party to any organization that had as its aim the overthrow of my government. I am not ashamed, nor do I regret, what I did for these groups of young people, or what I have been able to contribute to my country my attempt to arouse my people, and all Americans, to a greater realization of the part we must play together to make ours a free democratic nation, and to set the pace for world peace."

"Gems of hate cut through glass,
Time or space, rank or class;
Spreaders most feel their pass!"
— Foster Heart.

Notes

Introduction

1 "Get on Board the Freedom Train: Proceedings of the Founding of the National Negro Labor Council," Cincinnati, October 28, 1951.

2 Lydia Lindsey, "Black Lives Matter: Grace P. Campbell and Claudia Jones—An Analysis of the Negro Question, Self-Determination, Black Belt Thesis," *Africology: The Journal of Pan-African Studies* 12, no. 10 (March 2019): 117.

3 Claudia Jones, *An End to the Neglect of the Problems of the Negro Woman!* (New York: National Women's Commission, CPUSA, 1949).

4 By "Communist-adjacent," we mean women who belonged to organizations in the Communist orbit, who worked alongside or in collaboration with the CPUSA, and/or who were fellow travelers, but who never officially became members.

5 See Dayo F. Gore, *Radicalism at the Crossroads: African American Women Activists in the Cold War* (New York: New York University Press, 2011); LaShawn Harris, "Running with the Reds: African American Women and the Communist Party During the Great Depression," *Journal of African American History* 94, no. 1 (2009): 21–43; Gerald Horne and Margaret Stevens, "Shirley Graham Du Bois: Portrait of the Black Woman Artist as Revolutionary," in *Want to Start a Revolution?* ed. Jeanne Theoharis et al. (New York: New York University Press, 2009), 94–114; Robin D. G. Kelly, *Freedom Dreams: The Black Radical Imagination* (Boston: Beacon Press, 2002); Lydia Lindsey, "Black Lives Matter: Grace P. Campbell and Claudia Jones—An Analysis of the Negro Question, Self-Determination, and the Black Belt Thesis," *Journal of Pan-African Studies* 12, no. 9 (2019): 110–43; Minkah Makalani, *In the Cause of Freedom: Radical Black Internationalism*

from Harlem to London, 1917–1939 (Chapel Hill: University of North
Carolina Press, 2011); John H. McClendon III, "Claudia Jones (1915–
1964): Political Activist, Black Nationalist, Feminist, Journalist," in
Notable Black American Women, vol. 2, ed. Jessie Carney Smith (Detroit:
Gale Research, 1996), 343–6; Erik S. McDuffie, *Sojourning for Freedom:
Black Women, American Communism, and the Making of Black Left
Feminism* (Durham, NC: Duke University Press, 2011); Mark Naison,
Communists in Harlem During the Great Depressions (Urbana: University
of Illinois Press, 1983); Mark Solomon, *The Cry Was Unity: Communists
and African Americans, 1917–1936* (Jackson: University of Mississippi
Press, 1998); and Mary Helen Washington, *The Other Blacklist: The
African American Literary and Cultural Left of the 1950s* (New York:
Columbia University Press, 2014). On biographies, see Gerald Horne,
Race Woman: The Lives of Shirley Graham Du Bois (New York: New York
University Press, 2000); Gregg Andrews, *Thyra J. Edwards: Black Activist
in the Global Freedom Struggle* (Columbia: University of Missouri Press,
2011); Carole Boyce Davies, *Left of Karl Marx: The Political Life of Black
Communist Claudia Jones Justice* (Durham, NC: Duke University Press,
2007); Keith Gilyard, *Louise Thompson Patterson: A Life of Struggle for
Justice* (Durham, NC: Duke University Press, 2017); Imani Perry, *Looking
for Lorraine: The Radiant and Radical Life of Lorraine Hansberry* (Boston:
Beacon Press, 2018); Barbara Ransby, *Eslanda: The Large and
Unconventional Life of Mrs. Paul Robeson* (New Haven, CT: Yale University
Press, 2013); and Sara Rzeszutek, *James and Esther Cooper Jackson: Love
and Courage in the Black Freedom Movement* (Lexington: University Press
of Kentucky, 2015).
6 See Charisse Burden-Stelly, "Claudia Jones, the Longue Durée of
McCarthyism, and the Threat of US Fascism," *Journal of Intersectionalities*
3, no. 1 (Summer 2019): 46–66.
7 McDuffie, *Sojourning for Freedom*, 191–2; Gore, *Radicalism at the
Crossroads*, 132–3.
8 See Gore's account of the organizing around the Ingram case, *Radicalism
at the Crossroads*, ch. 3. Gore illuminates the wide array of groups and
tactics involved in the struggle. These included the Civil Rights Congress
(a party-affiliated legal defense organization), its National Committee to
Free the Ingram Family, the United Women's Committee to Save the
Ingram Family, the Women's Committee for Equal Justice, Sojourners for
Truth and Justice, and publications such as Paul Robeson's *Freedom*
newspaper.
9 "Reds Try to Stir Negroes to Revolt," *New York Times*, July 28, 1919, p. 4.
10 Charisse Burden-Stelly, "Constructing Deportable Subjectivity:
Antiforeignness, Antiradicalism, and Antiblackness During the
McCarthyist Structure of Feeling," *Souls* 13, no. 3 (2017): 342–58.
11 Mike Gonzalez, "Black Lives Matter Leader Resigns, but This Radical
Marxist Agenda Will Continue," Heritage Foundation, June 4, 2021,

heritage.org; Keeanga-Yamahtta Taylor, "'Wokeism' Is Not the Democrats' Problem," *New Yorker,* November 19, 2021; Andrew Atterbury, "DeSantis Pushes Bill That Allows Parents to Sue Schools over Critical Race Theory," politico.com.

12 Ch. 8, p. 60, this volume. The treatment to which Burroughs is referring concerns a US government invitation to the mothers and widows of soldiers killed in World War I and buried in Europe to make a pilgrimage to visit their graves. These trips—the travel and housing arrangements—were segregated.

13 Quoted in McDuffie, *Sojourning for Freedom,* 108.

14 Ch. 32, p. 224, this volume.

15 Ch. 32, pp. 223–4, this volume.

16 See the discussion in Jodi Dean, *Comrade: An Essay on Political Belonging* (London: Verso, 2019), ch. 2.

17 Ch. 19, p. 154, this volume.

18 Ch. 21, p. 172, this volume.

19 Ch. 22, p. 187, this volume.

20 Ch. 20, p. 170, this volume.

21 Ch. 9, p. 68, this volume.

22 Ch. 10, p. 71, this volume.

23 Ch. 22, p. 195, this volume.

Section I: Struggle in the Early Years

1 Mark Solomon, *The Cry Was Unity: Communists and African Americans, 1917–1936* (Jackson: University Press of Mississippi, 1998), 11, 28.

2 Quoted in Erik S. McDuffie, *Sojourning for Freedom: Black Women, American Communism, and the Making of Black Left Feminism* (Durham, NC: Duke University Press, 2011), 34–5.

3 Minkah Makalani, *In the Cause of Freedom: Radical Black Internationalism from Harlem to London, 1917–1939* (Chapel Hill: University of North Carolina Press, 2011), 148.

4 Minkah Makalani, "An Apparatus for Negro Women: Black Women's Organizing, Communism, and the Institutional Spaces of Radical Pan-African Thought," *Women, Gender, and Families of Color* 4, no. 2 (Fall 2016): 250–73, 262.

5 McDuffie, *Sojourning for Freedom,* 56.

6 Ch. 2, p. 24, this volume.

1. Two Articles on the Women's Day Court

1 The editor's note appears in the original publication. The editor is identified as Maybelle McAdoo.
2 Incomplete in the original.

2. Negro Work Has Not Been Entirely Successful

1 Report submitted as "Mary Adams" before the Comintern Congress. Reel 104, Delo 1366, CPUSA archives, Library of Congress. We are grateful to Minkah Makalani for providing us with this text.

4. Trade Union Work Report

1 Thanks to Minkah Makalani for providing us with this text from the Russian State Archive of Sociopolitical History, fond 495, reel 155, delo 177. For further details on accessing these archival sources, see Minkah Makalani, *In the Cause of Freedom: Radical Black Internationalism from Harlem to London, 1917–1939* (Chapel Hill: University of North Carolina Press, 2011), 271.

5. Three Reports on Negro Women Workers

1 Thanks to Minkah Makalani for providing us with this text from the Russian State Archive of Sociopolitical History, fond 495, reel 155, delo 87. For further details on accessing these archival sources, see Makalani, *In the Cause of Freedom*, 271.

Section II: Organizing, Labor, and Militancy

1 Erik S. McDuffie, *Sojourning for Freedom: Black Women, American Communism, and the Making of Black Left Feminism* (Durham, NC: Duke University Press, 2011), 54.
2 McDuffie, *Sojourning for Freedom*, 65.
3 Ch. 6, p. 48, this volume.
4 Ch. 7, p. 53, this volume.
5 "Dual unionism" was a tactic associated with the Communist Party's "Third Period" analysis of the early 1930s. Looking at the Depression affecting advanced economies across the world, Communists interpreted collapsing

capitalism as heralding a new revolutionary period. From this vantage point, they assessed the AFL as too reformist in its orientation. Communists advocated forwarding demands that would radicalize workers, not just provide incremental improvements in their conditions.

6 Ch. 11, p. 79, this volume.
7 McDuffie, *Sojourning for Freedom*, 100–1; see also McDuffie's discussion of the engagement of Black Communist women with the Spanish Civil War and its importance for their understanding of the links between fascism and women's subordination, p. 109.
8 Ibid., 109.
9 Gregg Andrews, *Thyra J. Edwards: Black Activist in the Global Freedom Struggle* (Columbia: University of Missouri Press, 2011), 105.

11. Attitudes of Negro Families on Relief—Another Opinion

1 In January 1935 there were 13,058,215 unemployed, according to A.F. of L. figures. These figures are of necessity conservative since in the United States there are no central Labor Exchanges or Federal machinery for a continual and accurate check of unemployment figures.
2 These figures are taken from "Incidence Upon the Negro" by Charles S. Johnson, *American Journal of Sociology*, May 1935. Relief statistics of 1933 used as the percentage base for computation.
3 See *The Compass*, February 1936, 10.

16. The Negro Woman Domestic Worker in Relation to Trade Unionism

1 "Domestic Workers in Private Homes," *Social Security Bulletin* 2 (March 1939),12.
2 Ibid., 16.
3 Lucy M. Salmon, *Domestic Service* (New York: Macmillan, 1897), 72.
4 Lorenzo Greene and Carter Woodson, *The Negro Wage Earner* (Washington, DC: Association for the Study of Negro Life and History, 1930), 337.
5 Ibid., 80.
6 Hazel Kyrk, "The Household Worker," *American Federationist* 39 (January 1932): 36.
7 Evelyn Seeley, "Our Feudal Housewives," *Nation* 146 (May 29, 1936): 613.
8 "The Servant Problem," *Fortune* 17 (March 1938): 81–3.
9 *Household Employment, Lynchburg Study, 1936–1937*, Lynchburg, Va., Y.W.C.A., p. 3.
10 *Household Employment in Philadelphia: Women's Bureau Bulletin, No. 93*, U.S. Department of Labor (1932), 7.

11 Unpublished report, "Domestic Workers," Social Security Board (1936, 1937, 1938).
12 Washington State, 60-Hour Bill. I.W.C. Order No. 33, Industrial Welfare Committee, Washington.
13 Wisconsin Minimum Wage Regulation, C-5a Industrial Commission, Wisconsin.
14 Leila Doman, "Legislation in the Field of Household Employment," *Journal of Home Economics* 39 (February 1939): 92.
15 Salmon, *Domestic Service*, 158.
16 "A Domestic Employees Union," *Woman's Press* 8 (September 1934), 421.
17 *The Need of Organization Among Household Workers*, Negro Workers' Council, National Urban League (May 1937), 6.

Section III: Fighting Fascism

1 Ch. 17, p. 137, this volume.
2 Ch. 18, p. 150, this volume.
3 We are grateful to Erik Gellner for providing us with this manuscript and for his expert historical sleuthing. See also Dayo F. Gore, *Radicalism at the Crossroads: African American Women Activists in the Cold War* (New York: New York University Press, 2011), 59.
4 Jadwiga E. Pieper Mooney makes a powerful argument for the importance of the WIDF and the anticommunism and Cold War binarism that resulted in its scholarly neglect: "Fighting Fascism and Forging New Political Activism: The Women's International Democratic Federation (WIDF) in the Cold War," in *De-Centering Cold War History: Local and Global Change*, ed. Fabio Lanza and Jadwiga E. Pieper Mooney (Abingdon, UK: Taylor & Francis, 2012), 52–72.

18. Reconversion and the Negro People

1 *Negro Workers After the War* (New York: National Negro Congress, 1945).
2 Dr. Robert C. Weaver, *Seniority and the Negro Worker* (Chicago: American Council on Race Relations, 1945).
3 See *Southern Frontier*, issued by Southern Regional Council—June and July issues, 1945, and Wm. A. Caudill's *The Negro G.I. Comes Back* (Chicago: American Council on Race Relations, 1945). [*Negro G.I.'s Come Back*: ed.]

19. On the Right to Self-Determination for the Negro People in the Black Belt

1 Joseph Stalin, *Marxism and the National and Colonial Question* (New York: International Publishers, 1942), 8.

Section IV: Winning Peace at Home and Abroad

1 See Dayo F. Gore, *Radicalism at the Crossroads: African American Women Activists in the Cold War* (New York: New York University Press, 2011).
2 Ibid., 115–17.
3 Garvin is extending an argument that Cyril Briggs made in the *Crusader* in the 1920s; Briggs proposed as an "acid test of white friendship" the question of whether a white person was willing to see Black people kill white people in defense of Black rights. See Jodi Dean, *Comrade: An Essay on Political Belonging* (London: Verso, 2019), 44–5.
4 Ch. 25, p. 205, this volume.
5 Imani Perry, *Looking for Lorraine: The Radiant and Radical Life of Lorraine Hansberry* (Boston: Beacon Press, 2018), 47.
6 Ibid., 57.
7 Erik S. McDuffie, *Sojourning for Freedom: Black Women, American Communism, and the Making of Black Left Feminism* (Durham, NC: Duke University Press, 2011), 173.
8 Carole Boyce Davies, *Left of Karl Marx: The Political Life of Black Communist Claudia Jones* (Durham, NC: Duke University Press, 2008), 214. "On the Right to Self-Determination for the Negro People in the Black Belt" was also listed, Davies, p. 212.
9 Ch. 22, p. 195, this volume.
10 Ch. 32, p. 224, this volume.

Section V: The Struggle Continues: White Supremacy and Anticommunism

1 Ch. 33, p. 241, this volume.
2 Ch. 33, p. 250, this volume.
3 Ch. 34, p. 253, this volume
4 Jadwiga E. Pieper Mooney details how treatment of the WIDF as a communist front group has led to its being neglected as a site of women's international organizational power: "Fighting Fascism and Forging New Political Activism: The Women's International Democratic Federation (WIDF) in the Cold War," in *De-Centering Cold War History: Local and Global Change,*

ed. Fabio Lanza and Jadwiga E. Pieper Mooney (Abingdon, UK: Taylor & Francis, 2012), 52–72.

5 Mary Helen Washington, *The Other Blacklist: The African American Literary and Cultural Left of the 1950s* (New York: Columbia University Press, 2014), 146.

6 Ibid.

7 Ch. 38, p. 268, this volume.

8 Ch. 41, p. 288, this volume.

Index

Robinson, Earl, 294
Rochester, New York, 110
Roosevelt, Franklin D., 49, 129, 131, 133,
    135, 138, 141, 168
Russak, Mary, 213
Russell, Clayton D., 294
Russia, 82, 253, 258–9
Russia/Soviet Union, 82, 138, 192–3, 253,
    258–9
Ryan, Neva, 72

S
San Diego, California, 112–13
San Diego Domestic Employees' Union,
    113
Sargeant, Winthrop, 184
"Save the Peace-Outlaw the A-Bomb" peace
    ballot, 182
Schulze Baking company, 55
Schwartz and Dorfman shop, 46
Scottsboro Boys, 5, 44, 91–102, 242
Scranton, Pennsylvania, 117–18
Scrota, Roslyn, 77
seamen, Negro, 135
Seamen's Union, 29
searching party, 82
Seattle General Strike, 8
Section VII Blue Discharge, 147
segregation, 101–2, 162, 224
self-determination, 158–9, 160, 161, 162,
    164
Sellins, Fanny, 191
seniority, 143–4, 145
sentencing, 19–20
separation, 158–9
service industry, 274. See also domestic
    service/domestic workers
sewing industry, 85
sex antagonism, 11
sex discrimination, 165
sex work, 13
Shafik, Doria, 207
shame, 258
Shapley, Harlow, 294
sharecroppers, 34, 70, 154, 217–19
Shaw, Artie, 295
Shepherd, Samuel, 208, 227
Simpson Avenue, Bronx, New York, 62–9
Sims, Annie Warren, 209
Sims, George, 209
skilled trades, 52
slave labour, 34
slavery, 104–5
Smith, Bessie, 178, 220–2
Smith, Darr, 294
Smith, Elsie, 191
Smith, Ferdinand C., 295

Smith, Howard W., 236
Smith Act, 179, 236, 252, 266, 282
Social-Democrats, 159, 161, 162
social insurance, domestic worker exclusion
    from, 110–11
Socialism, 160–1, 188, 192–3
Socialist Women's Congress, 59
Social Security Act, 111
social services, 173, 175
social workers, 79
Sojourners for Truth and Justice (STJ), 179,
    180, 202–3, 204–5, 208–9, 285
Sopkins, Ben J., 49–58
South. See also Black Belt
    capital investments within, 163
    challenges within, 149
    conditions of, 32
    domestic work within, 105–6, 114
    education within, 39
    industrialization within, 163
    legislation within, 155
    organization within, 276–7
    semi-slavery within, 155
    voting exclusion within, 169
    wages within, 38, 108
    war orders within, 163
South Africa, 36, 253, 254, 287
South African Indian Congress, 288
South America, 33
South Carolina, 217
South Chicago, Illinois, 189
Southern Negro Youth Congress
    character building within, 137
    Citizens Committee for Army Welfare of,
        134
    financing of, 139–40
    generational connections within, 139
    James Jackson and, 246–7
    leadership training school for, 136
    leadership within, 133
    membership within, 128, 139
    motto of, 243
    organizational problems within, 139
    origin of, 127, 242–3
    printed material from, 129
recreation within, 137
South Nashville Civic League, 115
South Women's Days Workers' Union, 29
Soviet Union/Russia, 82, 138, 192–3, 253,
    258–9
Spain, 87–90, 89
Spengler, Oswald, 184
Stalin, Joseph, 6, 82, 191–2
Stanly, Nellie, 281
Stanton, Elizabeth Cady, 191
starvation, 257
State Industrial Commission, 111

About the Contributors

Ella Baker (1903–86). Born in Virginia. Major activist in the civil rights movement of the 1960s: organizer with the National Association for the Advancement of Colored People (NAACP), the Southern Christian Leadership Conference (SCLC), the Mississippi Freedom Democratic Party; mentor to the Student Nonviolent Coordinating Committee (SNCC). In the 1930s Baker was active in the Harlem Communist milieu, opposing the Italian fascist invasion of Ethiopia and supporting the Scottsboro Boys campaign. Honored with a US postage stamp in 2009.

Charlotta Bass (1874–1969). Owner and publisher of the *California Eagle*, the most influential Black newspaper on the West Coast for nearly forty years. First African American woman to be a candidate for vice president of the United States (nominated by the Progressive Party in 1952). Had leadership roles in Los Angeles branches of the United Negro Improvement Association (founded by Marcus Garvey) and the NAACP. National chair of Sojourners for Truth and Justice (STJ). Under constant FBI surveillance as a suspected Communist although she was not a member of the party.

Dorothy Burnham (1915–). Lifelong activist and organizer with the Communist Party. Attended Brooklyn College. Taught biology at City University of New York. Education coordinator for the Southern Negro Youth Congress. Married to CPUSA leader Louis E. Burnham. On the board of *Freedomways* magazine. Leader in multiple organizations, including Women for Racial and Economic Equality, Women's International League for Peace and Freedom, and Sisters Against South African Apartheid.

Williana Burroughs (1882–1945). Born in Virginia to a formerly enslaved mother. Attended Hunter College. Teacher in New York City public schools. Recruited into the Communist wing of the New York City Teachers Union. Joined the Workers Party (Communist) in 1926. Served as a delegate to Comintern's Sixth Congress. Wrote for the *Daily Worker* under the name Mary Adams. Active in Harlem Tenants League and the League of Struggle for Negro Rights. Director of the Harlem Workers School. Enrolled her children in school in Leningrad so that they would not have to grow up in a racist society. Worked for ten years at Radio Moscow.

Grace P. Campbell (1883–1943). Born in Georgia. Worked as a parole officer, court attendant, and social worker. Active in New York City politics. Cofounder of the African Blood Brotherhood, the American West-Indian Association, the People's Educational Forum, the 21st Assembly Branch of the Socialist Party, and the Harlem branch of the Workers Party (Communist). Left the party in 1929. Leader of Harlem's Tenants League. First woman to run for public office in New York State.

Alice Childress (1916–94). Born in South Carolina; her family moved to New York when she was a child. Successful actor, novelist, and playwright. Influential in the Harlem Left. Active in the progressive Negro Theatre Youth League of the Federal Theatre Project. Part of the American Negro Theatre cooperative (which included Sidney Poitier, Harry Belafonte, Ruby Dee, and Ossie Davis). Columnist for Paul Robeson's *Freedom* magazine. According to her FBI file, a member of the Communist Party (as well as the Civil Rights Congress, Congress of American Women, Sojourners for Truth and Justice, and other Communist-adjacent organizations). Blacklisted in 1956.

Marvel Cooke (1903–2000). Born in Minnesota; graduated from University of Minnesota in 1925. Worked for W. E. B. Du Bois at *Crisis* (the magazine of the NAACP). Actively engaged in the Harlem Renaissance. Worked to draw attention to conditions facing Black women domestic workers. Reporter for the *Amsterdam News* where she organized the first union of Black workers at a Black newspaper. Later worked at the *People's Voice* and the *Daily Compass*. Member of the Communist Party. Called to testify in the McCarthy hearings.

Esther Cooper Jackson (1917–). Born in Virginia. Studied at Oberlin and Fisk. Joined the Communist Party in 1939. Executive secretary of the Southern Negro Youth Congress, headquartered in Birmingham, Alabama. Founding and managing editor of *Freedomways* (1961–85), a magazine important for building connections between Black communists active during the Popular Front era and the next generation of activists in the struggle for Black liberation.

Thelma Dale Perkins (1915–2014). Born in Washington, DC; attended Howard University. Cofounder of the Southern Negro Youth Congress. National secretary of National Negro Congress. Member of the Communist Party. Delegate to the founding meeting of the Women's International Democratic Federation. Served on executive board of the Congress of American Women. Managing editor of *Freedom* newspaper. Founding member of Sojourners for Truth and Justice.

Thyra Edwards (1897–1953). Born in Texas. Worked as teacher, social worker, and journalist. Active labor organizer. Deeply engaged in struggle against fascism, traveling to and writing about Republican Spain during the Spanish Civil War. Raised money for the American Medical Bureau to Aid Spanish Democracy and supported the Abraham Lincoln Brigades. Editor of the left newspaper *The People's Voice*. Harassed by the FBI during the 1940s and '50s.

Vicki Garvin (1915–2007). Born in Virginia. Family moved to Harlem. Graduated from Hunter College. Earned master's degree in economics from Smith College. Worked as wage-rate analyst in National War Labor Board. Joined Communist Party in 1947. Active union organizer. Vice president of National Negro Labor Council. Served on *Freedom* newspaper editorial board. Called to testify before the House Un-American Activities Committee. Active in Pan-African and Third World Liberation movements, living in Nigeria, Ghana, and China during the 1960s.

Yvonne Gregory (1919–71). Born in Washington, DC. Studied at University of Michigan and New York University. Staff writer for *Freedom* newspaper. Deeply engaged with Rosa Lee Ingram campaign.

Member of Sojourners for Truth and Justice. Executive secretary of the Women's Committee for Equal Justice. Contributor to the Civil Rights Congress book edited by William Patterson, *We Charge Genocide: The Historic Petition to the United Nations for Relief from a Crime of the United States Government Against the Negro People*, published in 1951.

Lorraine Hansberry (1930–65). Born in Chicago. Studied at the University of Wisconsin, Madison, where she became a member of the Communist Party. Moved to Greenwich Village, then Harlem, where she wrote poems and joined the staff of *Freedom* newspaper. Achieved widespread cultural prominence for her play, *A Raisin in the Sun*, the first play authored by an African American woman to be performed on Broadway. Member of the Daughters of Bilitis, a lesbian organization. Published short stories and letters in the organization's magazine, the *Ladder*.

Dorothy Hunton (dates unknown). Born in New York City (?). Political activist in several radical organizations including the Southern Negro Youth Congress, the Council on African Affairs, and the Civil Rights Congress. Cofounded Sojourners for Truth and Justice in 1951. Signatory of the historic *We Charge Genocide* petition. Worked on the *Encyclopedia Africana* with her husband, William Alphaeus Hunton Jr., after relocating to Accra, Ghana, in 1962. Author of *Alphaeus Hunton: The Unsung Valiant*, the only full-length biography of her late husband.

Claudia Jones (1915–64). Born Claudia Cumberbatch on February 21, 1915, in Port-of-Spain, Trinidad, British West Indies. Immigrated to the United States, to Harlem, in 1924. Joined the Communist Party and the Young Communist League in 1936. Wrote for party publications including the *Daily Worker*, *Spotlight*, and the *Weekly Review*. Elected to the National Committee in 1946 and later served as secretary of its Women's Commission. On January 19, 1948, arrested with other party leaders and indicted under the Smith Act. Deported on December 9, 1955. Continued her activism and journalism in England, editing the *West Indian Gazette and Afro-Caribbean News* and organizing the first London Caribbean Carnival.

Maude White Katz (1908–85). Born in Pennsylvania. Joined the Workers Party (Communist) in 1926. Studied at the Communist University of the Toilers of the East (KUTV) in Moscow. Organizer with the Needle Trades Workers Industrial Union. National administrative secretary of the National Committee to Free the Ingram Family. Led public education struggles in New York City in the 1960s as president of the Concerned League of Harlem; organized boycott of West Harlem's P.S. 125.

Louise Thompson Patterson (1901–99). Born in Chicago. Graduated from University of California, Berkeley. Taught at Hampton Institute. Joined the Communist Party in 1937. Organized Harlem writers, artists, and intellectuals in a visit to the Soviet Union. Organizer in the campaign to free the Scottsboro Boys. Founding member of Sojourners for Truth and Justice. Member of National Women's Action Committee.

Eslanda Goode Robeson (1895–1965). Born in Washington, DC. Graduated from Columbia University. Worked as business manager for her husband, Paul Robeson. Wrote several books and hundreds of articles, acted in films, and earned a PhD in anthropology. Outspoken supporter of anticolonial struggles. Founding member of Council on African Affairs. Surveilled by FBI for subversive activities. Forced to testify in McCarthy hearings.

About the Editors

Charisse Burden-Stelly is associate professor of African American Studies at Wayne State University. She is the coauthor, with Gerald Horne, of *W. E. B. Du Bois: A Life in American History* (ABC-CLIO, 2019); the coeditor of *Reproducing Domination: On the Caribbean Postcolonial State* (University of Mississippi Press, 2022) with Percy C. Hintzen and Aaron Kamugisha; and the guest editor of "Claudia Jones: Foremother of World Revolution," a special issue of the *Journal of Intersectionality*, published in 2021. Her writings appear in peer-reviewed journals including *Small Axe, Souls, Du Bois Review, Socialism and Democracy, International Journal of Africana Studies*, and *CLR James Journal*, and her public scholarship can be found in *Monthly Review, Boston Review, Black Perspectives*, and *Black Agenda Report*. Her commentary has been featured on NPR and the Real News Network and popular podcasts such as *Bad Faith, Millennials Are Killing Capitalism, The Dig*, and *Useful Idiots*.

Jodi Dean teaches at Hobart and William Smith Colleges in Geneva, New York. Her books include *The Communist Horizon, Crowds and Party*, and *Comrade*, published by Verso.